Does Khaki Become You?

Cynthia Enloe teaches at Clark University, Massachusetts. She is the author of many books, including *Ethnic Soldiers: State Security in Divided Societies*, *Ethnic Conflict and Political Development* and *Comparative Politics of Pollution*. She is the co-editor (with Wendy Chapkis) of *Of Common Cloth: Women and the Global Textile Industry*. Cynthia Enloe's next book, a feminist analysis of international relations, will be published by Pandora in 1989.

DOES KHAKI BECOME YOU?

The Militarization of Women's Lives

CYNTHIA ENLOE

PANDORA

London Boston Sydney Wellington

First published in Great Britain by Pluto Press in 1983.
This edition published by Pandora Press, an imprint of the Trade Division of Unwin Hyman Limited in 1988.

PANDORA PRESS
Unwin Hyman Limited
15/17 Broadwick Street, London W1V 1FP

Unwin Hyman Inc
8 Winchester Place, Winchester, MA 01890, USA

Allen & Unwin Australia Pty Ltd
8 Napier Street, North Sydney, NSW 2060, Australia

Allen & Unwin New Zealand Pty with the Port Nicholson Press
60 Cambridge Terrace, Wellington, New Zealand

British Library Cataloguing in Publication Data

Enloe, Cynthia H., *1938–*
Does Khaki become you?: the militarization of womens lives.
1. Women. Influence of militarism – Feminist viewpoints
I. Title
305.4
ISBN 0–86358–301–6

Printed in Finland by Werner Söderström Oy

CONTENTS

For my mother,
Harriett Goodrige Enloe

Preface

It was a warm June afternoon, so my mother and I took our glasses of ice tea out on her porch. We also carried several of my mother's diaries. I wanted to know more about what her days had been like during the second world war, those years when my father had been in the Army Air Corps and she had been left to manage the household and my brother and me. My mother began keeping a diary in 1923 when she was a teenager in California and she hadn't missed a day since then. My brother and I were always asking her to read bits from her diaries, but this was the first time I had ever imagined that I could learn a lot about militarisation from those small leather-bound books.

So much of military history and current commentary on weapons, wars and defence spending is written as though women didn't exist, as though the Second World War (or the Falklands war or the Vietnam war) depended solely on men in war rooms and in the trenches, as though my mother didn't need to be mentioned at all. But by the time I listened to excerpts from her diaries, I was coming to realise that armed forces both thought about women and tried to control and use women; and they did not want to admit that preoccupation and reliance. As I sorted through the experiences of women like my mother who had been married to soldiers, and women who had worked in weapons factories, in massage parlours near bases, and in navy or army hospitals, it became my goal not only to reveal how military policy-makers past and present used women, but to figure out why they were so afraid to admit it. For it seemed to me that by revealing both how military forces had depended on women and had tried to hide that dependence, we, as women, could expose a vulnerable side of the military which is usually overlooked.

I began writing this book in 1980, just as the US Supreme Court was taking up the question of whether it was constitutional for the government to institute a military registration system that excluded women (a year later, the Court decided it was). Midway in my research I became involved in an effort by feminists in Boston, Massachusetts, to ensure that issues of concern to women, such as abortion and sexual harassment, were not purged from the nationwide organising campaign for disarmament. As the last chapter was being written, 30,000 women were converging on Greenham Common, one of the sites for US cruise missiles in Britain, to protest at the further escalation of the arms race and against the notions of manliness and masculinity that are embedded in so much of the official thinking that attempts to justify this escalation.

More than perhaps any other writing projects I have set out upon, this book has been affected by daily interactions with the women whose experiences I have been trying to understand. Some days it felt as though every woman I talked to had been or was currently affected by attempts by military planners to use her energies, intelligence or symbolic value. I am indebted to literally scores of women who generously shared their experiences and their insights with me over the last three years.

Jane Hawksley first suggested I tackle this issue of women and militarisation and stuck with me as editor and friend as the project took unexpected twists and turns. Myna Trustram opened my eyes to how important the history of military wives was to the whole question of how soldiers and officers think about women. Wendy Chapkis brought me together, at the Transnational Institute, with a wonderful group of European and North American feminists concerned with the military recruitment of women. All the women in the Boston-Cambridge Feminists against Militarism helped me to understand the often subtle ways in which militarist ideas depend on notions of masculinity and femininity and how such insights can be translated into political action. The students in my seminar on women and militarisation at Clark University pushed me to clarify my hunches.

Karen Shephardson and Peg Harrington turned scrawl and

tapes into legible typescripts. All of the women at Modern Times Café (where much of the first draft was scribbled) and at New Words Bookstore—that constantly revitalising source of so much information about and by women—contributed to this book. Gilda Bruckman and Lois Brynes read many of these chapters not just once but twice and offered invaluable friendly support and criticism. Serena Hilsinger, Mary Lowry, Kathleen Barry, Lena Sorenson and Rita Arditti read drafts, shared ideas and pushed me to take the risk of saying what I thought as clearly as possible.

In Britain, Judy Lown, Myna Trustram, Carole Jordan, Jennifer Gould, Hilary Land, Nira Yuval-Davis, Jalna Hanmer, Lillian Tetzlaff, Chris Smith, Dan Smith, Hilary Wainwright and Gill Rogers all provided information, press clippings and encouragement. In the US I was the beneficiary of experiences shared by Cindy Chin, Jean MacRea, Helen Horigan, Kate Rushin, Susan Schecter, Cheryl Conron, Robin Becker, Dorothy Johnson, Lisa Leghorn, Margie Chaset, Judith Dameworth, Paula Rayman, Winnie Cowan, Shauna Whitworth, Nina Gilden, Kip Cherutas, as well as Marlis, Louise and the women who served on the US Navy ship *Vulcan*.

Wellesley, Massachusetts, January 1983

Introduction to Pandora Edition

I began thinking about the surprising ways in which women's lives have been made to service the military while listening to my mother read from the diaries she'd kept during the second world war. My mother's diaries are on my own bookshelves now, but I'm still puzzling.

As the snow was falling this morning and the thermometer outside my kitchen window plummeted, I thought back to this time last January in Helsinki. Eva Isaksson and her energetic co-workers in the Finnish Peace Union had invited 30 women from a dozen countries to come together and discuss 'Women and Military Systems.' Unlike Boston, where snowy streets turn to freezing slush within hours, Helsinki's city streets remained white; each morning the night's fresh powdering crunched beneath our boots. And there were other unexpected experiences awaiting me.

One evening Eva took me to a beautiful nineteenth-century townhouse, its walls lined with photographs of early Finnish suffragists, to meet with local feminists interested in the issue of women in the military. Finland's Socialist government recently had proposed that Finnish women be permitted to volunteer for the currently all-male military. The women sitting on couches and the floor that night, with their foremothers looking down on them from the walls, clearly were astonished that any woman imagined that joining the military could be a step towards liberation. The women there spanned several generations and a range of political parties, but they seemed in agreement on this: governments that offered women a place in their militaries were not doing their women citizens a favor; they simply were filling their own military needs. In the 1980s, Finland may be one of the least militarized societies and yet, one woman told me, as others chuckled approvingly, 'In Finland, women are a demilitarized zone.'

I went out into the cold, clear Helsinki night shaking my head. There was no such cross-party, cross-generation feminist concensus in most other countries, and certainly not in the United States. So many women's relationships to their military and to their own soldiers were wrapped in memories, myths, aspirations, fears and confusions.

Just as I was about to raise Finns onto a pedestal, I was warned that patriarchy was still alive and well, if subtly operative, in Finland. During our subsequent conference women noted, for instance, that for many Finnish men the second world war remained a vital reference point for constructing their sense of manliness and national identity. Furthermore, even some of the men active in the peace movement wished women would stick to things they allegedly knew about and leave the rest to men. After one of our sessions one man was overheard asking another why these women thought they could discuss 'military systems'. Of course, he conceded, women might have insights into 'militarism', that is, into a set of beliefs and values. But 'military systems' – structures, technology, doctrines, strategies? That wasn't something women could shed any light on!

Many men – inside defense ministries and within peace movements – are reluctant to take seriously militaries' dependence on ideas about feminity. And, admittedly, it is hard to see how such abstract military doctines such as 'mutually assured destruction' or the newly popular 'low intensity conflict' rely on concepts such as motherhood and homemaking. How many men would pursue careers as civilian national security advisors or devote themselves to peace movement work if they thought that they would have to spend time thinking about nursing and alimony?[1] But what the women gathered together in Helsinki revealed over and over was that these 'feminine' things have indeed been made parts of the military system in the 1980s in societies as seemingly disparate as Chile, Algeria, Britain, Canada, the United States, Italy, Yugoslavia, Ethiopia and Norway. We didn't fool ourselves into imagining that life for women in Chile is the same as life for women in Britain; but when we compared our histories and our everyday experiences, we discovered that in each country government officials had tried very hard to harness women's labor and women's sense of self-worth to the military's wagon. Sometimes their efforts have succeeded; often they have failed. But each time a government has tried to make women's sense of duty, vulnerability, security, or pride enhance the military's influence in that country, women have had to reassess just what it means to be a 'sweetheart', a widow, a daughter, a wife, even a feminist.[2]

A 'system' is a set of relationships between several things that has reached such a point of interdependence that a change in one part can't help causing changes in other parts. If we reveal that women as people and feminity as an idea have been made integral parts of a military system, we are suggesting that if women withdraw their labor, their sexual services or their emotional support they will set off ripple effects – even waves – that could crack the very foundations of that military system. Some people have told me that after reading this book they have felt a bit overwhelmed: the military seemed to be creeping into every nook and cranny of what they had thought of as their 'civilian' lives. Yet when our Helsinki gathering came to an end last January everyone was in high spirits. Not only had we spent five days amongst women who challenged and laughed with each other. We all, I think, had come away from our discussions more than ever convinced that if women do pull back the curtain with which militaries try to camouflage their increasing dependence on women, we stand a good chance of limiting militarization; we might even chip away at patriarchy itself. We didn't leave Finland cocky. But we certainly weren't depressed. I try to keep that sense of confidence alive as I continue to sort out the latest twists and turns in the militarization of women's lives.[3]

Private Benjamin Becomes a Lobbyist

When Jane Hawksley, my editor, and I first thought through the politics of ordering *Khaki's* original chapters, I knew that I didn't want to start off with the chapter on women as soldiers. At the time, London newspapers were full of photos of women in uniform shipping off to the Falklands; they were pictured smiling pluckily and hugging their favorite stuffed teddies. In the United States during the early 1980s, feminists were divided over what to make of so many women volunteering for the post-Vietnam War military. Goldie Hawn was telling us cinematically that joining the military didn't mean killing Asians or even defending democracy from the communist menace: *Private Benjamin* instead showed a new American way for a girl to cope with youthful widowhood, escape clinging parents and stay physically fit: go to boot camp.

The question of women-in-the-military seemed to be only the tip of the gendered iceberg of militarization. I was afraid that if I became preoccupied with debates over whether women could or should be soldiers in 'this man's army', I would just thicken the smokescreen already making it so difficult for us to take seriously the experiences of other women on whom militaries past and present depended. I also had a sneaking suspicion that the image of women in fatigues aiming rifles at cardboard enemies was becoming a bit *too* enticing to many male commentators. Iranian women, Nicaraguan women, Libyan women, even white South African women – their photos were popping up too frequently in the press. It seemed as though an army rifle made a woman especially exotic – and maybe erotic – and the military for which she was fighting particularly fearsome. So we decided to leave the discussion of women as soldiers until later in the book; readers, I hoped, would puzzle over the experiences of women soldiers as they reflected – or maybe subverted – the ways women as wives, mothers, nurses and prostitutes were used by militaries. Thinking about the connections *between* militarized women seemed the most promising way to reveal how militaries have come to rely on women to be 'feminine', and how confounded militaries become when women refuse to live according to that artificial standard.

Today, in 1988, more women than ever are in military uniform, most as volunteers (though a few as conscripts) in regular state armed services. Sandinista women publically criticized Nicaragua's new post-revolution conscription law that exempted women from compulsory military service; many

Nicaraguan women showed their displeasure by immediately volunteering to serve in the local armed militias so that no one could roll back the social clock and reinstitute the assumption that men fight for their country while women stay home. A significant number of women in other countries continue to join anti-state guerrilla armies. Elsewhere, women are enlisting in state armies out of a mix of patriotism and economic need. In the United States alone, there are 220,957 women in uniform on any given day. Still, I'm not convinced that whether women donning khaki is good for women or for militaries is the most crucial issue with which we need to tussle. In a sense, perhaps the very inclination to dwell on women as soldiers is a reflection of our own militarized imagination: are women as soldiers – even for those of us trying to reduce the influence of military values – perhaps more interesting, more 'serious', a topic than women as wives of soldiers?

Despite my reluctance to dwell on women soldiers, I must confess that this book's discussion of women in the military has generated some intense conversations, especially among young women with whom I have talked during the last five years. One reason why so many women feel strongly about women's entrance into and rights within the military is that many women are fighting hard to make their country's military a place where they are accepted on equal terms with men. Those women exerting so much energy inside the military establishment to overcome barriers to training and promotion may find it insulting when a civilian feminist like me argues that a military is so fundamentally masculinized that no woman has a chance of transforming that military into a place where women and men can be equal. At first I was puzzled when several young American women told me how angry this book had made them. I recalled how I had tried not to blame women for their society's militarism, even women in the military. But gradually I've come to understand that when a 'feminist-in-khaki' hears another woman arguing that the military is basically misogynist, she hears someone telling her that she can't accomplish what she's set out to do, that she's letting herself be duped if she persists in trying. The message reeks of condescension. No woman of any age wants to be told by another woman that she's crazy to try to make the world less sexist. She and her anti-militarist sister both agree that the military is one of the most powerful institutions in their country. They agree that it has been founded on ideas and practices that marginalize women for the sake of exalting masculinity. What they disagree about, however, is what it's worth doing about those conditions. The anti-militarist feminist believes that women have the most to gain by cutting back the military's role in society. Her sister in uniform believes that women can work from inside to make the military less hostile to women and thereby less socially distortive.

One young woman who most forcefully made this point to me described how she and her mother both attended meetings of the US Defense Department's women's advocacy commission, DACOWITS (the Defense Advisory Committee on Women in the Services). Barbara spoke movingly about how she resented her mother having been pushed out of the army after the second world war, like so many other American, British and Canadian women, for the sake of remasculinizing the army in the name of peacetime 'normalization'. Today Barbara is getting through college on a military scholarship; she has endured a painful divorce and is determined to make her career in the US army. She has her own share of shocking stories to tell of sexist practices which still are daily fare in US military life. But that was the point, she insisted to me and the rather skeptical students in our seminar. This wasn't the 1940s, this was the 1980s, and today women aren't going to accept the old sort of marginalization lying down, literally or figuratively. Barbara and women like her were prepared to fight it on the military's own turf – for the sake of their own careers and for the sake of their mothers' memories.

There is evidence that their efforts are bearing fruit. DACOWITS is compelling Congressional armed services committees to hold public hearings on military sexual harassment, for the first time making links between the disrespect shown by American male officers towards American military women and the disrespect routinely shown by those same men toward Filipina women around US bases. DACOWITS and its allied pressure groups also have embarrassed a reluctant Secretary of the Navy to open up more posts on 'non-combat' ships to women. American military women are meeting regularly with their counterparts in other NATO militaries to insist that women are used to their full capabilities in the alliance. In 1983 their bureaucratic agility was such that they had forced a reluctant Defense Department to allow 170 white and Black American women to take part in the US invasion of Grenada. Military women had successfully pressed their Washington superiors and won the right to serve on underground missile teams in Comiso, Italy and elsewhere, thereby overcoming the previous insinuations that a woman serving with a male partner underground would have her eyes only on the man and not on the control panel.[4]

If Goldie Hawn's Private Benjamin had stayed in the military, by now she probably would be a savvy lobbyist. Over the last several years women have become formidable adversaries for those male policy-makers who naively presumed that they could use women in just the numbers and ways that were comfortable for military men. These women speak in terms of 'jobs' and 'equality'. They see patriotism and 'public service' as compatible with soldiering. They rarely talk about 'militarism'. Yet these women know how their legislative military affairs committees work. They have learned who to call with what information about the latest sexist outrage. They know how to set their complaints against sexism in the sort of national security context even a conservative policy-maker can't turn a deaf ear to. Over the past decade they have become at home in the official corridors of Ottawa, Washington and Brussels. And when the inside track hasn't worked, they have taken their cases to the press and the courts. These are smart women. They see themselves as doing feminist work. They have made a lot of women proud and a lot of men nervous.

In 1987, most governments in the NATO alliance told its Brussels headquarters that they intended to recruit more women into their regular forces in the near future. The British government stands out as one of the few that says that it plans no increase. Women comprise about 5% of all British military personnel today, and that suits the Thatcher government just fine. Maybe this satisfaction reflects the Conservative government's persistent reluctance to press for women's rights generally. The government's desire for women to see themselves fulfilled through marriage and domesticity has most recently been spelled out in its 1988 budget, which makes it harder than ever for a woman to buy a house on her own or with other women. The Thatcher regime can afford this luxury of dreaming of the domesticated wife so long as Britain's unemployment rates remain stubbornly high among young men, a situation that lightens the task of military recruiters in an era when there is no compulsory male conscription. They still can attract the male enlistees they need without resorting to bringing in more women. They can even persuade young mens' mothers that it's better for their sons to be playing war games in West Germany than to be on the dole and on the streets in Birmingham. While the Prime Minister and her Cabinet proclaim their desire to reduce unemployment, drastic reductions in joblessness among young men in the declining factory towns and mining communities of Wales, Scotland, Northern Ireland and the north of England might compel them to reassess either their commitment to a large standing army or their satisfaction with that 5% female proportion.

Elsewhere in Western Europe, military manpower planners are more anxious than ever about their women citizens deciding to have so few children. Declining birth rates translate into fewer young people, especially fewer young men, to conscript or recruit into the armed forces. The French military under both Conservative and Socialist governments has urged policies that will encourage French women to have more than two children. But at the same time they have been recruiting more women into their services: currently they need to have 20,000 French women in uniform, but there are plans to enlist more. Next door, the West German military has only 141 women in uniformed jobs. But it relies on another 48,000 women to perform important civilian jobs for the military. Portugal's government today has a mere 9 women in its military, but it is promising NATO officials that soon it will bring in more women. That policy is part of the Portuguese policy-makers' effort to prove to their allies that

Portugal is a 'modern' country worthy of NATO membership.[5]

Thus there are thousands of women soldiers who need advocates, especially lesbians, women veterans and women of color.[6] Since 1983, for example, Canadian women have been organizing to protest the treatment of lesbians – and women accused of being lesbians – in the Canadian military. Nervousness about women's femininity isn't new. Canadian historian Ruth Pierson recently has revealed in stunning detail the lengths to which the country's military went during the second world war to ensure that Canadian women in khaki would remain conventionally feminine.[7] But Daryl Wood, a Canadian veteran, reports that discharging women in groups on charges of lesbianism has been the US military's way; their Canadian counterparts typically have preferred to accuse and discharge women as isolated individuals, thus keeping a lower public profile. That is, until 1984.

Between April and November that year, 17 women at one navy base, Shelbourne, Nova Scotia, were investigated for lesbianism; five were dismissed; others were transferred. None of the women was given reasons. What the Canadian military had not counted on was these military women's access to activist women, lawyers and the media. Some of these women wanted to stay in the military. They had enlisted as young women, worked hard to get their ratings, saw a future in the military. And even those women who came out of the months of interrogation seeing the military for the first time as a patriarchal institution inherently hostile to women believed that women who wanted to stay in should be able to. Today the Canadian forces still have the right to exclude or expel people they accuse of homosexuality. But the new Canadian Charter of Rights has made it harder to justify this discrimination, and even National Defense Department officials in Ottawa have had to admit publically that many gay men and lesbians serving in the military perform their jobs well.[8]

As Washington presses the Canadian government to devote more resources to its military and as the country's slow climb out of its economic recession makes it harder to attract young male volunteers, the logic of Canada's new Charter of Rights might start to make military sense as well as civilian sense to defense policy-makers. But if in the 1990s Canadian military 'manpower' planners do start to allow lesbian women to pursue careers in the armed services, how should we understand that change? Should we see it as progress for women or as one more step towards the militarization of women's lives? And how should we explain that change? We might interpret it as the consequence of gutsy political lobbying by an alliance of civilian and military feminists. Or we might see this change as merely the consequence of patriarchal men's refining their tools for using women's best energies. My own hunch is that the latter explanations are more realistic. Still, I've become more conscious recently of how complex the relationships are between the state and women who engage with the state: those women are not mere puppets.

Race, Ethnicity and Signing Up

Who are the women who join a military? Most are volunteers, at least according to the law, though many may feel as if in reality they have little choice. Few governments have passed genuinely 'universal' conscription laws, although both the United States and the Soviet Union have contingency plans allowing for the compulsory service of female nurses. Canada and the United States began counting women and men in the military by ethnicity and race in the 1970s.

Surprisingly, for instance, figures from Ottawa show that Francophone women are joining the Canadian military in the same proportions as Anglophone women. This is despite the Canadian military's historic connections with the English-speaking community and the French community's traditionally more conservative attitudes toward the role of women. The Canadian military appears to have started to keep track of the proportions of French-speaking and English-speaking women and men in the military as a result of the emergence of French-Canadian nationalism in the 1960s and 1970s and, with it, an insistence that all federal institutions be explicitly monitored in their efforts to reflect Canada's demography. Francophones comprise approximately 27% of the country's population. In October, 1987, French-speaking women comprised 27% of all

NATO WOMEN

Among the 15 governments in the NATO alliance, the United States and Canada pride themselves today on having the highest proportion of women in their militaries: the US, 10.2%; Canada, 9.1%. And 'pride' is the term these governments use, for while they may have been pushed at first by recruiting needs and later by local women's advocates, they now are holding up their higher percentages as evidence of their being 'civilized' nations.

Women in the NATO armed forces, 1987

Country	# of women	women as % of total	expected to increase?
Belgium	3,496	3.8	yes
Canada	7,724	9.1	yes
Denmark	821	2.98	yes
France	20,470	3.7	yes
West Germany	141*	0.028	no
Greece	1,640	.96	yes
Italy	none	0.0	no
Luxembourg	1st recruits, '87	–	yes
Netherlands	1,644	1.5	yes
Norway	540	1.4	yes
Portugal	9**	0.0012	yes
Spain	none	0.0	no
Turkey	(no data)	0.0084	yes
United Kingdom	16,323	5.1	no
United States	220,250	10.2	yes

* All are medical officers; approximately 48,000 women work for the West German military as civilian civil servants, as typists, laboratory technicians, translators, lawyers.
** All are air force nurses.
Source: Figures supplied by the Public Information Advisor, International Military Staff, NATO Military Committee, 1110 Brussels, Belgium, November, 1987.

women in the Canadian regular forces; English-speaking women comprised 73%. Among men the proportions were roughly the same: French-speaking men comprised 29% of all men in the regular forces; English-speaking men comprised 71%. We still need to know what has been happening within Quebec to have attracted a growing number of French-speaking women to join the military. Is it a deepening job crisis? Is it perhaps a spill-over from the earlier French Canadian nationalism which, oddly, has inclined today's French-speaking women to break from conservative patriarchal traditions and enlist in a national military? The Canadian defense officials do not yet have the incentive to count proportions of women and men of color who join the military, so discovering why a Canadian West Indian woman or a Native Canadian woman might consider enlisting will call for a less quantitative approach.[9]

It's even harder to know *which* women make up the 16,000 in the British armed forces. The British military today includes an estimated 5,000 Black and Asian men and women. But officials claim it does not count its personnel by race and ethnicity, although Black male soldiers have been strangely under-represented in some of the more elite units. 'After all', the officials seem to say, 'how can you tell a West Indian's name from a white Briton's name?'. We don't know whether Black British women or Northern Irish Protestant women are more or less likely to seek a job in the military than white English women. Nor do we know whether poor working-class women are less likely to be accepted as volunteers because of the Royal Navy's and the nursing corps' preference for middle-class women. And because in Britain, as in Canada and the United States, it remains an offense to be a homosexual in the military, we also have a hard time knowing how many young lesbians are drawn to the British military in search of a life with other women or of less traditionally feminine job skills.

We do know, on the other hand, that Black women in the United States have continued to join the military in ever greater numbers in the last five years. By September 1987, there were 59,166 Black women in all uniformed branches of the country's military; Black women comprised 28.6% of all women in the US military. In the enlisted (non-officer) ranks of the Army, Black women's prominence is even more striking. By mid-1987, Black women made up 44.3% of all enlisted women in the US Army. That is 4 *times* their proportion in the civilian female population.

This represented a rise of 2% since 1982. Yet Black women's particular experiences continued to attract little political attention, hostile or friendly.[10]

One Black civil rights organization did host a brief meeting to explore the conditions causing so many women to seek out the military as an employer. At that meeting, Betty Woode, whose research focuses on the barriers facing Black women in the American job market, suggested that the answer might not have much to do with patriotism or the desire to keep physically fit. A young Black woman may go to an army recruiting interview at her high school thinking about how she might obtain a full-time job which has medical benefits and the promise of training. In the 1980s this sort of job isn't readily available to 18-year-old American Black women. Neither the Black community nor the women's movement has taken up the question of the US military's growing reliance on Black women. At the same time, Black women appear in American opinion polls as the social group most opposed to US military interventionism abroad, more so than white women, more so than Black men, and, of course, far more so than white men. So what are we to make of young Black women increasingly looking to the military to provide the security and dignity denied to them in the civilian economy? To make sense of the role that the military is playing in American society today, we need to listen to what Black women soldiers and Black women veterans are saying. What would be a Black woman soldier's description of the US invasion of Grenada?[11]

Wives, Mothers and the INF Treaty

Military recruiters skilled in playing on young men's desire to prove their manliness by soldiering still don't have an easy time meeting their 'manpower' quotas. For recruiters in the NATO countries, the next several years could bring even greater pressures: those aided by male conscription laws have to worry about falling birth rates – women choosing to have fewer children; those without conscription (including Britain, Canada and the US) have to worry about improvements in the male civilian job market. Even before the ink was dry on the 1987

Gorbachev-Reagan intermediate range nuclear missile treaty, NATO security strategists began calling for a build-up in so-called 'conventional' armies to compensate for what they believed was the Soviet Union's greater strength in non-nuclear forces in Europe.

We now understand that these sorts of urgings translate into efforts to militarize more women's lives. If more women who are married to soldiers can be made to feel happy with the life of a military wife, they might encourage their husbands to stay in the service. If more women can be persuaded to have more children out of a sense not only of personal satisfaction, but of national duty and pride, militaries will have an easier time filling their manpower quotas. If more mothers can be convinced that their own sons' problems with leaving the nest, with drug abuse or joblessness can be remedied by joining the military, then military commanders will have more societal support for their policies.[12]

Today, however, these governmental efforts are colliding with new budgetary constraints and a spreading collective consciousness among military wives in the United States and Canada. In the late 1980s, most militaries are facing the prospect of lower ceilings on their budgetary expansions. This is coming at a time when more military manpower planners have recognized that keeping women satisfied enough so that they will urge their husbands to stay in the service requires better housing, better social services, better medical care. One way, some policy advisors suggest, to resolve this dilemma is to offer military wives more of the jobs that keep overseas bases running, jobs that now go to local residents: military wives will cost less. This is one of the arguments being made by Britain's National Audit Office in its report to Parliament. The authors of the report conducted their study of the costliness of British bases in West Germany by comparing British policies towards dependents' wives and children with those of the Americans. This represented a change: until recently, policies regarding military families seemed to be one area of military policy-making that wasn't considered exportable. But tighter budgets and NATO's sprawling social science network may be breaking down these barriers. The British National Audit Office noted with approval, for instance, that the Americans don't allow such a high proportion of soldiers to bring their dependents with them to Germany: 'the US army has only about 50,000 married quarters for some 205,000 soldiers [in West Germany], whereas the British army and the RAF keep 37,000 quarters for 67,000 men'.[13] Let more spouses and children stay behind when their soldier husbands (occasionally wives) are sent abroad. If such a policy is implemented to save money, more British military wives may press their husbands to leave the service after their next tour of duty.

In the last five years the collective consciousness of military wives has been growing, their political skills have increased and their alliances have widened. American ex-wives of military men have won some of the battles they were only gearing up to fight in the early 1980s. Working through two new activist organizations and making alliances with the Women's Equity Action League (a Washington-based group that also is lobbying for an end of discrimination against women soldiers), divorced wives of servicemen persuaded Congress to pass a law compelling their ex-husbands to share their extensive military retirement benefits with them. At the same time, women still married to men in active service began to object to the long-standing military assumption that they were first of all 'military wives', women who would put their husbands' military careers before their own job aspirations and the military's own need for unpaid community work before their own educational and economic needs. The Department of Defense had continued to expand their bureaucratic services for military families between 1983 and 1987. But these policies did not resolve the fundamental tension between women and the military. In 1987, the wives went to Congress after one Air Force wife, backed by her husband, refused to quit her paid job when her husband was offered a promotion:

> In many communities commanders' spouses are still held responsible for recruiting volunteers to maintain these family support services. This expectation can become a virtual albatross around their necks. Spouses' efforts to

> address the issue are rebuffed by senior leaders. The women who were commanders' wives and wives of senior military personnel at Grissom [Air Force base] tried to address this issue for one solid year with no results. The message they got was, 'Play the game or your husband will suffer'. The message their husbands were sent was, 'Control your wife or your career is over'.[14]

For the first time, women working for the military as soldiers' wives began to make common cause with women in the military as soldiers, though this happened more at the senior than at the lower ranks. In making these links, military wives exposed the depths of the military's reliance not just on wives, but on the entire conventional sexual division of labor:

> It is well known in all of the military services that many commanders still refuse to accept officers and senior non-commissioned officers who have been selected for command positions if they are unmarried, or if the spouse will not accompany the officer to his assignment. Women officers can be in a double bind because, quite obviously, they will not have a wife. Even if they are married, their husbands will not be expected to assume the same duties or responsibilities of a female spouse.[15]

The Canadian Department of National Defense is being sued for the first time by military wives who are charging that its treatment of women married to soldiers violates the Canadian Charter of Rights. Lucie Richardson, mother of five children and military wife for 18 years, together with several other young military wives with children, began meeting at each other's houses on the Penhold military base in Red Deer, Alberta, to plan a day care center and a women's center. They drew up a constitution, got a small public grant and won the right to join the local video club without their husband's consent. Then they began thinking about dental care. Their husbands' cavities and gum care was looked after by the military, but wives' childrens' dental work had to be paid for out of limited family funds.

Dental care, in these women's minds, was linked to other issues they were discussing: traffic lights, pensions, rape. But at this point, the women were contacted by the base commander: pensions and dental care were 'political' issues; military wives were prohibited from participating in politics. Lucie and her friends were told to stop their activities. They began to wonder what other political rights they were denied. They wrote to the Department of National Defense only to be told that their political rights weren't protected under the new national Charter of Rights, despite the fact that they were civilians. In the meantime, some military commanders told officers under them to 'control your wife – or else'. Some men pressured their wives to stop attending the wives' group meetings. Other men were angry and supported their wives' efforts to improve conditions on the base, though they realized that such support might jeopardize their own careers.

Currently there are 50,000 military wives in Canada, 24,250 of whom live on bases. A small group of them have formed the Organizational Society of Spouses of Military Members – OSSOMM, which Lucie Richardson and her allies pronounce 'awesome'. By early 1988, OSSOMM activists had contacted military wives and military women advocates in the United States to learn of their problems and strategies and were planning a conference at which Canadian and American women would examine the legal restrictions and rights of women inside and dependent on the two militaries.[16]

Rambo, Rape and 'Low Intensity Conflict'

When I finished writing this book in 1983, Sylvester Stallone's cinematic 'Rambo' had not yet replaced John Wayne as the globalized shorthand for militarized masculinity, a standard of manliness that men are supposed to live up to and women are supposed to look up to. *Rambo III* is upon us now, with Rambo foresaking Vietnam and turning his muscular, monsyllabic vengeance toward Afghanistan. Feminists report that *Rambo* videos have become popular among men in Helsinki, Manila and Santiago, as well as Los Angeles. John Wayne and John Rambo aren't carbon copies, even if both seem embedded in individualistic American culture. This may forecast some important transformation in the ways that masculinity – and thus femininity – are being militarized.[17]

Over these same five years the militarization of the Caribbean and Central America has been intensified by the policies of the US government and those of governments in the region. The Rambo-esque sort of 'low intensity conflict', rather than the John Wayne-ish battalions-on-the-move, characterizes this new militarization. Half a globe away this same 'post-Vietnam' doctrine is informing the campaign against popular insurgency in Corazon Aquino's Philippines.

'Low intensity conflict' ('LIC') is a refurbished counterinsurgency strategy intended to protect existing Third World governments from urban poor people and landless peasants who have been organizing to improve their lives. Not all American or British military officials find LIC attractive. Some even wage bureaucratic warfare against the adoption of LIC ideas because they assign less importance to heavy armored warfare and because they shift the foreign policy limelight away from more conventional battlefields of Europe. If one adopts the LIC doctrine, slum dwellers who organize a handicraft cooperative begin to appear dangerous: they are as likely to upset the fragile political order as armed guerrillas in the mountains. LIC is designed especially to allow the local regime to carry on counterinsurgency operations without drawing the forces of foreign supporters, particularly the United States, directly into the conflict. This has 'post-Vietnam' appeal for its American advocates. In its reliance on irregular militarized groups such as vigilantes, and its stress on the manipulation of popular imagery, low intensity conflict is meant to give even the local government's military protective camouflage. This is the sense in which LIC is low intensity. In another sense it is not low intensity at all. For the women and men in countries like El Salvador and the Philippines, who have taken the brunt of these operations, the consequences are very intense indeed. Anyone who attempts to organize poor villagers or members of an urban squatter community will be labeled a 'Communist terrorist' by vigilante or military leaders. Once turned into a 'Communist terrorist', that person will be subjected to daily harassment, dislocation or even murder.[18]

Despite the growing alarm about the uses and consequences of low intensity conflict, most human rights and progressive critics don't appear curious about whether – and why – women and men may be experiencing this new sort of militarization differently. It has been Third World feminists who have been spelling out how presumptions about women and about feminity have been shaping this kind of warfare.

It is almost two years since Corazon Aquino, backed by an historic popular upsurge of political activism, replaced Ferdinand Marcos as the President of the Philippines. Filipino feminists hoped that this political change would bring about a fundamental demilitarization of their society. They had a realistically broad notion of what genuine demilitarization would have to entail. They saw the rollback of local commanders' influence as integrally connected not only to the empowering of local communities but also to the end of massive prostitution around American military bases. Hopes ran high; many women in North America and Europe looked to the women of the Philippines, Brazil and Argentina – whose militarized governments also had fallen – for inspiration in what otherwise appeared a world ever more permeated by the presumptions and priorities of militarized security.[19]

But by mid-1987, it was obvious that something was going terribly wrong. The government of Corazon Aquino appeared intent upon remilitarizing Filipino life with the support of the American administration. The sorts of ideas and tactics shaping that trend seemed to be borrowed from Central America. Philippines and Latin American feminists have noted, however, that this new kind of counterinsurgency warfare deliberately targets civilian neighborhoods and family households for 'anti-terrorist' operations. Even the myth of the dichotomy between 'homefront' and 'battlefront', a dichotomy which has been a pillar of military thinking about women and about men, disintegrates in a low intensity conflict sweep. But for the counterinsurgency strategist, it is the woman herself who has torn apart the social fabric when she has begun to stretch the confines of feminized domestic space to organize with other women. Moreover, a woman who helps organize a day care center, a soup kitchen or a literacy class comes to be seen by military commanders and anti-communist vigilantes as doubly subversive: not only is she challenging the government to provide adequate services, she is questioning the very sexual divisions of labor on which the current political order rests.

Rape has become integral to the implementation of low intensity conflict doctrine insofar as it is meant to punish a woman for defying rules of respectability. For feminine respectability which serves to hold up the existing political order as well as the existing domestic order.[20]

Lourdes Ignacio

Date of Incident: April 19, 1987
Place of Incident: Paco, Flora, Kaling-Apayao
Perpetrators: unidentified soldiers
Circumstances: Victim is a farmer suspected as an NPA. Her body was already decomposing when discovered. She was raped.

Gina Isidro
Rosie Paner
Edna Velez
Susan Ubamos

Date of incident: April 26, 1987
Place of Incident: Sitio Munungka, Brgy. Celestino C. Villacin, Negros Occidental
Perpetrators: 57th and 61st IB-PA under Col. Pablo Sencil
Circumstances: Victims are teenage girls raped by their military captors. They were suspected NPAs. Col. Sencil denied any knowledge of his men's killings in Cadiz and EB Magalona. He said the deaths resulted from his men's battles with the NPA.

So reports Gabriela, the coalition of Filipina women's organizations.[21]

There is a tendency to make rapes just one more offence in a litany of atrocities that accompany these coercive actions: 'dislocations, assassinations, interrogations and rapes.' But Third World feminists are developing quite a different analysis. They are contending that the fact that so much of low intensity conflict is accompanied by rape may not be merely a 'side effect' of a kind of militarization that relies on men not directly under a formal chain of command. Rape, they tell us, is being used as a tool of this kind of warfare. As part of village 'sweeps' or as a systematic part of torture while under arrest, rape may be integral to the very strategy of sustaining the existing social order in the face of women's growing 'subversiveness'.[22]

I didn't foresee this sort of militarization in 1983. Nor did I grasp initially how this new US-designed and exported military doctrine depended as much as the others before it on presumptions about women's relations to men. The Third World women living in the midst of, and organizing against this demoralizing form of militarization are taking the lead in creating a feminist understanding of low intensity conflict. What this suggests is that whenever we hear of a new military doctrine, no matter how abstract or arcane it may sound at first, we should presume that there may be gendered ideas at its very core. Expectations about what it means to be 'masculine' and what it means to be 'feminine' are more than likely to be among the pillars holding up the newest, as well as the oldest, military ideas.

Condoms in Khaki

Seven thousand American soldiers were rotated in and out of Ecuador's interior region last year. They were men and women enlisted not in the regular US military, but in the National Guard, which acts as the military's reserve force. Most of the troops came from Puerto Rico and southern states, with a high proportion of soldiers able to speak Spanish, and thus more easily 'blend in' to Latin American society. Their official mission was to build a road through the jungle. But some commentators speculated that these operations were part of the Pentagon's emerging low intensity conflict strategy of using the military in what normally would be civilian projects and in such a way as to encourage local governments to be more energetically involved in counterinsurgency efforts.

Although this area of Ecuador is sparsely populated, Archidona, the market town nearest the American military encampments, soon attracted poor women willing to work as prostitutes servicing the male soldiers. One reporter heard that the Ecuadoran women were earning up to $30 per American customer. That compared favorably with the average $65 per month that an Ecuadoran factory worker was paid, if she could get such a job. Aside from the location, none of this is surprising. The pattern has roots back to ancient Greece, roots nourished by assumptions about militarized masculinity and by women's landlessness. But this is 1988, and there is a new and deadly twist to the age-old pattern: AIDS. The townspeople of Archidona are afraid that this sexualized low intensity conflict operation will spread AIDS throughout Ecuador.[23]

AIDS is changing the militarized sexual politics of bases, not only of American, but of British and French bases. In 1983 only a few scientists knew the phrase 'acquired immune deficiency syndrome'. Five years later it has become a household – and war room – nightmare. AIDS is drastically altering the ways that military commanders are thinking about their male soldiers' sexual needs and about the prostitutes in Latin America, Asia and Africa who are supposed to keep morale high by fulfilling those presumed needs. To feminists, however, the militarization of this devastating disease may look strangely familiar. As I read about Filipino and Honduran women's efforts to critique their own and foreign governments' policies regarding prostitution, my thoughts return to Britain's 19th century Contagious Diseases Acts, laws that were meant to keep British soldiers safe from 'unclean' English, Indian and Egyptian women. As different as some of the politics of ordinary venereal disease and AIDS are, both have been dealt with by male officials as if they were threats to 'national security'. This has been especially so when policy-makers have thought about the implications of stationing their male soldiers in a foreign country. In 1988, as in 1878, military commanders have sought to protect their men by controlling the women with whom they might have sex.

The French military long has contested the British and American practice of treating male soldiers' sexual needs with an arms-length policy marked by ambiguity and secrecy. Instead, the French have made a practice of sanctioning and supervising what the French military calls 'field brothels'. By early 1987, however, the threat of AIDS had added a new dimension to that control strategy. In Bangui, capital of the Central African Republic and site of one of France's several African military bases, the French officers were saying that no French soldier stationed in the Central African Republic had yet died of AIDS. Still, some 800 local citizens had died of AIDS, and the incidence of AIDS infection among local prostitutes was estimated at 19%. The French military wasn't being sanguine. Its medical officers already had adopted a policy of compelling African women in the two military field brothels to undergo AIDS antibody tests. The report did not say whether French soldiers were being subjected to tests before being allowed to visit a field brothel. The implication was that it was the women of the Central African Republic who posed the military threat.[24]

One of the newest of the United States' overseas military base sites is in Honduras, a country supposed by Washington officials to be as critical to its support of the anti-Sandanista 'contra' campaign in Nicaragua. Between 1981 and the end of 1986 approximately 60,000 American soldiers – mostly men, but some women – had been sent to Honduras to build roads and airfields and to conduct joint military exercises with Honduran soldiers.[25] Palmerola airforce base, near the town of Comayagua, has become the biggest US base in Honduras. Roxanne Pastore, a Honduran feminist, estimates that more than 1,000 women come into Comayagua every weekend to work as prostitutes to the American military men on leave.[26] Many of these women have children to support but no land to farm. Some of the women work 'freelance' in the center of town, others work in organized brothels, at least several of which reportedly are owned by Honduran military officers.[27] Before 1985, Honduran doctors had become alarmed at the spread of venereal disease, which had become popularly labeled 'Vietnam rose'. Hondurans traced the increasing number of cases to the American bases.

Since 1985, AIDS has replaced VD as the cause for most alarm.

Between 1985 and mid-1987, 17 cases of AIDS were reported in Honduras. Four of those suffering with AIDS (whose Spanish acronym is 'SIDA') were women. Hondurans began suggesting that AIDS entered their country with American soldiers. But the Honduran government, which has been closely allied with the United States, refused to question the effects of that alliance on its citizens' health. The Health Ministry, however, has allowed some Honduran women to be taken to the United States for AIDS testing.[28] The American military commander at Palmerola airforce base, Colonel Charles Carlton, seems to be taking a more activist stance, but he shares the assumption that it is the Honduran prostitute who is the threat; he couches his policy in the language of moral uplift rather than physical health. Upon arriving at Palmerola in September 1987, the colonel announced a policy of prohibiting soldiers from going to local brothels; he stopped the regular bus service between the base and the brothels in Comayagua. It isn't clear what such a policy is doing to the relations between American male soldiers and the small number of American women serving with them on the base. Are the women under more pressure now to become sexually involved with their male colleagues? We don't know how the American women soldiers think of their relationships to the Honduran prostitutes. It also isn't clear whether Colonel Carlton still follows his predecessor's policy of having US military doctors give local prostitutes medical examinations. Some local residents have welcomed the new policy, seeing it as helping to restore the town's respectability. The mayor, assured that medical examinations have kept the prostitutes clean, only worries that closing the brothels will be bad for business. Still other Hondurans note that the women working in Comayagua's brothels are landless and are often the sole supporter of children.[29]

'Yanki basura fuera!' Yankee trash go home. This has been a growing demand heard from Central Americans. Now one is more likely to hear 'Yanki basura con SIDA fuera'. Honduran feminists argue, however, that the entire militarization policy, of which the American bases are a central part, has served to deprive women of genuine security. Being deprived of farming land by an armed local elite and its soldiers and being infected with AIDS by an American soldier are part of a single militarizing process.

The Philippines Ministry of Health announced in January, 1987 that it knew of 25 people in the country who tested positive for the AIDS virus. All were women. 22 of the 25 infected women were entertainers working in bars around the Clark, Subic Bay and Wallace US military bases.[30] Gabriela, the coalition of Philippines women's organizations, has argued that the US military has been the vehicle through which AIDS has come to the Philippines and that, therefore, it was more urgent than ever that the newly installed government of President Corazon Aquino refuse to renew the leases for the bases when they expire in 1991. Leaders of Gabriela were insistent that the Aquino government should not adopt the US military's attitude that it was Filipinas who posed the threat and thus had to be controlled.

We demand therefore, that:

> . . . Solutions to poverty and unemployment, under-education and job marginalization of women, the real causes of prostitution, be undertaken. Meanwhile, immediate attention should be given to the rights, health, safety and welfare of prostitutes. They too are citizens of this country, not criminals . . .
>
> . . . While the US bases are still on Philippine territory, all servicemen or base employees with any finding of AIDS not be allowed on Philippines soil. In the same way that American servicemen demand VD clearance from the women, the Filipinas have the right to demand AIDS and VD clearance from the servicemen.[31]

At the same time, American military officials seem caught in a quandary. Quandaries, in fact, are the very stuff of militaries' attempts to make use of women for militaristic ends. It has never been easy. Military men and their civilian superiors repeatedly have tripped over themselves trying to devise ways to keep the military a bastion of masculine honor while still controlling women, on whom every military depends. Now the puzzle confronting military officials is how to sustain male soldiers' morale, a morale long imagined to require legitimation of their alleged sexual needs, when either the women with whom they have sex in foreign countries are considered a threat to the men's health or the men themselves will have to be seen by their commanders as a threat to national security.

In the 1870s the Ladies National Association, created by Josephine Butler and other British feminists, concentrated on repealing the Contagious Diseases Acts, militarily inspired laws that harmed and humiliated English women. Butler herself did become actively involved in repealing similar acts imposed on Indian women, whose infection with venereal disease was alleged by British commanders to threaten their imperial troops. But for the most part the protests against the policing of women for the sake of the health of soldiers were organized country by country. Today there is the beginning of an effort to create a feminist organizing network as global as the basing networks of the major powers. It is called CAMP – the Campaign Against Military Prostitution. It sprang out of conversations between Kenyan and Philippines women during the United Nations End of the Decade on Women conference in Nairobi in 1985. Kenyan women were concerned and angry about the growing prostitution business in the Kenyan port city of Mombassa due in large part to the port's increasing use by the United States navy. Their concerns dovetailed with those of Filipina feminists. CAMP's network is fragile and dependent on the stretched energies of a few women. But already it includes women from South Korea, Japan, Thailand, Sri Lanka, West Germany, Ireland, Iceland, the United States, Greece and Honduras.[32]

The very activism of organizations like CAMP, a member of the Gabriela alliance, may compel the American military to radically rethink their gendered policies for insuring soldiers' morale. Could it be that in the next few years American military strategists will move away from large foreign bases because they no longer can provide their men with the sexualized 'rest and recreation' that they have come to expect? Might they instead opt for more reliance on what are called 'rapid deployment forces', men based in the home country but able to be transported quickly abroad to the latest hot spot? Maybe this would have the added advantage of pacifying soldiers' wives, a group about whom military planners have become more nervous.

What would these decisions do to the relations between first and third world women? Militarization has long relied on women of different countries seeing each other as competitors, if not outright enemies. If American – or French or British – women married to soldiers become persuaded that Filipino, Kenyan or Honduran women threaten their husbands' and even their own health to such an extent that the military was considering cutting back on overseas stationing, basing logistics would become awkward. Yet such beliefs in the minds of American or European military wives could simultaneously refuel a xenophobia that would perpetuate global militarism.

Conclusion

This is a book about sexuality. This is a book about racism. It is about the family and about work. Any sphere of any woman's life can be militarized. But what continues to surprise me is how dependent the military is on women to make this happen and yet how we as women often believe that we don't know very much about militaries. Most of us and most of our mothers and grandmothers haven't ever donned khaki. Most of us don't read military histories, play battlefield games or build model fighter planes. Many of us take little pleasure in arguing about our military's latest manuevers when we're out for dinner with friends. As a result, we think we aren't qualified to critique our own or anyone else's military. And since all too often the men we know are eager to show that they can talk confidently about such matters, we're inclined to let them have the floor.

But during the years in which I worked on this book and in the years talking with people about their own reactions to it, I've come to realize that a lot of women, maybe most women, in fact know a great deal about militaries, even 'military systems'. We know how a woman friend struggles with the idea that her son joining the army might get him off drugs or equip him with a marketable skill. Some of us have taken care of men whose minds and bodies have been damaged by military service. A lot of us have lived in towns dependent on a nearby military base or a defense contractor. Some of us have had jobs there. Some of us have been tempted to join the military ourselves in order to delay marriage, to work with other women or to get the kind of job training that is so hard for women to acquire in the civilian sector. Each of these experiences is as valuable for understanding how and why militaries work the way they do as being able to distinguish between a Cruise and Pershing missile. Maybe we can redefine what it means to do 'military research'. Perhaps our new definition will prompt us to listen to more women from more countries tell *their* 'war stories'.

In addition to all the people who helped me think through the ideas that appeared in the first edition of this book, I am grateful to Philippa Brewster for imagining that there was a need to bring out a new edition. Candida Lacey brought her skill and humor to its redesign. And in the five years since it first appeared I have been helped in my ongoing education about the militarization of women's lives by Joni Seager, Sister Soledad Perpinan, Eva Isaksson, Ruth Pierson, Harold Jordan, Ed Dorn, Daryl Wood, Margaret Bluman, Julie Wheelright, Ann Holder, Carolyn Becraft, Lucie Richardson, Elisabetta Addis, Lois Wasserpring, Saralee Hamilton, Julia Perez, Kristin Brooks, Jennifer Schirmer, Lauran Schultz, and the students at Clark University who took part with me in women's studies seminars. Perhaps most of all, I have been educated by my good and courageous friend, Ximena Bunster, who is working with other Chilean women to demilitarize their country. It is to Ximena that I dedicate this new introduction.

Notes

Introduction

1. One of the most perceptive descriptions of the ways men working as military security intellectuals are using language to distance themselves from the destructive realities of their enterprise is: Carol Cohn, 'Sex and Death in the Rational World of Defense Intellectuals,' in Jean Bethke Elshtain and Shiela Tobias, eds., *Women, Militarism and War: Essays in History, Politics and Social Theory*, Totowa, New Jersey, Roman and Littlefield, 1988.
2. Two sensitive and disturbing feminist descriptions of precisely how some women – in Nazi Germany and in Pinochet's Chile – have been coopted into active support of militaristic regimes are: Claudia Koonz, *Mothers in the Fatherland*, New York, St. Martin's Press, 1987; Ximena Bunster, 'Watch Out for the Little Nazi Man That All of Us Have Inside: The Mobilization and Demobilization of Women in Militarized Chile,' *Women's Studies International Forum*, vol. 11, no. 5, 1988.
3. Papers from the Helsinki conference are published in: Eva Isaksson, ed., *Women and the Military System*, Brighton, England, Wheatsheaf Books and New York, St Martin's Press, 1988.
4. Two of the best sources for the latest information on women in the US military are: Women and the Military Project, Women's Equity Action League, 1250 I Street N.W., Suite 305, Washington, DC, 20005; Defense Advisory Committee on Women in the Services (DACOWITS), Department of Defense, The Pentagon, Washington, DC. A good overview of trends between 1952–1976, appears in Judith Stiehm's 'The Generations of US Enlisted Women,' *Signs*, vol. 11, no. 1, Autumn, 1985, pp. 155–168. See also Stiehm's 'Women's Biology and the U.S. Military,' in Virginia Sapiro, ed., *Women, Biology and Public Policy*, Beverly Hills, Sage Publications, 1985, pp. 205–233.
5. Public Information Office, International Military Staff, NATO Headquarters, 1110 Brussels, Belgium, correspondence, November, 1987.
6. First-hand accounts of experiences by women of color and white women veterans of the American military are included in: Julia Perez, 'Women Veterans Speak Out at First Women in the

Military Conference,' *Minerva, Quarterly Report on Women and the Military*, Summer, 1987, pp. 44–59. A video film including many of these Black, Asian, Jewish, Latina, Native American and white women veterans is: 'Invisible Force,' obtainable from Julia Perez, the Joiner Center, University of Massachusetts, Harbor Campus, Boston, MA, 02125, USA. Julia Perez is currently producing a second video film, 'Sisters in Arms,' which explores Black women's experiences in the US military from the 1940s through the 1980s. The experiences of American Women who are veterans of military and Red Cross service in Vietnam are recounted in Katherine Marshall's *In the Combat Zone: An Oral History of American Women in Vietnam*, Boston, Little, Brown and Company, 1987.

7. Ruth Pierson, *'They're Still Women After All': The Second World War and Canadian Womanhood*, Toronto, McClelland and Stewart, 1986.
8. Daryl Wood, 'Women and the Military,' *Kinesis*, July/August, 1985, p. 8; Pat Spencer, *The Body Politic*, No. 113, April, 1985, p. 9 and p. 14; Heather Robertson, 'A Lesbian Ordeal,' *Saturday Night*, August, 1986, pp. 22–25. American women describe some of their experiences with military accusations of lesbianism in the video 'Invisible Force,' *op. cit.* and in 'False Note,' a true story that appears in a new anti-militarism comic, *Real War Stories*, issue No. 1, published by Eclipse Comics, PO Box 1099, Forestville, CA 95436, USA.
9. For a world map that graphically reveals many countries' varying policies towards conscripting women and towards excluding them from posts considered to be 'combat,' see: Joni Seager and Ann Olson, *Women in the World: An International Atlas*, London, Pan Books; New York, Simon and Schuster and Toronto, Collins, 1986, map no. 32. Canadian military figures come from the Director of Information Services, National Defence Headquarters, Ottawa, Canada, correspondence, December, 1987. By early 1988, the Canadian military had opened 100 of its 135 occupational posts to women. The Canadian Air Force had opened all posts to women with the exception of helicopter pilot posts aboard naval destroyers. David Francis, 'Canada is Looking for a Few Good Women – To Take Combat Roles,' *Christian Science Monitor*, February 25, 1988.

   The source of the British figures is Ministry of Defence, 'Defence Manpower Strengths,' April 1, 1987, supplied by the British Information Service, Washington, DC, November, 1987. For a brief discussion of the experiences of Black British men in the British army, see John Sweeney, 'The Thin Black Line,' *Observer Magazine*, London, January 24, 1988. A new historical account of relations between Black American soldiers and white

British women in Britain during World War II increases our awareness of the uneasy relationships between racism, military alliances and sexuality: Graham Smith, *When Jim Crow Met John Bull*, London, I. B. Tauris and Co, Ltd, and New York, St Martin's Press, 1988.

10. 'Distribution of Active Duty Forces: September, 1987,' US Department of Defense, Washington, DC. Reports on American military manpower distribution by gender and ethnicity are issued twice annually and may be obtained from the Defense Management Data Center, Department of Defense, Washington, DC. Also useful is *Military Women in the Department of Defense*, volume 5, Office of the Secretary of Defense, Department of Defense, Washington, DC, July, 1987.
11. A report on the meeting held by the Joint Center for Political Studies, a Washington-based Black research organization, can be found in James R. Daugherty, 'Black Women in the Military,' *Focus*, vol. 13, no. 7, July, 1985, p. 3. More information can be obtained from Edwin Dorn, director of the JCPS project on Blacks in the military, 1301 Pennsylvania Ave., N.W., Suite 400, Washington, DC, 20004. The Women in the Military Project of the Women's Equity Action League (see address above) also monitors participation of Black women and other women of color in the military. In its 'Minority Women in the Military' fact sheet, WEAL reports that 1) 'Black women are less likely to leave the services before the end of their enlistment term and are more likely to sign up for additional service than any other group, including white men;' 2) 'Black women, more often than white women or black men, occupy the five lowest pay/rank grades, and Black women officers are concentrated in lower ranking administrative positions;' and 3) 'Minority women who are veterans are 1.4 times more likely to be in a higher income category – defined as earnings of $300 per week or more – than non-veteran minority women in the general population.' Regarding this last figure, it is important to note that US military only accepts women who have secondary school diplomas. Thus it may be the very pool from which the military obtains its Black women volunteers, rather than what Black women gain from their military service, that explains this difference. Other articles on Black women in the US military include: Cynthia Enloe and Harold Jordan, 'Invisible Soldiers of the 80's: Black Women in the Military,' *Militarism Resource Project Newsletter*, Philadelphia, PA., vol. 1, no. 3, Spring, 1985, pp. 4–5; Cynthia Enloe, 'Black Women in the Military,' *Sojourner*, Boston, MA, Nov., 1985, pp. 15–16. Julia Perez, of University of Massachusetts, Boston, is writing a book based on oral histories of Black women veterans.

12. Linda Forcey includes interviews with American women who describe their hopes and ambivalences in turning to the military to help them make their sons grow up in her book *Mothers of Sons*, New York, Praeger Publishers, 1987, pp. 117–135. Mary Wertsch's interviews with women and men who have grown up with fathers serving in the US military and mothers coping with military family life will appear in her book, *Military Brats: Legacies of Childhood Inside the Fortress*, forthcoming. Mary Wertsch is including a chapter devoted to children of color who have grown up in military families; she can be contacted c/o Department of Psychology, Clark University, Worcester, Massachusetts. Feminists in Iran, Israel, Zimbabwe, Japan, Italy and other countries reveal how presumptions about marriage and femininity are sometimes strained and sometimes reentrenched by militarizing governments in a special issue on 'Women and Militarism,' of the magazine *Connexions*, no. 11, Winter, 1984.
13. 'Army Dependents: Relatives Come Cheaper,' *The Economist*, January 23, 1988, p. 56. A new play explores tensions between women in the paternalistic world that British military wives inhabit: *The Last Waltz*, by Gillian Richmond, performed at the Soho Poly Theater, London, November, 1986. An interview with Gillian Richmond, herself an 'army brat,' appeared in *The Guardian*, November 19, 1986. Further information about *The Last Waltz* can be obtained from Valerie Hoskins, Jeremy Conway Ltd, Eagle House, 109 Jermyn Street, London SW1Y 6HB, England. Another recent play portraying the lives of British Army wives – and widows – after the Falklands War is *Taken Out* by Greg Cullen, directed by Sue Glanville and performed at the Drill Hall theater, London, 1986. An interview with Sue Glanville appears in *Women's Review*, no. 16, 1986, pp. 40–41. A novel describing what it was like to become a military wife to a man serving on the homefront in Britain during World War II recently has been reissued: Betty Miller, *On the Side of the Angels*, London, Virago, 1985.
14. Carolyn Becraft, Director of the Women and the Military Project of the Women's Equity Action League, testimony before the US House of Representatives Armed Services Committee's Subcommittee on Military Personnel and Compensation, Washington, DC, October 1, 1987. In March, 1988, the US Air Force announced a new policy holding that 'military wives' decisions to work outside the home are none of the service's business,' and that a spouse's job choices should have no bearing on the promotion criteria applied to the service member. Wives' advocates welcomed the new policy, though some voiced skepticism about its enforcement in practice. *New York Times*, March 20, 1988.

15. *loc. cit.* For more information on the status of ex-wives of US military personnel, contact Lois Jones, National Action for Former Military Wives, 1700 Legion Drive, Winter Park, FL 32789, USA.
16. I'm indebted to Lucie Richardson for sending materials giving the background to her court suit and to the formation of OSSOMM. For more information concerning the group's activities, contact Lucie Richardson, c/o the Law School, Queens University, Hamilton, Ontario, Canada.
17. I've tried to think about the culturally different ways in which men's senses of 'masculinity' becomes militarized in: 'Beyond "Rambo": Women and the Varieties of Militarized Masculinity,' in Eva Isaksson, ed., *op. cit.*; and 'Beyond Steve Canyon and Rambo: Toward Feminist Histories of Militarized Masculinity,' in John Gillis, editor, *The Militarization of the World*, New Brunswick, New Jersey, Rutgers University Press, 1988.
18. Sara Miles, 'The Real War: Low-Intensity Conflict in Central America,' *NACLA Report on the Americas*, vol. 20, no. 2, April/May, 1986, pp. 17–48; Michael T. Klare and Peter Kornbluh, eds., *Low Intensity Warfare*, New York, Pantheon, 1987; Enrique Delacruz, Aida Jordan and Jorge Emmanuel, *Death Squads in the Philippines*, PO Box 170219, San Francisco, CA 94117, Alliance for Philippine Concerns, September, 1987.
19. Sonia Alvarez, *Politicizing Gender and Engendering Democracy: Comparative Perspectives on Women in the Brazilian Transition to Democracy*, Boulder, Colorado, Westview Press, forthcoming; Sonia Alvarez, 'A Feminist Success Story? Women's Movements and Gender Politics in the Brazilian Transition,' in Jane Jacquette, ed., *Women, Feminism and Transitions to Democracy*, Boston, Allen and Unwin, forthcoming.
20. 'Women Victims of Militarization,' *Gabriela Women's Update*, vol. 3, no. 7, August–September, 1987, p. 6. See also Gabriela, 'The Women's Movement and the Militarization Issue,' *Proceedings*, Fourth Annual Conference, March, 1987. For further information on Gabriela's work on militarization, contact Gabriela National Office, PO Box 4386, Manila 2800, Philippines.
21. Ximena Bunster, 'Surviving Beyond Fear: Women and Torture in Latin America,' in June Nash and Helen Safa, eds., *Women and Change in Latin America*, South Hadley, MA, Bergin and Garvey Publishers, 1986, pp. 297–325; Sister Mary John Mananzan, chair of Gabriela, informal talk, Cambridge, MA, June 29, 1987; Jennifer Schirmer, Women's Studies Program, Wellesley College, in discussion of her forthcoming publication on women and the doctrine of national security; Cynthia Enloe, 'Bananas, Bases and Patriarchy,' *Radical America*, vol. 19, no. 4,

July–August, 1985, pp. 17–23 and reprinted in *Trouble and Strife*, no. 9, 1986, and in Elshtain and Tobias, eds., *op. cit.*.
22. Paul Little, 'Blazing a Road to Nowhere,' *In These Times*, January 13, 1986, pp. 14–15.
23. James Brooke, 'AIDS Danger: Africa Seems of Two Minds,' *New York Times*, January 4, 1987. A report implying a close relationship between the spread of AIDS and Ugandan soldiers and prostitutes: Mary Anne Fitzgerald, 'Unrest "spreads" Aids in Uganda,' *The Independent*, London, January 31, 1987.
24. NARMIC, *Militarization, Central America and the US Role*, Philadelphia, American Friends Service Committee, 1987, p. 6.
25. Roxanne Pastore, 'Militarization of Women in Honduras', talk given at Roxbury Community College, Boston, June 12, 1986. Roxanne Pastore's work can be obtained through the Honduras Information Center, 1 Summer Street, Somerville, MA 02143.
26. Lucy Komisar, 'White Slavery in Honduras?' *Honduras Update*, vol. 3, no. 9, June, 1985. *Honduras Update* is a publication of the Honduras Information Center.
27. Sandra Avila and Luis Sierra, 'US and Contra Troops in Honduras: Programmed Death,' *Resist Newsletter*, May, 1987, reprinted from *Honduras Update*, March, 1987.
28. Alan Gottlieb, 'The US Presence in Honduras and the Politics of Prostitution,' *In These Times*, September 16, 1987, p. 2. For a description of the problems facing American women soldiers stationed in Honduras, see Charles C. Moskos, 'Female GIs in the Field,' *Society*, vol. 22, no. 6, September/October, 1985, pp. 28–33.
29. Gabriela Network on Violence Against Women, 'AIDS is Here! Fight AIDS!' in Isis, *Women's World*, no. 14, 1987, p. 37–38.
30. *Ibid.* p. 38. Starting April 18, 1988, according to the Philippines Immigration Commissioner, all American military personnel and all foreign sailors arriving in the Philippines will be required to present certificates showing that they are free of AIDS: *Christian Science Monitor*, February 18, 1988.
31. Campaign Against Military Prostitution, Third World Movement Against the Exploitation of Women, PO Box SM–366, Manila, Philippines. Philippines feminists are making the links theoretically and organizationally between military prostitution and tourism prostitution and in so doing are forming alliances with Japanese feminists. See, for instance, Tono Haruhi, Tsukamoto and Iyori Naoko, 'For a Song', *Trouble and Strife*, no. 12, Winter, 1987, pp. 10–15; *Cast the First Stone*, joint publication of the Women's Desk of the World Council of Churches and the National Council of Churches in the Philippines, Quezon City, the Philippines, 1987. New historical accounts that compare British and American wartime anti-VD

campaigns' criminalization of women thought to be prostitutes and the current politics surrounding AIDS and prostitution include: Barbara Meil Hobson, *Uneasy Virtue: The Politics of Prostitution and the American Reform Tradition*, New York, Basic Books, 1988; Allan M. Brandt, *No Magic Bullet: A Social History of Venereal Disease in the United States Since 1880*, New York and Oxford, Oxford University Press, 1987.

1. The Military Needs Camp Followers

> As woman was created to be a helpmate to man, so women are great helpers to armies, to their husbands, especially those of the lower conditions; neither should they be rashly banished out of armies; sent away, they may be sometimes for weighty considerations...[1]

Looking back on his years of European military campaigning, Sir James Turner offered the above advice in 1683. Women have been of concern—as a threat, an annoyance, a useful resource—to military men for centuries.

Military men have sought to control women in order to achieve military goals. Yet, as Sir James Turner's ruminations suggest, men commanding military forces have been uncertain whether they are better off exerting that control directly or indirectly. Should women (as morale boosting wives, reserve labour, prostitutes) be made integral cogs of the military machine, 'on base'? Or will the military's masculine image, mobility and customary ways of operating be better protected by devising less direct structures of control, keeping women available but 'off base'?

Long before the military had women's corps, married quarters, VD classes and legions of civilian clerical workers, they had women 'in tow'. In the mid-seventeenth century, one European army was reported to have had 40,000 male soldiers and '100,000 soldiers' wives, whores, man servants, maids, and other camp followers'.[2]

'Camp followers' are kept ideologically marginal to the essential function of militaries—combat. The archetypal image of the camp follower is a woman outcast from society, poor but tenacious, eking out a livelihood by preying on unfortunate soldiers. She is a woman intruding in a 'man's world'. Skirts dragging in the battlefield mud, she tags along behind the troops, selling her wares or her body, probably at unfair prices. If by chance she falls in love with a soldier, she is destined to be abandoned or widowed.

According to this classic formulation, women camp followers were barely tolerated by military commanders. So long as they provided supplies and services that the military didn't want to bother with itself, so long as they kept rank and file men satisfied enough not to desert, they were allowed to follow the armies from battle to battle. But as soon as a commander decided that they were slowing down the march or tainting his troops' reputation as an efficient fighting force, camp followers were summarily purged.

The periodic purge required the discrediting of women who followed and serviced the troops, for it was far easier for commanders to send the women out of camp if they could be portrayed as rootless, promiscuous, parasitic and generally a drag on the military's discipline and battle readiness. 'Camp follower' was commonly equated with whore. The very fact that she was a woman who allegedly *chose* to make her life among 'rough' men was presumed proof enough of her loose character. So, whatever useful functions they might temporarily provide the military, a commander who wanted to rid himself of the women in his trains could claim that camp followers were fundamentally nothing more than whores. Furthermore, they could be replaced by other women when the need again arose. (In the late twentieth century women mobilised to serve the military's needs are still vulnerable to the stereotype of camp follower—whore—no matter how the professional their formal position in the military. Men in the US Air Force jokingly translate WAF—Women's Air Force—as 'Women All Fuck'.)

Even when they were not driven out of camp, women who followed and serviced armies were reminded of their ideologically marginal and despised position within the military pecking order by the punishments imposed on the grounds that they were 'unruly'. Camp followers were not army regulars, but they were thought of as within reach of officers' authority. One military historian described a typical punishment to which camp followers and other marginal people in camp were subject in Britain's seventeenth-century army:

> In garrisons where martial law prevails, the followers of an army are liable to the military punishments; one formerly very common, for trifling offenses, commited by petit sutlers [traders in food, usually women], Jews, brawling women and such-like persons, was the whirligig; this was a kind of circular wooden cage, which turned on a pivot; and when set in motion, whirled around with such an amazing velocity that the delinquent became extremely sick, and commonly emptied his or her body through every aperture.[3]

Armies travel on their stomachs

Women travelling with an army (unless she travelled disguised as a man) ran the risk of being disciplined or disparaged as a common whore. In reality, these thousands of women were soldiers' wives, cooks, provisioners, laundresses, and nurses. Sometimes they served in all of these roles simultaneously. When they weren't being reduced verbally or physically to the status of prostitutes, camp followers were performing tasks that any large military force needs but wants to keep ideologically peripheral to its combat function and often tries to avoid paying for directly. Sir James Turner, in cautioning his fellow officers not to be too quick to rid themselves of women, reminded them that camp followers:

> provide, buy and dress their husbands' meats, when their husbands are on duty or newly come from it; they bring in fuel for fire; a soldier's wife may be helpful to others, and gain money to her husband and herself, especially they are useful in camp and leaguers, being permitted (which could not be refused them) to go some miles from the camp to buy victuals and other necessaries.[4]

Individual male soldiers also recognised that women could ease their hardships. A seventeenth-century soldier with a wife in camp who proved a skilled sutler, cook and nurse was envied by the other soldiers. If the husband was killed, his comrades vied to gain her services for themselves.

> I should have mentioned that one of my comrades was married to a pretty Scotchwoman, who lived in camp with him, and got a good deal of money by keeping a scuttling tent for the officers. The man was killed. In such a situation, the woman must not remain a widow and with such qualifications, she was a prize to any man. Another comrade said to me, 'I advise you to marry Kate Keith. If you won't, I will. But there's no time to be lost, for she'll have plenty of offers.'
>
> I took a few hours to consider of it, and determined upon soliciting the hands of Kate Keith... The little black-eyed Scotchwoman accompanied me to the chaplain of the regiment the second day after her husband had fallen.[5]

Some women become totally dependent on the military. At the end of the Thirty Years War, one camp follower asked plaintively: 'I was born in war; I have no home, no country, no friends; war is all my wealth and now whither will I go?'[6]

Today's military forces are such complex organisations administratively and technologically that they demand ever greater support services. Napoleon is routinely quoted as observing that armies travel on their stomachs. But this scarely captures the range of support services commanders and their government superiors require to keep their forces prepared for battle. First, they need *troops*: men, preferably, and men from the class, ethnic and racial groups most trusted by the government.[7] But many men will not stay in the military if they cannot marry and/or otherwise have ready sexual access to women. Women, therefore, must somehow be brought under sufficient military control so as to enlist thousands of raw male recruits and keep seasoned veterans.

Second, troops must be kept healthy, or at least well enough to follow their officers' orders. They must have their clothes washed, their wounds bandaged, their spirits mended so they can return to battle. Women, stereotyped as uniquely fitted to perform these sanitary and caring tasks because of their innately 'sympathetic' natures and housekeeping proclivities, provide the military with a useful pool of cheap labour, often unpaid if it can be incorporated into the expected role of 'military wife'.[8]

Soldiers' lives are hard. Even away from the dangers of the battlefield, they are subject to and possibly made discontented by hierarchical command structures and perpetual uprooting. Yet commanders need men who will soldier with a sense of fervour and a willingness to sacrifice. 'Morale' preoccupies officers, and a good commander is one who can create 'good morale' in the ranks. To portray the soldier's regiment as a 'family' which cares for him and to whom he owes loyalty is one solution. But without women, this is a difficult enterprise. If women can be made to play the role of wives, daughters, mothers, and 'sweethearts', waving their men off to war, writing them letters of encouragement and devotion in the field, reminding them that women's and children's safety depends on men's bravery, *then* women can be an invaluable resource to commanders.

At times, some women are deliberately exploited by the military for the sake, allegedly, of protecting other women (or other women as the valued possessions of men). Thus Sancho de Londono, a Spanish officer, explained in 1589 how prostitutes were integrally necessary to well-run militaries:

> For, accepting the fact that well organized states allow such persons (prostitutes/camp followers) in order to avoid worse disorders, in no state is it as necessary to allow them as in this one of free, strong and vigorous men, who might otherwise commit crimes against the local people, molesting their daughters, sisters, and wives.[9]

Finally, women can provide a 'reserve army of labour' for military men and their civilian allies. So long as women are kept on the margins of the civilian waged labour force, they can serve as a pool of underused, readily available labour when a war necessitates massive male conscription, with its resultant drain of labour from fields, factories, and offices. Best of all in the eyes of military planners, these reserve labourers won't jeopardise governmental post-war planning: being women, people whose 'natural' role is to supply free labour within the household, they will passively accept the post-war need to demobilise them in order to make way for returning male soldiers who will expect to get their jobs back in return for having served their government and their country.

All of these support services, however, can be provided to the military by women *only* if the military can be assured of sufficient control over women. The key to that control is their defining of women as creatures marginal to the military's core identity, no matter how crucial in reality are the services they perform (and the symbolism they provide) to the smooth operations of the military. When women begin to act in their own interests, military commanders suspect that their control is slipping, there begins a search for alternatives. But some especially astute military commanders have tried to continue using women, even at a time when women are self-consciously striving for autonomy. They have tried to camouflage women's service to the military as women's *liberation*.

Why should a feminist study the military?

The life of a camp follower does not seem strikingly different from the life of any woman in a male-dominated society: she is financially dependent on men; her labour is used but she does not control it or reap its rewards; she is expected to be nurturing and self-sacrificing; but if she steps out of line, she can be labelled a 'common whore' and marginalised even further.

To demystify the military and to uncover all the ways it resembles the rest of a society in which being male carries power and privilege makes it possible for women, normally excluded from military affairs, to shed light on aspects of the military ordinarily overlooked. Any woman, then, who is working to dissect and explain the myths and reality of family structures, the way sexuality is constructed or the way women's labour has been exploited can contribute to the analysis of the military.

As the following chapters reveal, the military has employed a variety of notions of 'the family' in order to control both the men and the women it needs to achieve its goals. Likewise, as the experience of camp followers demonstrates, the military relies on particular idea of sexuality to mould women and men into the kind of organisation it needs, and military elites have been as self-conscious as any factory manager about designing and redesigning sexual divisions of labour. Debates in the media and legislatures over just what constitutes 'combat' and the 'front'—as versus 'support' and the 'rear'—are nothing less than arguments over how to make use of women's labour without violating popular notions of femininity, masculinity and the social order itself.

A common assumption has made the armed forces almost immune to feminist investigation. That assumption is that the military, even more than other patriarchal institutions, is a *male* preserve, run by men and for men according to masculine ideas and relying solely on *man* power. The military has been presented to women as inaccessible, a secret order that doesn't *need* women (except as sweethearts, pin-ups or prostitutes). The great majority of women have had no first-hand experience inside the military. The very language of military life uses a vocabulary that is foreign to most women.

In contrast, women *have* had access to the ideology of *militarism*. Though 'the military' as an organisation has been relatively closed to women, 'militarism' as an ideology (a set of beliefs and values) has been vulnerable to women's critique because it presumes a concept of 'masculinity' that only makes sense if supported by the complementary concept of 'femininity'.

Women in groups such as Britain's Women Opposed to the Nuclear Threat (WONT) and the Women's Peace Camp at Greenham Common, and Women's Pentagon Action in America have deliberately devised actions that have avoided top-down relationships, maximised people's spontaneous participation and drawn connections between militarism and women's ordinary lives. They have done this because they saw the qualities of equality, spontaneity and connectedness as the opposites of the quintessential characteristics of both patriarchy and of militarism.[10]

When 500 Australian women defied police directives and marched through Canberra on ANZAC Day in 1982, 'in memory of all women of all countries in all wars who were raped', they were intent on revealing and rejecting one of the underlying assumptions of militarism: that societies must be composed of the dominant and the subordinate and that conquest 'civilises'.[11]

Women in Portsmouth, England, who leafleted against the Falklands war emphasised the same connection, a factor they understood to be at the heart of militarism. Women who sprayed anti-rape slogans on walls in this navy town were subject to increased vigilance by the police during the war. Did the police suspect that anti-rape activism might be part of a scheme to subvert Britain's war effort?[12] At almost the same time, in Boston, USA, women were arguing within the local disarmament movement that militarism couldn't be fully understood if links with the issues of abortion and sexual harassment were not made. The underlying forces that have created the arms race, they explained, would continue to exist so long as the objectification of women and the control over women's bodies is deemed a male prerogative and a testimony to 'manhood'.[13]

So feminists have argued a particular position on militarism, the ideology. But, the military as an *institution*, with its own history, its own resources and bureaucratic rivalries, its peculiar organisational dilemmas and contradictions, often escapes women's analytical scrutiny. This is due partly to defence officials' deliberately technocratic and bureaucratic obfuscation. An added obstacle placed on women's path is the penchant of so many men within *anti*-militarism groups to adopt precisely the same sort of technical, abstract, off-putting terms of reference as defence experts themselves—as if they have to prove their own 'manhood' by talking the military's language.

The military in the 1980s is commonly portrayed as a weapons-laden behemoth: it is what it launches. This narrow concept of the military makes it all the more impenetrable for women (and for most men, too). The portrayal is inaccurate as well. Revealing the military to be 'just one more patriarchal institution' is healthy, for it strips the military of its 'high tech' protective camouflage. Even the military organisations of the most advanced industrial societies depend on man and woman power.

The nuclear age has *not* made military worries about how to recruit and keep quality 'manpower' redundant. The concerns voiced by Sir James Turner in 1683, quoted at the beginning of this chapter, and the fears prompting officers to employ the tortuous whirligig, still plague military commanders and their political supporters. They worry about birth rates, masculinity, unemployment trends, racial tension, and the women's movement at the same time as they think about the 'state of the art' in guided missiles.

Examining officers' worries allows us to learn a great deal about the military as an institution. In turn, what we learn from both examining the military's manpower policies and exploring the experience of women who have coped with those policies can build a bridge to what feminists are already revealing about the ingredients and implications of the ideology of militarism. The military as an institution and militarism as an ideology are distinct phenomena, but women's lives are deeply affected by their interaction and can, indeed, begin to show just *how* the two interact.

Women are being used by militaries to solve their nagging problems of manpower availability, quality, health, morale and 'readiness'. This book seeks to expose the character and operations of the military as an institution, not by concentrating on the usual topic—male soldiers—but by focusing on those women most subject to military exploitation: military prostitutes, military wives, military nurses, women soldiers, women defence industry workers and 'civilianised' defence workers. Looking at these women, who straddle military and civilian positions, shows how more and more of us are becoming 'militarised'. Militarisation can be defined as a process with both a material and an ideological dimension. In the material sense it encompasses the gradual encroachment of the military institution into the civilian arena —for example, if a textiles plant becomes dependent on military contracts for its survival, then its workers have become militarised, ultimately dependent on the military for their livelihoods. Likewise, if the state begins to organise schemes to send unemployed youngsters on military 'adventure' holidays run by the armed forces, the military institution has become a solution to the civil problems associated with youth unemployment. Almost imperceptibly, the ability of society to deal with its civil responsibilities becomes dependent on military intervention.

The ideological dimension is obviously closely linked to this. What we are looking at here is the degree to which such developments are acceptable to the populace, and become seen as 'common-sense' solutions to civil problems, such as in the case of army intervention to restore services in public sector strikes. If women who seek freedom from traditional sex roles begin to see military decisions to recruit women soldiers as triumphs for women's liberation, then they too have become open to ideological militarisation.

Different societies at different times experience different levels of militarisation. Nazi Germany during the 1930s is an obvious case, where more and more civil institutions merged with or become dependent on the military, supported by an ideological *militarism* which identified manhood with soldiering and defined a woman's role as the mother of soldiers. But there is a much less obvious kind of militarism which is happening in many 'peacetime' societies today; and this is what this book describes.

This book argues that by looking at women we can reveal, not only the spreading institutional encroachment of the military, but also the processes by which that spread becomes publicly legitimised. Equally important, scrutinising the ideological difficulties armed forces have in coping with women can reveal contradictions, gaps and cracks in the militarising process into which a politics of resistance can intervene.

More than just one more patriarchal institution

Women wiring the electronic circuitry of guided missiles have a lot in common with a woman working on the wiring of cars destined for civilian sales lots. Each group consists largely of women who know about dead-end jobs, lack of day care, and husbands who think of their own jobs as naturally more important than their wives' jobs. Similarly, women who have joined the army to acquire training as mechanics only to find themselves sexually harassed by their supervising officers can identify with women secretaries who feel pressured to go out to lunch, or be 'friendly' with their male bosses in order to insure a pay rise. In a multitude of ways, all of which affect women, the military resembles other patriarchal institutions. On the other hand, the military is distinctive, and the experiences women have had in coping with military efforts to use them demand special attention.

Perhaps most important is the military's intimate relationship with the state—with the central government and the laws and ideologies which sustain its authority. No other public or private institution comes so close to being the *sine qua non* of a state. Some states (Costa Rica, Japan), have made token attempts at disestablishing their armed forces; but in each instance, under different guises, military institutions have re-emerged (a very powerful one in the case of Japan).[14] The claim that a state isn't a genuine state unless it has its own instrument of organised coercion—an army—carries a lot of weight, even in a society not usually considered highly militaristic.

The close identification of the military to the state thus gives the military a kind of influence and privilege rarely enjoyed by a large corporation or a Ministry of Health. This special status permits the military to exercise powers denied to other institutions. For instance, in formulating Britain's 1967 Sexual Offences Act the Parliament decriminalised adult male homosexuality in all areas of British life but exempted the military. Likewise, the US Supreme Court has repeatedly shied away from imposing those civil liberty requirements on the military that it demands of the rest of American society.

The military can use this extraordinary status in relation to the state to define 'national security'. This concept—'national security'—in turn, has been used to define the 'social order' supposedly necessary to ensure that national security. In this circular process, 'national security' can come to mean not only the protection of the state and its citizens from external foes but, perhaps even primarily, the maintenance of the social order. The social order includes in its turn those gender definitions which bolster ideological militarism. It follows naturally that, in 1980, American senators drafting the oppressive Family Protection Act went to the Defense Department first to get a stamp of approval even before submitting their bill to Congress.

Out of this same expansive concern for the social requisites of 'national security', military professionals and defence bureaucrats keep track of demographic trends, worrying not only about overall birth rate declines, but about high birth rates among those ethnic groups that the current government does not trust. Racism and militarism become mutually supportive in such a 'national security state'. In the process the lives of all women are militarised.

Consequently, the behaviour of the military as an institution —in particular, how it treats women and women's own capacity to react to military control—cannot be simply deduced from our studies of and experiences with other patriarchical institutions such as the family, church or business firm. Those analyses do give women an invaluable vantage point from which to pose questions, make connections, see hidden implications. But the military's use of its privileged status within the state has to be taken into explicit account if we are to fully understand how it can penetrate women's lives.

Few other institutions can command such vast financial, labour, and material resources as the military. With its expanding budgetary appetite, the military can distort a country's whole public spending structure—as well as its trade relations with foreign countries. Public services intended to reduce society's economic inequalities are cut when military funding proposals outstrip the government's current revenues. Women are especially vulnerable to economic recessions; they are usually the first to be laid off or cut to part-time and the first affected by service and welfare cuts. Some economically vulnerable women may even enlist in the military in order to compensate for the loss of jobs and economic security resulting from spiralling military spending. This connection may help explain why, by 1981, 42 per cent of all enlisted women in the US army were *black* women.[15]

Patriarchy and militarism

The military plays a special role in the ideological structure of patriarchy because the notion of 'combat' plays such a central role in the construction of concepts of 'manhood' and justifications of the superiority of maleness in the social order. In reality, of course, to be a soldier of the state means to be subservient, obedient and almost totally dependent. But that mundane reality is hidden behind a potent myth: to be a soldier means possibly to experience 'combat', and only in combat lies the ultimate test of a man's masculinity.

'Combat', however, is usually left conveniently vague in definition. Are bomber pilots, a thousand feet above their helpless targets, engaged in manhood-testing combat? Is an infantryman, shooting in blind frustration at an enemy he can't see in the distant foliage, engaged in combat? Are sailors, sitting in front of a computer control panel aboard a ship in a war zone, doing something that qualifies as 'combat'?

The myth of combat dies hard. In today's highly technological societies, there is still the widespread presumption that a man is unproven in his manhood until he has engaged in *collective*, *violent*, *physical*, *struggle* against someone categorised as 'the enemy'—i.e. combat. For men to experience combat is supposed to be the chance to assert their control, their capacity for domination, conquest, even to gain immortality. Or this, at least, is what men are taught to believe as young boys:

> With all my terror of going to the Army—because I figured that I was the least likely person I knew to survive—there was something seductive about it, too. I was seduced by World War II and John Wayne movies...
>
> One way or another in every generation where there was a war, some male in the family on my father's side went to it. I never had it drilled into me, but there was a lot of attention paid to the past, a lot of not-so-subtle 'this is what a man does with his life' stuff when I was growing up...
>
> Even in the midst of the terror after the induction notice came, there was a part of me that would lie in bed at night and fantasise about what it would be like if I went.[16]

To be masculine is to be *not* feminine. To prove one's manhood is imagined to be to prove (to oneself and to other men and women) that one is not 'a woman'. Consequently, experiencing military combat and identifying with that institution totally committed to the conduct of combat is, for those men trying to fulfil society's expectations, part and parcel of displaying and proving their male identity and thus qualifying for the privileges it bestows.

Not all men, of course, grow up learning this catechism of militarism and patriarchy. An American draft resister of the 1960s recently interviewed one of the young men refusing to register under the new draft of the 1980s. The older man found his younger compatriot apparently far less worried about 'the John Wayne thing' than he had been.[17]

Drill sergeants, those masters of military socialisation and psychological manipulation, know that not all men come to basic training fully instilled with the belief that military performance is the key to their identities as men. But drill sergeants have not only military authority but the entire arsenal of patriarchal ideas to draw on in order to turn civilian male recruits into 'soldiers'. A drill sergeant is trying to devastate a resistant young man when he contemptuously shouts into his face, 'Woman!' To be prepared for combat, to soldier, a man must be stripped of all his 'feminine' attributes:

> 'The only way I'm going to get through this,' I said to myself, 'is to do everything right and not cause any trouble.' That's what I tried to do, but you can't help but get in trouble.
> 'What'd you do in college, boy? Learn to push a pencil?'
> 'Yessir.'
> 'What do you mean by that?'
> 'Nossir.'
> 'You like me, don't you, boy?'
> 'Yessir.'
> 'You're a queer for me.'
> 'Nossir.'
> 'You don't like me?'
> 'Yessir, nossir.'
> 'All right, ladies, you look like shit, so we're going to do a little PT now. Bends and mother-fuckers, many, many of them...'

> I saw a couple of guys snap. But by the time you get to the end of that whole process, you feel you're the baddest thing that ever walked the earth. When they call you Marine in graduation ceremony, there's tears in your eyes.[18]

Men are taught to have a stake in the military's essence—combat; it is supposedly a validation of their own male 'essence'. This is matched by the military's own institutional investment in being represented as society's bastion of male identity. That mutuality of interest between men and the military is a resource that few other institutions enjoy, even in a thoroughly patriarchical society.

This mutuality of interests has the effect of double-locking the door for women. Women—because they are *women*, not because they are nurses or wives or clerical workers—cannot qualify for entrance into the inner sanctum, combat. Furthermore, to *allow* women entrance into the essential core of the military would throw into confusion *all* men's certainty about their male identity and thus about their claim to privilege in the social order.

We know, of course, that women *are* at 'the front'; women do experience violent confrontation: as nurses in MASH units, as Vietnamese prostitutes flown in to service French troops in the forward trenches in the Indo-Chinese war, as civilian women whose homes are bombed from above or whose bodies are raped by rapidly advancing soldiers on the ground. And, yet, the military believes it must categorise women as peripheral, as serving safely at the 'rear' on the 'home front'. Women *as women* must be denied access to 'the front', to 'combat' so that men can claim a uniqueness and superiority that will justify their dominant position in the social order. And yet because women are in practice often exposed to frontline combat (see Chapters 4 and 5) the military has to constantly redefine 'the front' and 'combat' as wherever 'women' are not. Women may serve the military, but they can never be permitted to *be* the military. They must remain 'camp followers'.

Liberation militarised

British and American military recruiters, faced with many women's decision to have fewer children, are running short of their preferred white male recruits. Recruiters are responding in part by urging young women to seek enlistment into selected military posts as their path to 'first-class citizenship', to financial independence and upward mobility.

It is a cruel hoax: militarism and the military, those instruments of male ideological and physical domination, are riding on the backs of individual women's genuine desire to find ways to leave oppressive family environments, delay or avoid marriage, acquire 'unfeminine' skills. It also is a hoax in that it covers up the armed forces' continued capacity to *reverse* that campaign, to purge ('demobilise') women as soon as women appear to threaten military interests.

Are women running a battered women's shelter near an army base being militarised if they co-operate with base commanders in order to give military wives access to the shelter? What about a woman married to a man who enlists because he has no job prospects? Is a woman who goes through nursing school on a military scholarship being militarised? Is a woman supporting herself and her children by working as an electronics assembler being militarised when her employer wins a big government defence contract?

And does a militarised woman unavoidably become a 'camp follower'—used by the military only so long as it can control her and keep her on the periphery of the military's core identity? There are complex issues of autonomy and co-operation, independence and exploitation for all women in an era of military expansion.

When one learns how women are transformed into camp followers, it is tempting to insist angrily that women should *not* be marginalised: women should be allowed access to the power and privileges that flow from weapons industry jobs and combat experience. Yet such well-meaning efforts may only reinforce the military as an institution and militarism as an ideology. So we face a dilemma: putting our efforts into gaining equal opportunity for those women who are used most directly by the military only *perpetuates* the notion that the military is so central to the entire social order that it is only when women gain access to its core that they can hope to fulfil their hopes and aspirations.

The experience of women who have been militarised—women who have serviced the military as wives, prostitutes, nurses, soldiers, clerks and electronics assembly workers—suggest quite a different direction than suggested by the equal opportunity approach. All women are affected by the military's need to exploit and yet ideologically marginalise women. Women will remain society's 'camp followers' so long as the military as an institution and militarism as an ideology are widely accepted as guarantors of the social order. Loosening the now tightly tied knot between the military and the social order may be the goal that will do most to reverse women's oppression. But the knot cannot be untied unless we can understand just how dependent the military is on the oppression of women.

2. The Militarisation of Prostitution

Portsmouth is one of England's most thoroughly militarised towns. Britain's navy, army and air force all have bases here. The naval dockyard is Portsmouth's largest employer. Sir Reg Scott, Lord Mayor of Portsmouth, told reporters proudly,

> This is probably the most service-minded city in the country... We have all three services here and almost every person you meet has a relative in some connection with the services.[1]

In the spring of 1982 the media descended on Portsmouth to capture in print and on film the mobilisation of the 25,000-man Falklands task force. Overnight the media transformed most Portsmouth women into brave, patriotic and accepting military sweethearts and wives. Soon, as war in the South Atlantic escalated, these same women would be transformed again, this time into grief-stricken, abandoned military widows.

But meanwhile, out on the high seas, soldiers and sailors who had just waved farewell to their wives, standing brave and tearful on the Portsmouth quay, were being entertained by other visions of women, visions intended to make them perform as 'men' when they confronted the Argentinian foe. The British women's newspaper *Outwrite* (May 1982) reported that pornographic films were shown to the Falkland-bound troops. The films ranged from the officially sanctioned soft-porn *Emmanuelle* to the unofficially condoned hard-core pornographic video tapes. Male correspondents aboard the task force ships described some of the porno films shown to the soldiers and sailors as 'hair-raising'.

Back home in Portsmouth, other women were being portrayed not as brave or weeping, but as poor and idle. For centuries Portsmouth has been home for prostitutes dependent on armed forces. But with its military men embarked for the Falklands, Portsmouth, according to press reports, now had 'the appearance of a ghost town':

> It is haunted by stories of the nocturnal ladies of Union Street who reputedly have dropped their prices, but very little else, since their customers disappeared to the South Atlantic.[2]

The prostitutes of Union Street, the wives waving on the quay and the women displayed on the ships' screens knew very little of each other, but they were linked by British military policy on sexuality.

Sexuality and military policy

In Portsmouth—or any town long used as a military base—you can trace the history of the relationship between militarism, sexuality and military policy. Through wartime mobilisation, postwar demobilisation and peacetime 'preparedness', sexuality and militarism have intertwined. They have been constructed and reconstructed together. And *together* ideologies of militarism and sexuality have shaped the social order of garrison towns and the lives of women in those towns.

This chapter will explore militarised prostitution, not because military policy on prostitution is so much more significant than its policy on other sexual practices, but because the history of the military's preoccupation with and control of prostitution is so intimately related to military policy on rape, homosexuality, pornography and marriage. On the other hand, prostitution stands out because it is the sexual area (along with homosexuality, to be discussed in Chapter 5) over which military officials have tried to exert the most formal control. Finally, prostitution deserves special attention because, as we have seen, each time a military establishment reasserts its 'masculine' identity, it is inclined to do so by purging or marginalising women, and it does this by insinuating that women are essentially whores. The prostitute becomes the paradigm for the marginalised yet militarised woman, the camp follower.

The history of the various attempts to control the sexual behaviour of soldiers and the women whose bodies they buy has yet to be written. It is a history that is especially hard to chart because so many women who have been subjected to such control have lacked the resources—money, literacy, fluency in the language of military officialdom, access to other women's support—that have given some select women a 'voice' and a place in written histories.

Tracing military prostitution policies is made doubly difficult by the common practice of denying that there even is a formal policy on prostitution. Military elites frequently pass the 'messiest', the most 'unmilitary' responsibilities down the chain of command to the level of field officers, where politicians and citizen groups have great trouble monitoring and holding the military as a whole accountable.

Yet an absence of a written, centralised prostitution policy does not mean that a military elite has no policy. It may only suggest that the military is aware that its attitudes and practices surrounding sexuality are fraught with contradictions and political risks. Those risks can be strategically minimised by a combination of decentralised responsibility, informal decision making and official acknowledgement only of 'health issues'.

Under certain circumstances, and at rare times, however, militarised prostitution does become visible and does acquire the status of a public issue. The women of Portsmouth have lived through such a time.

The Contagious Diseases Act: using women to control soldiers
In 1857, William Acton described the daily life of a woman working (often to escape rural poverty) as a prostitute in an English military town such as Portsmouth:

> (Her) daily gains are not large. The generous and prodigal Son of Mars who had lately received his pay or his loot money will, perhaps, bestow half a crown in return for the favours granted to him, but the usual honorium is one

> shilling. [To obtain a] subsistence a woman must take home with her about eight or ten lovers every evening, returning to her haunts after each labour of love... to dance or drink beer until a fresh invitation to retire is received by her.[3]

Despite their poverty and dependence on tavern keepers and soldiers, however, the prostitutes were not totally without resources of their own:

> For help when her own resources fail her, she depends on the contributions of those of her companions, whom chance has for the time being more befriended; and in justice to these women, it must be said that they are always ready to afford each other this mutual assistance.[4]

After 1864, women compelled to earn shillings from sex with soldiers would need each other's support all the more. For in that year the British parliament passed the first Contagious Diseases Act. This was followed by the Acts of 1866 and 1869, so that eventually 18 towns were brought under the Acts. The government formula was this: the military could control male soldiers' sexuality by controlling the poor women with whom they were most likely to have sexual relations. The Acts applied only to women in specific navy ports and garrison towns such as Portsmouth. Local police and judges in those towns were given wide-sweeping powers to compel any woman vaguely suspected of prostitution to undergo a humiliating, painful genital examination. Any such woman could be officially categorised as 'prostitute' by the health and police authorities. Thereafter she would be subjected to surveillance, treatment and repeated medical examination. By contrast, the men who engaged in procurement and who ran the pubs that the women used were left outside the Acts' control.

Not only poor women but local police, health and court officials were militarised by the passing of the Contagious Diseases Acts: all were made to serve the needs of the Victorian British military.

The Contagious Diseases Acts were a post-war reform. Both the US and Britain the 1860s and 1870s witnessed efforts to digest the social 'lessons' of costly wars. In America, the emergence of 'General Joe Hooker's girls'—later to be known simply as 'hookers'—during the civil war led to a post-war flood of anti-vice literature, condemning 'loose women' who preyed on men.[5] In Britain, the Crimean War prompted many social commentators to conclude that the disappointing British military performance was due to the moral and physical degeneration of its male soldiery. To reverse this distressing trend, critics urged reforms covering all aspects of soldiers' lives: housing, health, recreation, punishment, diet, marriage—and sex.

Military reformers were especially worried about reconciling soldiers' presumed male 'sex drive' with military efficiency. Left uncontrolled, soldiers' 'natural sex drive' led them into a vicious downward spiral of indebtedness, drunkenness, illness and poverty. If men serving the military were allowed to satisfy their sexual needs with greedy, unclean women, so the reformers reasoned, they would continue to undermine the country's military capabilities:

> Clearly the [Victorian] army was fostering a certain kind of man and this had crucial implications for the treatment of the women with whom the men were permitted to consort. It would appear that the attitude was that military life called for a special kind of man reared away from the distractions of women... Women threatened a man's loyalty and vigour and were a financial drain.[6]

Military reformers in the 1860s and 70s presumed that, to be real men, soldiers had to satisfy their sexual 'appetites'. But military commanders saw each of the various outlets for sexual activity as potentially threatening to military effectiveness as they imagined it. For instance, commanders, especially those responsible for sending sailors on long sea voyages, feared homosexual relations between men confined to each other's company, frequently in close quarters. They imagined then, as now, that homosexuality somehow made men less able and willing to serve as effective fighting men. On the other hand, commanders were nervous when their male soldiers sought sexual relations with women, fearing that those women would dilute the men's loyalty to the military as well as ruin their health. So military officials faced a dilemma: how could they reconcile their ideas about soldiers' manly sexual appetites with their ideas about the impact of sexual relations on military operations?

While commanders believed that women drained men's military vigour, the justification for the Contagious Diseases Acts was narrowed initially to the deleterious effects of venereal disease on the military. In effect, VD became the stalking horse for a far more expansive military misogyny, which had many believers among Britain's civilian elite as well.

Prior to the 1864 Contagious Disease Act, however, British commanders had tried to prevent venereal disease in the ranks by compelling soldiers themselves to undergo genital examinations performed by a military medical officer. Under this system militarisation was relatively contained; military criteria and military objectives were imposed mostly on formal members of the military itself: officers, rank and file men and the military's own doctors. Married soldiers were exempted from the compulsory genital examinations. Commanders and military doctors reasoned that married rank and file soldiers—a very small proportion of all soldiers at the time, since marriage was presumed to divide a soldier's loyalties—were not as tempted by prostitution as were their bachelor comrades. Furthermore, in Victorian Britain married men generally were considered more respectable and thus deserved to be spared such humiliation as the examinations entailed.[7]

But this relatively confined control system proved ineffective. British officers, as *men*, seemed loath to inflict what they saw as a humiliating and degrading ordeal on other men.[8] Officers exercised clear authority over rank and file men, but the British military worked best when that authority could be cushioned by a mix of paternalism and male bonding.

The armed forces, especially as portrayed by heavy-handed enthusiasts of militarist ideals, may seem simplistically hierarchical. But in reality most military institutions are like that of Victorian Britain insofar as male bonding cuts through and often contradicts the more formal concepts of the chain of command and centralised control. On the other hand, most armies, including that of mid-nineteenth-century Britain, are built on a patriarchal bonding between men *as men*, cutting across class, ethnic and rank divisions. On the other hand, most are stratified by rank in a way that in fact accentuates those inequities of class and ethnicity that already exist in civilian society at large.

It is, therefore, the dynamic—and often tense—interaction between shared masculine identities and the division of rank, ethnicity, race and class in any military that shapes official policies toward soldiers' sexuality.[9] So, for instance, prior to the enactment of the Contagious Diseases Acts, rank and file men and men in the officer corps were expected to consort with different sorts of women, the former having relations with poor and marginalised women (in the colonies this meant 'native' women), whereas the latter would have relations with respectable (and white) women whom, in fact, they might marry.[10] As we will see later, this stratified notion of military men's sexual relations structured prostitution systems during wartime.

In Britain the Contagious Diseases Acts of 1864, 1866, and 1869, established a state policing system for *compulsory* periodical genital examinations of any woman that local police and judges suspected of being a prostitute. Josephine Butler was among the feminist leaders of the campaigns in the 1870s and 1880s to repeal the CD Acts. In the midst of what became one of nineteenth-century Britain's most explosive political controversies, Josephine Butler described how these military acts subjected women to men's control:

> I recall the bitter complaint of one of those poor women [picked up under the Acts]: 'It is *men*, *men*, *only men*, from the first to the last, that we have to do with! To please a man, I did wrong at first, then I was flung about from man to man. Men police lay hands on us. By men we are examined, handled, doctored... In the hospital, it is a man again who makes prayers and reads the Bible for us. We are had up before magistrates who are men, and we never get out of the hands of men till we die!' And, as she spoke I thought, 'And it was a parliament of men only who made this law

> which treats you as an outlaw. Men alone met in committee over it. Men alone are the executives. When men, of all ranks, thus band themselves together for an end deeply concerning women, and place themselves like a thick impenetrable wall between women and women... it is time that women should arise and demand their most sacred rights in regard to their sisters.'[11]

Led by Josephine Butler and other women who were to become key figures in the subsequent British suffragist movement, the campaign to repeal the Acts can be understood as a successful feminist movement against militarisation, against a collusion between the military and the state to control women. Judith Walkowitz, in her book *Prostitution and Victorian Society,*[12] shows that the feminist campaigners argued that what began as a regulation of poor women to serve supposedly narrow military needs—i.e. to prevent VD among rank and file soldiers—quickly became a springboard for the expanding state control of *all* women's sexuality.

Underlying the Contagious Diseases Acts was the belief that women must serve men and male institutions, not just by providing cheap or unpaid labour, but by providing 'clean sex'. Only if women were sexually healthy, so it was implied, could men's presumably uncontrollable sexual drives be allowed full rein without society's male institutions being jeopardised. Victory for the Contagious Diseases Act repealers in the 1880s was a significant step towards building a national political women's movement in Britain. But repeal did not end militarised prostitution. Rather it moved policy out of public view, to be administered by base commanders in co-operation with local civilian administrators.

Many town councillors do not relish the creation of a military base in their area. They are afraid that, with soldiers, will come more drinking places and consequent disorderliness. A town's reputation may be tarnished if it becomes known as merely an 'army town' or a 'navy port'. We know little about how bargains are struck between influential civilians in a garrison town and the local military commanders. The objective is for the town to get the social order and revenue its officials want, while, at the same time, the base or garrison officers get access to local women for their soldiers without jeopardy to those soldiers' health or finances.

Nor do we know what part the procurers of women into prostitution and their employers—often small-time publicans or, nowadays, massage parlour owners—play in this decentralised military policy process.

Even admitting how little information we have, there is clearly more to the process than simply the involvement of two individual actors: a woman making her own decisions (about how to earn her living, whom to have sex with and at what price) and a man who 'happens to be' in the navy or army.[13] We may learn much more about women in militarised towns such as Portsmouth—or Aldershot, Colchester, San Diego, Hong Kong—if we start with and then test this hypothesis: underneath seemingly individual actions there is a coherent pattern of military decision-making that determines local women's sexual relations with soldiers. It will also be useful to ask how, and when, do other male-run institutions (town councils, health departments, hospitals, courts, churches, taverns) play a part in that decision-making process.[14]

After the repeal of the Contagious Diseases Acts the British government gave local civilian authorities responsibility for controlling prostitution and women allegedly working as prostitutes. This was the decentralised, fragmented system that prevailed in Britain at the outbreak of the first world war. With the war, the effectiveness of soldiers and thus their health once again became a matter of grave official concern. Senior military men, however, claimed that they issued no uniform instructions to regulate prostitution. Lower-ranking field officers were left to make policy.[15]

British women foresaw the likelihood of the revival of the hated Contagious Diseases Acts and held a rally in 1914 to protest any attempt to re-establish such controls.

Prostitution became a formal political issue at the highest levels of wartime policy-making when the prime ministers of Canada and New Zealand came to London for a meeting of the

Imperial Defence Committee. Both men were outraged at what they claimed was the seduction of their innocent boys from the colonies by the aggressive whores of London's Soho. If the British government did not control their allegedly voracious women, the Canadian and New Zealand prime ministers threatened to pull their soldiers out of the British war effort. At the same time, field officers were complaining about the loss of soldiers due to the rampant spread of VD. While there was a running debate inside the government over how to control women, not until the latter days of the war did the government issue a formal directive. It simply directed local authorities to impose greater control over women in their areas.[16]

The picture remains sketchy indeed. During the second world war the connections between men's 'sex drive', soldiers' morale, VD, health requisites for victory, prostitution and women occupied official thoughts. But, once again, British policy was characterised by fragmentation and ambivalence. The politics of military sex were camouflaged as merely the politics of soldiers' health. And, again, officers directly in charge of rank and file troops were torn between their belief that any soldier who was a 'real man' needed sexual access to women and their fear that uncontrolled sexual relations with local or 'native' women would undermine the physical and moral vigour of men, making them less valuable in battle.

Military prostitution policy differed from one war zone to another, reflecting the varying dispositions of different field commanders, differing race and class origins of local women and how they affected relations with the British soldiers, and the lesser or greater opportunities soldiers had for recreation between battle manoeuvres. In Tripoli, North Africa, in the second world war, British army commanders permitted brothels to remain open but compelled women working as prostitutes to undergo military medicals. Some of Tripoli's brothels were even brought under direct control, with a Royal Army Service Corps non-commissioned officer placed in charge. Each of the army's different ranks and racial groups had its own brothel: one for coloured soldiers, others for white men in the ordinary ranks, still another for NCOs and warrant officers, and the most exclusive brothels reserved for British officers.[17]

One soldier described Britain's militarised prostitution system in Tripoli in the early 1940s:

> The army, with its detailed administrative ability, was able to organise brothels in a surprisingly short time and a pavement in Tripoli held a long queue of men, four deep, standing in orderly patience to pay their money and break the monotony of desert celibacy. The queue was four deep because there were only four women in the brothel. The soldiers stood like units in a conveyor belt waiting for servicing... Brothels for officers were opened in another part of town, where a few strolling pickets of military police ensured that the honoured ladies were not importuned by those who did not have the King's Commission.[18]

Who were these four women? We are told nothing, only that they were Italians.[19] They were probably products of Mussolini's earlier imperialist ambitions in North Africa. But how did they get to Tripoli? How were they compelled to stay there? What did they do to survive their hours of servicing those men fresh from desert battles, waiting 'like units in a conveyor belt'?

British army commanders stationed in India ran official brothels at the start of the war. Later, when orders from London shut down the brothels, prostitutes were moved elsewhere; officers claimed that VD rates soared as a consequence of the military's loss of direct control of the women.

As in Tripoli, Delhi's military brothels were differentiated so as to match the British army's own class and race stratifications:

> The officers' brothel was in Thompson Road and cost 75 rupees. Most of the women there were white, *some of them the wives of absent officers keen on a little money.* [emphasis added].[20]

British and American officers disagreed in their approaches to prostitution during the second world war. While the British adopted an attitude of relative resignation and fined a male soldier hospitalised for VD at the rate of one shilling and sixpence per day lost, their American counterparts treated men suffering from VD as criminals, often putting them behind barbed wire so they would feel humiliated.[21] Both militaries, however, officially filed all prostitution policy under the heading of male soldiers' health, as merely an off-shoot of their anti-VD programmes. This protected the military against criticism at home, while it made the military's dependence on the control of women invisible.

Throughout both world wars there ran a controversy that has yet to be resolved, a controversy that has its counterpart in civilian society as well. In both military and civilian corridors of power, women figure in this debate as allegedly passive creatures whose sexuality is merely designed to service individual men and male-defined institutions. The perpetual question is this: *How can women be controlled so that they can be made available to satisfy individual male soldiers' presumed sexual needs and yet cause no loss to military efficiency?*

Although British and American military establishments at various times have been directly involved in the organisation of women to sexually service soldiers, both traditionally deny any such direct involvement, and even deny they have any policy on prostitution at all. The British military especially likes to distinguish its 'non-policy' policy from what is commonly referred to as the 'continental system', the French policy of the direct military control of brothels. The distinction is more real on paper than it is in practice, but it has protected the military for civilian criticism. It has also served as a reference point from ongoing debates inside various armed forces and between military allies over how to satisfy the alleged needs of individual soldiers (and, importantly, thus how to continue to preserve the military's *masculine identity*) without jeopardising the organisational requisites of the military as a war machine.[22]

'Victory girls': controlling women on the home front

While American commanders were using their authority during the second world war to keep men fit to fight, civilian authorities were worried that wartime so disrupted the social order that home front women had to be placed under tighter control.

'Victory girls' were American women who supposedly 'pursued sexual relations with servicemen out of misplaced patriotism or a desire for excitement'.[23] Many of these 'victory girls' were in fact 'Rosie the Riveters', women able to get well-paying jobs outside the home for the first time.

The American government's response to women's seeming liberation was a programme which merged public health with military efficiency. From 1942 to 1945, local health and police officials were empowered to arrest any women they suspected of 'sexual delinquency' and to subject them to mandatory VD tests. The intent was not just to protect soldiers but to ensure that the exigencies of wartime did not radically alter gender roles in American society.

The anti-vice campaigns became part of the larger anti-Axis campaign in various American cities, though not all local authorities docilely compiled with the instructions of the government's Social Protection Division. (The SPD, perhaps not coincidentally, was headed by Eliot Ness, the legendary FBI gangbuster of the 1930s.) Baltimore officials, for instance, were reluctant to force anyone to take mandatory health tests and dragged their feet in creating a local social protection committee. Other cities did comply, often enthusiastically.

FBI statistics indicated a *95 per cent increase* in American women officially charged with moral violations between 1940 and 1944. In Seattle, zealous police and health authorities arrested 2,063 women on morals charges during 1944, but found only 366 (17.3 per cent) had venereal disease. All of the women arrested, nevertheless, were compelled to spend four or five days in jail awaiting the health test results; and during that time these so-called 'victory girls' were counselled by social workers to mend their ways.[24]

There was little protest by Americans against these violations of women's rights and the complementary militarisation of local police forces, courts, health services, and social workers. Protection of servicemen became a legitimising umbrella for the expansive state control of those women portrayed as the urban American equivalent of camp followers.

Thus, while wartime is frequently remembered nostalgically

as an era of new opportunities and liberation for women, it can also be a time of increased government control of women. The very changes brought by wartime mobilisation can make gender-defined military security presumptions all the more salient.[25]

Following the flag

Karayuki is the term used for Japanese women sold into debt bondage to brothel keepers throughout South-east Asia and North Asia during the period 1890-1945; they were most in evidence in the 1905-1930 era.[26] These were the decades of Japanese expansionism, following Japan's military victory in the Russo-Japanese war of 1904.

Karayuki were young women (often as young as 10 years old), from the agriculturally depressed northern regions of Honshu. They were sold to brothel brokers by fathers and brothers, peasants desperate for money and burdened with large families. The Japanese government reformers of the late nineteenth century, determined to modernise Japan so it could compete internationally, outlawed infanticide and abortion while at the same time banning the distribution of birth control literature. The *Karayuki* were the product of this convergence of rural impoverishment, the traditional devaluation of female children, government suppression of practices used to limit family size and energetic overseas military and trade expansion into countries such as Korea, Manchuria, China, Malaysia, Thailand and Singapore.[27]

Officials in Tokyo did little to prevent the sale of women into foreign prostitution. The export of rural women and girls helped relieve the otherwise dangerous and political pressures in the countryside.

By 1909 there were an estimated 3,500 Japanese prostitutes in Shanghai. In addition, approximately 30,000 young Japanese rural women and girls found themselves trying to pay off ever escalating debts to brothel keepers in Manchuria. Wherever Japanese political (military and trade) activities intensified, the number of brothels multiplied.

By the end of the first world war, however, the Japanese government became worried that this string of brothels throughout Asia tainted its image as an emergent world power. Thus in 1920 it persuaded Singapore's British colonial administration, which in 1913 had banned prostitution by *white* women, to extend the ban to Japanese women.

Yet, world image not withstanding, the Japanese military government in the 1930s and early 1940s continued to *use* prostitution, now of Korean women, as an integral tool of military expansionism:

> In every area Japanese conquered during World War II, prostitution was restored. In fact, in 1941, the Japanese authorities actually conscripted Korean women into a corps of 'entertainers' to 'comfort' the Japanese troops in Manchuria. With the beginning of the Pacific War, from 50,000 to 70,000 Korean girls and women were drafted and sent to the front to 'entertain' the Japanese troops.[28]

After 1945 the American military occupation authorities prohibited the practice of selling Japanese women into overseas prostitution. But now, 30 years later, the processes that are militarising Asia again are fostering prostitution once more, with the US military establishment itself an active participant.

Vietnam: from racism to rape and prostitution

The first Vietnam war, or 'Indo-China war' (1945-54), was fought by the French against the Communist-led, but broadly nationalist Vietnamese independence movement. The Vietnamese had endured the second world war and decades of French colonialism, and yet preserved enough social cohesion to resist coughing up dislocated, impoverished women to service the French military's sexual needs. French military officers resorted to imported non-Vietnamese women, who were turned into prostitutes for French soldiers. Asian women who could not speak French or any of the several languages common in Vietnam were preferred by the military: these women could have sex with the French troops without their commanders worrying about lonely soldiers whispering military secrets in moments of indiscretion.[29]

By 1954, when the French had withdrawn in defeat and

American soldiers had begun to fill the vacuum, war had so disrupted South Vietnamese society that local Vietnamese women were desperate enough to be available for a prostitution industry that grew ever more expansive as the war dragged on.[30] American military officials militarised local prostitution by degrees: 'First bar girls, then massage parlours for the Marines at Da Nang, then a shanty town of brothels, massage parlours and dope dealers known as Dogpatch soon ringed the bases.'[31]

Prostitutes were made officially welcome to US bases in Vietnam as 'local national guests'. The American base at Long Binn was a militarised city of 25,000 people. It employed hundreds of Vietnamese women on base as service personnel: 'There were mama-sans and hooch-girls all over the place. Everything was clean.'[32] In addition, there were other women just off base; soldiers could bring on base as 'local national guests' any of the 50 to 60 girls who waited outside the wire fences.[33] There were separate brothels for black and white soldiers. A Vietnamese woman who was a prostitute servicing white soldiers was likely to be murdered by soldiers if she was discovered providing services to black soldiers.[34]

By 1973, on the eve of the American military's withdrawal, between 300,000 and 500,000 women were working as prostitutes in South Vietnam.

The precise number of women engaged in prostitution was impossible to calculate because thousands of Vietnamese women worked as cleaners and servants for American troops and thousands more were raped by American soldiers. All of them were vulnerable to the label 'prostitute', because they were women and because they were at the bottom of the racial hierarchy that structured all relations in the Vietnam war.

One American soldier remembers how men made the links between racism, rape and prostitution.

> You take a group of men and put them in a place where there are no round-eyed women. They are in an all-male environment. Let's face it. Nature is nature. There are women available. Those women are of another culture, another colour, another society. You don't want a prostitute. You've

> got an M-16. What do you need to pay for a lady for? You go down to the village and you take what you want. I saw guys who I believe had never had any kind of sex with a woman before in that kind of scene. They'd come back a double veteran.[35]

'Double veteran' became a common slang phrase among American soldiers in Vietnam: 'Having sex with a woman and then killing her made one a double veteran.'[36]

Vietnamese women migrated to Saigon as the bombing and ground fighting escalated in their rural home areas. Some of them tried to band together to rent space and provide each other with some minimal protection. They were not officially 'on base', but they were being militarised, put at the service of soldiers:

> The place where I spent many an evening when I could get away from the war was the Hung Dao Hotel, a three-storey dilapidated shack in the middle of Tu Do Street, Saigon. The first floor was almost like a hospital ward, they had rolled about ten beds into it. The second floor was kinkier stuff, so they had little rooms. That was also for officers or people who just wanted to fuck alone. The whores cooked and lived on the third floor...
>
> There was one girl who was about twelve years old who was great. She was one of my favourites. Although there was another women there that I swore I'd marry. She stole a ring from me, so I didn't marry her... In fact we were at the Hung Do so much and they loved my team so much, they made us T-shirts—Hung Dao No. 1, Hung Dao No. 2. Each one of us had a numbered T-shirt.[37]

Vietnamese women struggled to make some sense of the war in order to protect themselves from the worst of the violence. But such efforts were often frustrated by the sheer rapidity with which confused, alienated American men equipped with the military's weapons and authority would merge their anger against their own commanders with their hostility toward Asian men. Asian women were abused as a way both to vent anger against their own officers and to humiliate Asian men. Women's bodies became mere pawns in this thoroughly militarised environment:

> These gooks are riding by in a Lambretta... we say, 'Hey, let's stop these gooks...
>
> 'What you got there? Hey, you VC? What you got?' It was a baby-san and a papa-san. I guess she was a teenager, maybe fifteen or sixteen.
>
> They had a can of pears!... We say, 'Isn't this some shit. Here we are in the field, we don't know what pears is. They got pears! And *we* don't have pears!' We are shit in the field and the guys in the rear have given these gooks pears, man...
>
> The GIs gave you pears? Oh yeah? For that, we're going to screw your daughter. So we went running, taking the daughter. She was crying. I think she was a virgin. We pulled down her pants and put a gun to her head...
>
> I was taking her body by force. Guys were standing over her with rifles, while I was screwing her. She says, 'Why are you doing this to me? Why?' Some of the gooks could talk very good. 'Hey, you're black, why are you doing this to me?'[38]

Rape is obviously not an exclusive preserve of military men. But it may be that there are aspects of the military institution and ideology which greatly increase the pressure on militarised men to 'perform' sexually, whether they have a sexual 'need' or emotional feelings or not. First, military men live more exclusively among other men than do most men (except perhaps prisoners), and thus are subjected 24 hours a day to pressures to conform to the standards of 'masculine' behaviour. Second, military officialdom seeks to make men feel secure within the cocoon of the 'military family', while it simultaneously encourages men as soldiers to see the rest of the world as chaotic, fearsome and needing to be controlled or conquered. Trying to cope with the confusion and dangers of warfare, military men, more than most men, feel the need to have 'buddies'. But to acquire buddies a soldier has to prove he is trustworthy, able to face death and violence while remaining 'cool'. Thus, while a militarised man needs a buddy, a friend to whom he can reveal his fears and vulnerability, he can only earn buddies by proving he is a 'man', that he isn't squeamish in the face of violence. Such contradictory pressures can make it especially hard to say 'no' to gang rape.

Turning some Vietnamese women into prostitutes did little to reduce the rapes of other Vietnamese women. Thus, one of the commonest justifications offered by authorities for officially organised and sanctioned prostitution finds little support in the experiences of women at the front in this war.

After the departure of the American military in 1975 and the establishment of a unified Vietnamese state, the Hanoi government introduced a programme to rehabilitate the thousands of women in the south who had been prostitutes. We have little information on how many Vietnamese women, however, were shipped out with the departing US forces to be made prostitutes in the growing international trade. Nor do we know how women in the rehabilitation camps were treated.

Visitors to Ho Chi Minh City six years later reported that prostitutes had been removed from bars, but that the government had not entirely abandoned the practice—though now in an apparently more benign form. Young Vietnamese women called 'Cinderellas' were paid by the government to dance with foreigners at a weekly ball held in the former American Officers Club. During the day these women were office workers or shop assistants, but on the night of the officially organised party, they wore Western jeans and blouses: 'They dance with French, Scandinavian and Russian partners, mostly technicians on projects, and they go home alone at night.'[39]

Post-war Vietnam is not demilitarised. An estimated one million Vietnamese—overwhelmingly males—served in the military in 1982. That same year an estimated 180,000-200,000 Vietnamese soldiers were posted across the border in Kampuchea. We know little about how Kampuchean women are experiencing the high level of militarisation in their impoverished country, though one foreign diplomat has reported that, 'So far Vietnam has been extremely careful with Kampuchean sensitivities, trying to ensure that Vietnamese troops do not plunder food or molest

Kampuchean women.'[40] While this official policy may be minimising the violence against women that seems so integral to any warfare, it still suggests that women in Kampuchea, as elsewhere, are abused *or* spared as the property of men, men whom other men, as military strategists, either want to hurt or to make alliances with.

Military bases, tourism and prostitution in 'post-Vietnam' Asia
Post-Vietnam Asia is witnessing a boom in the prostitution industry. Ten years after the end of the Vietnam war, Asian women are being sexually exploited by a powerful alliance of militarism and tourism. Both the expansion of the military and the massive development of tourist enterprises are being financed by foreign capital, which in turn is legitimised by insecure local governments eager to pay off foreign loans and suppress domestic opposition. Most affected are women in the Philippines, Thailand and South Korea, countries in which the militarism/tourism syndrome is especially potent.

The typical life cycle of a Filipino prostitute has been described this way.[41] A teenage girl grows up in a poor rural family which has failed in its struggle to hold on to land which could produce a sufficient income to sustain the family. The girl may have suffered sexual abuse by male adults in the family. To help her family pay off its rising debts, she is sent off to Manila. Sometimes the girl goes in the custody of an adult who promises her parents she will be trained for an income-producing job in the city. She may start by working as a domestic servant, still hoping to find work in one of Manila's many Japanese or American owned garment or microelectronic factories, whose managers are known to favour young girls on their assembly lines, but eventually she is put to work as a prostitute. She hits her peak right at the start, working in the city's expensive international hotels where Western men stay on their business trips. This peak is brief. The young prostitute one sees having drinks bought for her in the high-rise Hilton or Holiday Inn is soon pushed on to her second, distinctly less elegant and remunerative phase.

She leaves Manila for the sprawling towns that surround the

two large American military bases: the Subic Bay Base servicing the US navy's Seventh Fleet, or Clark Air Force Base. Created by the Americans during their colonial rule, both bases' leases were renewed by a 1979 agreement between the Marcos regime and Washington. The bases nominally came under Philippines authority for the first time, but in practice were still run as if on US territory. In return, the Marcos government received millions of dollars in American military and economic aid. The compromises and mutuality of interest that shaped the Clark and Subic lease negotiations directly affected Filipino women on and off the bases. These deals made women more subject to both economic and sexual exploitation with few avenues of redress or protection.

The American bases were cut back in the mid-1970s with the 'winding down' of the Vietnam war. But in the 1980s they are expanding once again as the US navy presses for domination of the Persian Gulf and Indian Ocean, presumed arenas for Soviet-US military confrontation in the coming decade.[42] *Insofar as the expansion or retraction of any foreign power's overseas bases increases or decreases the demand for women's sexual availability to male soldiers or sailors, the Pentagon's changing Asian strategy is a 'women's issue'.*

American officials claim that Clark Air Force Base injected $50 million into the Philippines economy in 1981, of which $13 million was spent on salaries for Philippine workers. Subic Bay reportedly spent $120 million in the Philippines that year, of which $47 million was in the form of salaries to local workers on the base.[43] The Marcos regime, desperate for revenues with which to pay off its mounting foreign debt and support its expanding police and military forces, welcomes such figures, pointing to them to justify its close collaboration with the US military base officials. Both governments fail to mention, however, that Philippine workers employed on the American bases earn the lowest wages of any local workers on American bases in Asia: Philippine workers average $65 per month, while Korean workers average $200 and Japanese workers average $400. Moreover, neither government acknowledges the degree of racism that Filipinos endure in order to keep these base jobs.

The Filipino women who work as cleaners, cooks, domestic servants and in other service capacities on the base are said to be subjected to strip-searches by US marine guards as they go out the base gates on the pretence that they are prone to steal US property. In addition, there are reports of Filipino women workers on the bases being sexually harassed by supervisors with minimal official interference.[44] Such treatment of local women base workers is scarcely surprising, given the fact that outside the base gates American military personnel take advantage of thousands of Philippine women who are offered to them as buyable sexual objects.

Olongapo is the Philippine town that is host to the US navy's Subic Bay personnel. The town has grown from 40,000 Filipino residents in 1963, just prior to the escalation of the American involvement in Vietnam, to 160,000 in 1982. Today, Olongapo is as militarised as Portsmouth, England. In addition, however, many of Olongapo's women are dependent on a foreign army with a long history of racist relationships with Asian civilians. Olongapo's Filipino mayor has complained that his town has acquired the reputation of a crime-ridden city in which prostitution is 'rampant', venereal disease is widespread and entertainers, pickpockets and pimps are the most influential entrepreneurs.[45]

When the rest and recreation ('R and R') industry began to expand rapidly in the late 1960s, spurred by the American military involvement in Vietnam, local businessmen in Olongapo made what has become a familiar argument to wary town officials:

> Instead of endangering our decent and respectable women to the possibility of rape and other forms of sexual abuse, better provide an outlet for the soldiers' sexual urge and at the same time make money out of it.[46]

By the end of the Vietnam war in 1976, Olongapo's town hall had 6,019 women officially registered as 'hostesses'. The town recorded no one in the category of 'prostitute'.[47] But the Filipino women working in the clubs and massage parlours catering to Subic Bay sailors knew what was expected of a 'hostess':

> The actual act of dropping one's panties, spreading one's legs and doing all possible motions during a sexual encounter with a customer in order to earn money is easy to do. What is difficult to do is to convince oneself to do it and to keep doing it.[48]
>
> Often times, I do not feel anything during sexual encounters. There are times when I am hurt. If I keep doing it, it is because I need money for myself and my children. I have learned to do the motions mechanically in order to satisfy my customers. If you do it very well, they will keep coming back—and that means money.[49]

During her years of providing sex to American servicemen, a Filipino woman will probably search for an avenue to escape from prostitution. Some women try to learn sewing skills in the hope of getting a job in Manila as a seamstress. Others try to return to their home villages, but are often rejected by their families who either are ashamed of them or need their continued flow of money. Some Filipino women try to transform the insecurity and degradation of prostitution into what looks to them to be the relative security of marriage to an American sailor or air force man.

Lily was a hostess in Olongapo in the mid-1970s. Her story is not unusual:

> Jim and I were already going steady for six months. So for six months I had not been working in the club. It was some kind of relief... Though I was not married to the serviceman, I had the feeling of being his wife. Besides, he promised he would marry me someday. I considered myself lucky, since most of us really look forward to a day when a serviceman proposes marriage. Many of us think marriage to a sailor is the only way out of this job... Little by little I was convinced that life was not that hopeless, even for a prostitute. Until my big disappointment came...
>
> ...Jim was to transfer to another place of duty back in the United States. He then told me he was going to marry me... I was ignorant about those papers so I just waited for what was going to happen...

> ...But a day before departure, he told me that the marriage papers could not be processed on time... he knew I was already six months pregnant...
>
> He said he would plead with his commanding officer. However, he did not come home that night. Neither on the following day... I found out he had already left for the United States. It was too late for me to realise I was fooled... Emotionally, because he made me believe that he loved me and I learned to give a loving response, which was difficult for me who had been used to an exploitative sexual relationship. Economically, because Jim took with him all my savings which he asked me to withdraw the day before... The more I am now convinced that men are all the same —manipulative and exploitative.[50]

And the Filipino interviewer adds:

> Since then Lily never trusted any of her customers. Instead, she cunningly handles them in such a way that she gets the most out of every transaction. In her own words, 'It is very likely that after some time working in the trade, a woman will really succumb to mistrust, pretense, and deception which characterizes prostitution.'[51]

Thousands of women do not find a way out of prostitution. Instead a Filipino prostitute is likely to be pushed on to the next stage along a path that leads ever downward. She will leave the outskirts of Subic Bay or Clark and return to Manila, often now with a child to care for. She will find work in one of the unfashionable but well-patronised dance halls, massage parlours or bars that have grown up within walking distance of the expensive international hotels. Her customers will primarily be Japanese businessmen, brought to Manila by the planeload on package sex tours. Japanese feminists have led the way in exposing the role of Japan's government-owned airlines and private tourist bureaus in promoting the prostitution industry—under the guise of tourism—in the Philippines and South Korea. They interpret the Japanese government's encouragement of these overseas sex tours as part of its more general policy of re-establishing

Japanese influence in Southeast and North Asia.[52]

The Filipino prostitute has not yet reached her nadir. Eventually she will move out of Manila for her last stop. She will be set up at a roadside tavern along one of Luzon's main highways. For the first time her clients will be mainly Filipino men, truck drivers.[53]

Bahai Zain, a Filipino feminist, has written a poem she says speaks for all Asian women in this era when militarisation and the tourist industry are thriving arm in arm:

What else can I give
all the frangipanis wilt in the fires of the blasts
you have filled all wombs
with your dollars
with your VD

What else
what else
you have left me
heir to germs and destruction
let me be

the prostitute at the Hotel Embassy
she cries,
'Hei, Jo, gip me your dolar
not your napalm, not your gonoria.'[54]

In Thailand, too, militarisation has laid the groundwork for tourism—and the exploitation of women's sexuality. In the 1980s, the tourist industry is a major foreign currency earner for Thailand's conservative government. Twenty years earlier the biggest flow of 'tourists' into Thailand wore khaki. Some were the American army and air force men stationed on the large US air force bases in Thailand, built as launching pads for bombing forays into Cambodia and Vietnam. Others were American soldiers who came from Vietnam combat zones to Bangkok and Thai beach villages to the south for rest and recreation.

On the US bases themselves, most of them located in Thailand's impoverished north-east, military commanders maintained an 'arm's length' approach to control of women by counting them officially as 'special job workers' (dancers, masseuses, entertainers). At Udon Air Force Base, the number of 'special job workers' grew from 1,246 in 1966 to 6,234 in 1972.[55]

By the end of the 1970s, an estimated 100,000 women in Bangkok were working as prostitutes; 70 per cent of them suffered from venereal disease: 'This means that 30 per cent of the female labour force in Bangkok suffer from venereal disease as a result of earning a living.'[56] Child slavery is also on the rise in Thailand. Though denied by the Thai Ministry of Labour, local and foreign investigators have documented the system by which young children from poor farm families are kidnapped and put to work to increase Thailand's gross national product. Some boys and girls end up working for little or no wages in small factories. Many of the girls are taken to work in brothels serving Thailand's booming tourist industry.[57]

Neither capitalist tourism nor local or imported militarisation alone can entirely explain the soaring numbers of Filipino and Thai women pressed into commercialised sex. The crisis is rooted in military and capitalist tourist exacerbation of the disasterous decline of Thai and Philippines agricultural and cottage industries over the last 20 years. The rural crisis was brought on by foreign advisers, investors and bankers who concentrated on urban and industrial development to the detriment of genuine rural development. As in English society a century earlier, an underdeveloped and economically destitute countryside produces 'expendable' women. If this coincides—as it so often does—with a period in which governments are going in for military expansion, then militarised prostitution will be one of the products of rural women's displacement.

In 1982, the US has 200 military bases and 500,000 military personnel overseas, 92 per cent of whom are male. Every foreign military base involves political bargaining. Bases must be leased. Lease agreements are the product of often complex, delicate diplomatic negotiations between governments. We know too little about exactly what goes on in these negotiations. It is likely that questions regarding distribution of policing powers between the foreign military and the local police of the proposed base town and questions of business zoning and of health regulations will not get on the table of the most senior government negotiators. They *will* be considered, but more likely at a bargaining session between lower level civilian and military officials whose arguments and compromises rarely get reported to the public. And yet each of these subjects for negotiation—police powers, business zoning criteria, health regulations—will affect the lives of women who live near or are brought into the towns that grow around the foreign base.

In September 1982, President Marcos visited the US. Top on his agenda was renewal of the leases for the Subic Bay and Clark air force bases in 1983. Those renewal negotiations will affect thousands of Filipino women. Similarly, as part of the same American military expansion of its strategic network from the Persian Gulf to the Pacific, US navy officials are taking steps to persuade the Sri Lankan government to open up Sri Lanka to 'rest and recreation' for sailors from the US Seventh Fleet (the same fleet that uses Subic Bay). Sri Lankan women have voiced opposition to such an arrangement, saying that R&R facilities would cause increases in prostitution, VD and drug abuse.[58]

The Royal Navy's face-saving expedition to the Falklands notwithstanding, the British government has reduced its global military responsibilities, often passing the baton to the all-too-eager US forces. In 1982, however, over 4,000 British soldiers are stationed in Northern Ireland, often imagined to be 'overseas' by many Britons. Being 'overseas', Northern Ireland has been more open to coercive military methods than would be popularly tolerated in Scotland, Wales or England. British soldiers are also stationed in large numbers in West Germany—in the British Army of the Rhine (BAOR). British troops are stationed in Belize. And Gurkha troops under British command still play vital internal security roles in Hong Kong and Brunei.

Until the 1970s the British military had authority over the small Indian Ocean island community of Diego Garcia. But, under pressure from Washington, the British government leased Diego Garcia to the US for use as a strategic naval air base. Diego Garcians themselves were forcibly moved to neighbouring Mauritius. Some Diego Garcian women are reported to be in such economic distress that they have resorted to prostitution. Whether or not they rely directly on sailors as customers, they are prostitutes as a result of their society's militarisation.[59]

At this point we can take an overview. As the British military and American military—as well as their NATO allies—continue to redistribute military power and responsibility over the globe women in various countries and towns will be differently affected by militarisation. Women in Ulster, the Philippines, West Germany and other militarised areas will not necessarily be the subjects of identical military policies. These policies will instead be shaped by a number of considerations: first, the imagined racial or cultural gap between troops and local women (a wide gap permitting soldiers and officers to treat the women as inferior and even more expendable); second, the level of local hostility, determining how much of a 'security risk' commanders presume local women to be; third, the length of overseas tour required for each soldier; fourth, the armed forces' policy regarding male soldiers marrying local women or bringing their wives with them to overseas posts; and fifth, the level of economic hardship and social displacement being experienced by working-class and peasant women, and thus their potential for dependency on the military and local pimps.

Nevertheless, despite variations from base to base or country to country, military commanders still appear uniformly uneasy about just how much direct control to exert over their male troops and local women mobilised to service those troops. Militarised prostitutes—women mobilised to provide commercialised comfort and sex for troops—will sometimes be brought directly on base, while at other times will be kept officially at arm's length, in makeshift shanty towns off base. Sometimes military commanders will try to control women; at other times they will make an unwritten pact with local procurers, pimps and police, leaving them to exert the direct control.

In this control process, military accountability becomes obscured and difficult for women themselves to trace. But it is a reasonable assumption everywhere that some military official is more than likely to be making decisions which affect how women are marshalled to serve military needs and goals.

3. Keeping the Home Fires Burning: Military Wives

> In short, it is evident that the presence of large numbers of women and children with a body of men intended for quick movements and for service in distant colonies, and for occasional fight is in the last degree inconvenient.[1]

In many ways, a woman married to a soldier experiences pressures and obstacles common to *all* women who are wives. She is presumed to be dependent on the man who is her husband, not only for her financial well-being, but for her very identity; her class or rank is derived from her husband's class or rank; she is expected to adapt her own life to whatever uprootings her husband's job requires; she is helpmate to her husband, regardless of her talents or waged employment; she is expected to be sexually available to her husband and to tolerate his occasional extramarital 'lapses'.

On top of these demands which all women-as-wives experience, a woman married to a soldier has to cope with the demands peculiar to being a 'military wife': she is defined by society not only by her relationship to a particular man, but by her membership in a powerful institution; she is seen not just as a particular soldier's wife, but as a military wife. She lives in a social world deliberately insulated from the 'real world' (as many military people call the civilian world) and thus loses much of the potential support from women in that wider, less tightly controlled world.[2] Many of the elements of economic well-being in the military come in the form not of cash wages, but of privileges (e.g. access to the base store, medical services) and these come to women solely by way of their soldier-husband's military status. Also, they are considered a part of an institution which to an extraordinary degree is infused with an explicitly masculine ethos.

As a 'military wife', furthermore, a woman is subject to the authority of the state more than most women (apart from women in prisons or in refugee camps). Yet, often with minimal state aid, she must cope with moving and long separations from her husband more than most women (except wives of prisoners and of migrant workers). As a military wife, she lives under the authority of an institution which often portrays itself as a 'family', thus making her subject to two patriarchal authorities: her husband's and the military commander's. A woman married to a soldier finds that daily interactions, friendships and social obligations are bound round by a military ranking system that usually exacerbates the class/racial stratification of the larger society. One white American woman who was a navy officer's wife in the 1960s when her first child was born remembers with dismay:

> We had a choice of going to a civil hospital which would charge us for the birth or to the Naval Hospital at Camp Pendleton. In the navy hospital there is no 'ranking' —mothers and babies are all inter-mixed. The problem was that the black woman in a ward of four with me hated officers because her husband, an enlisted man, hated officers, and her hostility transferred to officers' wives as well. I felt awkward because it never entered my mind before that one would be hated by 'rank'.[3]

Military commanders seem most comfortable when they can treat their troops as if they were permanent bachelors: energetic adolescents or worldly Beau Brummells. Controlling their troops' sexual encounters with those women whom the military can categorise as prostitutes (because they are poor and/or are racial outsiders) is a nuisance. But at least, in military commanders' eyes, those relationships are casual and commercial and can be useful in convincing their otherwise downtrodden male soldiers that they are 'real men', heroes and conquerors.

In contrast, when a soldier seeks a more permanent and socially established relationship with a woman, military officials get nervous. They envision his loyalties being divided and his mobility obstructed. The military foresees its own resources being diverted from military pay and weaponry to social workers and day-care centres. It visualises an alien presence—women and children—on base and 'manly' soldiers transformed into uncombative 'henpecked husbands'.

Military commanders and their civilian political superiors nevertheless *do* try to make use of those women who have married soldiers. If those women can be socialised to become 'military wives', they can perhaps further some of the military's own goals. For instance, women as military wives can help win civilian support and sympathy for the military by making it seem a less brutal or insulated institution. And military wives can—if controlled—give male soldiers emotional support and incentives to 'act like men' in battle.

Prior to the Crimean War, nineteenth-century British social opinion (and military official opinion as well) imagined the ordinary soldier as little more than a beast. But in the late nineteenth century there emerged a new appreciation of the fighting man as a moral creature, a man who would fight all the better if his moral dimension were cultivated—by a woman, and especially by a loyal, patriotic wife. As one Member of Parliament explained:

> I believe that if there is a time when the home affections press most strongly upon [soldiers], it is not only in the heat of battle, but in the silence and loneliness of the wards of the hospital. Having lost everything but their kit and knapsack, they have produced to me, over and over again, from the linings of their coats, letters from the families whom they have left in England... It is remarkable that every one of those letters which I saw, breathed the fondest affections; many of them expressed a woman's tenderness and a woman's fears; but not one of them invited the man to return home until the victory had been gained...[4]

Soldiers' wives can also provide cheap or unpaid labour for the dozens of social agencies on a modern base which in turn sustain the military as a self-sufficient 'community'. Moreover, if they will accept this identity as military wives, women married to soldiers can be taught to relate to other wives and male and female soldiers in ways that reinforce the ranking system and the competitive careerism that perpetuates that system. Finally, if women are socialised into acting like military wives, they can bear children and bring up those children—especially the boys—to imagine that enlistment into the military is a natural and rewarding thing to do, thereby providing the military with its most reliable manpower pool.

But all of these apparent benefits are only begrudgingly acknowledged by military officials. Transforming a soldier's wife into a useful resource for the military is, for officers, only making the best of a bad job. Furthermore, it is not always successful. Even under the pressures the military can bring to bear, many women refuse to act and think like the ideal military wife.

Women who marry soldiers experience a perpetual whiplash: one moment they are used as a resource by the military; the next moment they are treated as alien and expendable. In the midst of the 1982 Falklands war, British navy wives described what that whiplash felt like:

> My brother was at sea, and my sister-in-law was worried... she knew they wouldn't tell her for a while—that's typical of the Navy, war or peace, you're treated as though you don't exist, always kept hanging on...
>
> The Navy still haven't contacted me and I have no idea when he will get home, could be months. And that's so typical. Wives and families—the ones they say it's all for—have never been taken into consideration, and never will be. War is a man's job in a man's world.[5]

For feminists, military wives raise a classic dilemma: should women who are concerned about the exploitation of women married to soldiers press their own country's military establishment to pay *more* attention to, and provide *more* services to military wives?

Feminists are often caught between, on the one hand, protesting the ways in which welfare programmes extend state control over women while, on the other hand, fighting to prevent cuts in those state welfare schemes on which so many women depend for daily survival.[6] Military wives are subject to direct state control by the very fact of being officially categorised as appendages of the state's soldiers. They have experienced neglect precisely because of that 'appendage' status: they are expected simply to *adapt* to constant moves, separations and withheld information.

It is tempting, consequently, for feminists to press the military to pay *more* attention to the needs of military wives. But would this just accelerate the already advanced militarisation of those women's lives? Would such reforms only make thousands of women married to men in the military even more dependent on and more subject to the control of the state? And, finally, would such a feminist campaign gradually compel the feminists themselves to become involved in and imperceptibly part of a process ultimately controlled by the military?

Counting the forks and knives

The British army's Colchester garrison is built on the site of a Roman army camp. Remnants of the ancient Roman wall around the town still remind one of Colchester's long military history. The modern-day garrison is less fortress-like. It was in Colchester that Josephine Butler fought one of her toughest campaigns to repeal the Contagious Diseases Act just a century ago. Around town one sees young soldiers—'squaddies'—with their tell-tale short clipped hair wandering about at loose ends or clustered together in a pub.

The married soldiers' quarters are a short drive from Colchester's busy shopping centre. They look like dozens of identical British army post-war housing estates—two-storey brick semi-detached houses set out in neat rows along streets that snake their way through the estate. There is plenty of grass but few trees to break the suburban monotony. In the mid-afternoon on a spring weekday there are few soldiers to be seen. Women in their twenties and thirties are walking home from the bus stop carrying groceries or out walking with their small children.

Connie (not her real name) is a young white English woman in her mid-twenties. Already she has spent seven and a half years as a military wife. Her husband, Bill, has been in the army for ten and a half years. He joined the engineers corps soon after he left school at 17. Connie, who met Bill after he had joined, thinks that her husband is not exceptional in his reasons for joining. Bill was a teenager with no job prospects. He wanted to get away from home, acquire a skill and travel, though the latter is in fact rare for most young soldiers once they marry: Bill and Connie spent all their leaves while they were posted in Germany travelling back to England to visit their parents. Bill has moved steadily up through the non-commissioned ranks, so that today he is a sergeant.

Connie and Bill have a three-and-a-half-year-old son, who was born while they were stationed in Germany. Connie is pleased to be back in England, especially at the Colchester garrison, which they had requested because Connie's parents live nearby.

In her seven and a half years of marriage, Connie had moved seven times, sometimes moving twice during a single posting. She had always lived in army housing (unlike many wives of low-ranking American enlisted men, who are left on their own to find cheap housing off base). She and Bill pay a monthly rent as well as separate heat and light charges—'It's not for free like everybody thinks.' But at this stage in her life as a military wife Connie finds all army housing depressingly familiar, cut out of the same pattern. Even the few pieces of furniture they have been able to accumulate and bring to their newest posting doesn't hide the standardised look and feel of what she calls home.

Beyond the sheer monotony and bleakness, base housing means more military intrusion into Connie's life: 'The Army controls everything—your heat, your medical care, your silverware.' It is the base housing officer or family officer that Connie and other wives deal with concerning housing or other problems. Most galling to Connie is the patronising attitude with which she and her neighbours are treated. She points to the centre of the living-room carpet and describes how, at the start and finish of every posting, she has to lay out all the army-issued kitchen-ware in the middle of the carpet to be counted and checked off on a clipboard by a man from the housing office—' "Six spoons, six knives, six forks." It makes you feel like a child!'

From Connie's experience, it doesn't seem as though the

army really cares about soldiers' wives. It only does the minimum necessary to keep the women contented enough so they won't object to their husbands signing up for another tour.

Good-natured, wifely adaptations proved especially hard during their time in Germany. Connie says that she suffered from depression during the two years she spent with Bill stationed in West Germany. It was before Daniel was born and she felt very isolated. Many military wives have children in order to break the boredom, pregnancies coming in cycles that match their husbands' tours away and their returns. Some wives also hope that they will get more attention when they are pregnant, for instance that their husbands will be given extra home leaves.[7]

Connie sought out the base's 'SSAFA Sister'—the woman who is part nurse, part charity worker, part social worker, employed by the Soldiers', Sailors' and Airmen's Family Association. SSAFA was formed in 1885 and is now an integral part of every British army base community. Connie found the SSAFA sister on the base in Germany helpful in a 'motherly sort of way'. But her main function seemed to be to refer wives under stress to the appropriate army medical officer; she had very limited authority with which to solve problems herself.

Sometime later Connie began to suspect that, despite assurances of confidentiality, her entire medical record had been made part of her *husband's* career file. All military wives are aware that what they do—or don't do—affects their husbands' chances for promotion. It's one of the things that Connie thinks makes the women she's known on several army bases so reluctant to complain about housing or medical conditions: they might get picked out as 'trouble makers', and that would jeopardise their husbands' careers.

Connie was able to get a waged job while she and Bill were in West Germany. Like many enlisted men's wives, Connie worked for minimum wages at the NAAFI—the Navy, Army and Air Force Institution shop that has its counterpart in the American PX. Jobs at the NAAFI are easy to get overseas because of the high turnover and low pay: 'All the employees seemed to be wives—and daughters—of soldiers.' The NAAFI, like so many army base services, depends for its viability on the unwaged or low paid labour of soldiers' wives.

There were two other job possibilities for British wives stationed in Germany. Some women were lucky enough to get clerical jobs on base with the chance to earn more than their husbands. Other women Connie knew ventured off base to work in nearby German factories where the pay was higher than at the NAAFI. Working in the factories had the added attraction of making the British women eligible for German medical benefits, thereby allowing them to avoid their usual dependency on the army's medical services.

According to Connie, though, the best job she ever had in her seven and a half years in the army was back in England. Bill was posted at a base near enough to a town so Connie could go back and forth easily. This was before Daniel was born, so she didn't have home responsibilities to tie her down as she does now. Best of all, working off base had meant Connie could have civilian women friends, something she now misses. At the Colchester post Connie feels cut off. She is thankful that the base provides a day-care centre within easy walking distance, but she hasn't been able to get a job, is dependent on the bus to get into town and surrounded solely by other women whose lives are shaped by young children and military rules. Her only outlet is a course at the adult education centre in town where she enjoys discussion with civilian women.

Military wives try to help each other, 'But it's hard to make lasting friendships when you all move so often.' Then there are the divisions by rank which circumscribe one's range of possible friends. Now that Bill is a sergeant, Connie says, most of her friends are the wives of sergeants and corporals—'none are wives of privates and definitely I don't have friendships with wives of officers'. Officers' wives seem quite removed from rank and file men's wives altogether. One waits on them if working at the NAAFI or sits next to them, in mutual awkwardness, at the base's annual Christmas dinner. It's not just that women married to army officers are further up the military pyramid; they also appear to adopt a class style that makes them remote: 'They all seem to carry baskets when they shop and to wear scarves with horses on them.'

Wife beating and child abuse have until recently been taboo subjects in the armed forces in both Britain and the USA. To admit that either occurred would endanger the military's standing in society. Officially acknowledging such issues would compel the military to confront the implications of their own socialisation of men into violence. But in the last three or four years, in large part due to women activists within the US military (wives, civilian agency workers), the American Defense Department has instructed base commanders in all services to look into wife battering and child abuse and to take at least tentative steps toward preventing 'family violence' and punishing its perpetrators.

Connie does not think that either child abuse or wife battering are given much attention on the various British bases where she has lived, nor is she even sure that it is a widespread problem. Perhaps, she speculates, women married to soldiers enjoy a bit more protection from violence than the average women: 'It's such an enclosed community. A man who hit his wife would be picked up very quickly.' It may be one of the few benefits Connie sees flowing from the military's paternalistic intrusiveness into the lives of their soldiers' wives.

Connie knows she is going to face a difficult decision in the not-too-distant future. To earn full retirement benefits, Bill will have to complete his entire 20-year tour. Connie thinks this is what he would like to do if the decision were his alone to make. Connie believes her husband is quite suited to army life; he doesn't seem as rankled by the pressures to obey and conform as she is. Furthermore, he is doing a mechanic's job that he likes and sees little chance of getting such a job outside the army, on Civvie Street. Connie cannot imagine living as a military wife for another 13 years. The depression that overtook her while they were stationed in Germany is sharply etched on her memory. She knows she and Bill would have to do more tours abroad—Malta, Hong Kong, Belize, perhaps now the Falklands, and always Germany.

So Connie is placing her hopes on Bill's bad back. Perhaps he will be medically discharged and the two of them can avoid having to work out the difficult choice on their own. Their alternative is a '12 year compromise'. Connie says she will stick it out another five years for Bill's sake if he will agree to leave the army at the 12 year mark. At that point he would receive a £2,000 bonus and be eligible for a pension when he reaches 65. And perhaps, Connie thinks, in another five years the British job picture will look less gloomy and both she and Bill won't have to look upon the army as an employer of last resort.

Two hours' drive south of Colchester is another facility housing British enlisted men and their families. Ann (not her real name) is one of the 7.5 per cent of the residents on a housing estate built in the semi-rural countryside of Kent who lives there in military housing. Many of her civilian neighbours have been housed here because of housing shortages in London. They were expected to be pleased about moving to so idyllic a region, removed from the smoke and congestion of the city.

Unlike Connie, who is surrounded on all sides by other military wives, Ann has civilian neighbours. But this does little to cut through the basic isolation she also feels. It is not only that the Kent housing estate is removed from any busy town centre. Army life is so peculiar in its rhythms and demands that a military wife feels quite cut off from civilian neighbours who can't possibly share those circumstances. Ann even gets nostalgic for life on base:

> We've been on the estate about two years now and really it is worse than other Army accommodations, mainly because here, Army families are split up into smaller groups. That means you don't get any feeling of community spirit. In the normal Army community everyone's in the same situation and they all muck in together. Here, we're all split up and the civilians don't know the Army people.[8]

On or off base, it seems, military wives experience a sense of being cut off that isn't explained simply by the housing conditions or physical proximity to civilians.

And from women's viewpoint, it is they, not their soldier husbands, who feel the isolation most acutely. Their husbands are an integral part of an institution that is defined as essential to the meaning of manhood and that is deemed crucial to the nation's security. Military wives, on the other hand, are fundamentally *marginal* at least to the publicly articulated meaning of the military, even while they are *integral* to that same institution's day-to-day maintenance.

Ann, whose husband is stationed at a base in Kent, tries to accept the fact her husband has to be away for long stretches of time. Not only does she feel 'trapped'—so do many of her civilian women neighbours—she also cannot make and keep lasting friends due to the constant moving:

> I don't think men realise what it's like to be just stuck here for 24 hours a day, seven days a week. My husband says he doesn't know how I stick it all day and he's pleased to get back to work... The army have just started a mother and toddler group. [But] being in the army means that even if you put your child's name down, by the time her turn comes, you're on the move again or the child is too old...
>
> In the army people are mostly between 20 and 40 as men do their 20 years and then get out, so most army people are young with children. The officers might be older, but they are separate anyway and don't live on this estate. Their wives aren't interested in personal relationships, only in a 'Lady Bountiful' type of way. I've never seen any officers' wives down here... At least the officers don't come round to inspect the houses any more, and even if they did, I wouldn't open the door![9]

The military wife as a political 'problem'

Ann and Connie attract senior officials' attention only when they become 'problems'. When the Thatcher government ordered the rapid mobilisation of the large Falklands task force in April 1982, the Ministry of Defence sent extra chaplains and social workers down to Portsmouth, the major departure point, to cope with what it presumed would be the distress of thousands of military wives. But no ambitious officer was going to earn military prestige and influence by attending to the needs of women and their children. And, as military wives tried to tell those reporters who would listen, the military more often than not left them in the dark as soon as the war in the South Atlantic took precedence over mere 'family problems' back in Portsmouth.

For centuries military commanders have debated the question of how to deal with the wives of soldiers—and their children. In a well-documented and wonderfully detailed account,[10] Myna Trustram describes just such a debate. These debates and how they are (at least temporarily) resolved don't attract most military historians' attention, but they can mark as much of a turning point in an army's historical evolution as a victory at Waterloo or a defeat in Vietnam.

Myna Trustram traces the controversy in Britain during and after the Crimean War, in the period from 1850 to 1880, over whether to allow soldiers to marry. Marriage had been expected of British army *officers*, but considered by the Army Command to be inappropriate for all but a select few of rank and file soldiers. The marriage debate took place, not coincidentally, at the same time as the more celebrated controversy over the Contagious Diseases Acts.

The question was, as always: How can women whom military men have relationships with be controlled so as to minimise women's influence on military operations while at the *same time* maintain the morale and re-enlistments of the men themselves?

Good morale and steady re-enlistment—these are two preoccupations of military commanders. They are as relevant in the nuclear 1980s as they were in the gunpowder 1880s. So long as soldiers' morale and re-enlistment could be assured without taking responsibility for wives and children, most military officials tried to limit and discourage troops marrying. But this has proved a luxury the military could not sustain. Recruiting officers going from town to town in Britain once did entice young men to join the army in order to *escape* their wives:

> If any gentleman, soldiers or others have a mind to serve Her Majesty, and pull down the French King; if any prentices have severe masters, any children have undutiful

> parents; if any servants have too little wages, or any husband too much wife, let them repair to the noble Sergeant Kite, at the sign of the Raven in this good town of Shrewsbury...[11]

In 1871, only 1.5 per cent of the British army's rank and file soldiers aged 20 to 24 were married, as contrasted to 23.03 per cent of British male civilians at the time. Among older soldiers, aged 30 to 34, the marriage rate rose to 25 per cent, but this was still far below the male civilian marriage rate of 75 per cent.[12] By 1971, one-third of British male soldiers had wives and/or children, and by 1979 *two-thirds* of male soldiers were married. It was a slow process by which the British army accepted the necessity not only of allowing soldiers to marry, but of providing soldiers' wives with decent living conditions and soldiers with pay adequate to support a family.

The Royal Navy did not prohibit marriage, perhaps because naval commanders saw homosexuality among men so long at sea as a much greater threat to military morale and discipline than wives waiting in home ports. The British navy also set sailors' pay higher than soldiers' pay in recognition of their need to support wives usually unable to get waged employment.[13] Similarly today the navy seems quicker to launch studies of military families and to acknowledge problems, perhaps because navy ports are more stable where a sense of community can be encouraged.[14] This suggests that each branch of the armed forces may have a different strategy of dealing with wives, due to different sorts of missions and organisational structures, even if all branches share a common basic sense that women are alien to the military institution.

During the Victorian era the British army came to see the allowing of marriage as necessary if they were to persuade soldiers to re-enlist. This became more imperative as the tours of duty to which soldiers committed themselves were shortened and thus re-enlistment decisions became more frequent in the life of any soldier. In the 1860s and 1870s, additionally, the British army was coming under pressure to conform to Victorian social morality and ensure that soldiers were orderly, moral men civilised by domestic ties. This, in turn, meant that women relating to soldiers should be made into 'angels of the house', providing their husbands with comfort and moral uplift. For military commanders who had thought or soldiers' wives as 'useless sloths... miserable drabs who are seen sauntering and smoking in the yard', this required a radical change in gender ideology.[15]

It was not until 1960 that the British army surrendered its cherished pay concept of the *single* soldier. In that year the military salary structure finally removed the disincentives for ordinary soldiers to marry. But with this change came the military's increased control of women who were married to soldiers.[16]

In 1942 the US Congress passed a law that provided some obstetric care and minimal family allowances to American military wives. And according to military social workers, it is only in the last 20 years that the American military establishment has taken the matter of military families seriously.[17]

In the 1970s and 1980s the militaries in Britain and the US are still carrying on internal debates (they could undermine the military's popular support if they became too public) over who is really responsible for military wives' well-being and, if the military, then to what extent. Both military establishments appear very reluctant to take on more responsibility, but British officials seem particularly afraid that the military may turn into a 'social welfare' agency. The British army, for instance, rejected most of the recommendations of a 1976 official *Report of the Committee of Enquiry on the Welfare of Military Families*.[18] While the committee was created during a mini-economic boom in Britain which made enlistments and re-enlistment goals hard to achieve, its report was received in the latter half of the 1970s when unemployment was rising and enlistments were on the upswing. In addition, the senior army officer within the Ministry of Defence, who had lent his enthusiastic support to the Committee's enquiry out of a conviction that the army ought to be doing more for the military families, had left his policy post inside the Ministry of Defence by 1976. Thus a combination of economic and personnel changes made it possible for army senior professional officers in 1976 to dismiss a report which called on them to spend money, personnel and energy on matters they thought were essentially 'unmilitary'.[19]

The British debate has to do not just with the military concept of itself and its sphere of obligation, but has to do with central government's own notion of who should be taking care of military families. The growth of a relatively comprehensive state welfare system in Britain over the last 50 years allows the state's military to use those services and avoid much direct responsibility for the social dislocations caused by its policies. As part of that welfare system's process, the Treasury, as guardian of the central purse, argues that local authorities where military bases are located should provide services to the families of military personnel. In a sense, as during the period of the Contagious Diseases Acts, the British central government wants local governments to play support roles to the military. Not surprisingly, local authorities argue that they lack both the funds and the expertise.[20]

American military officials in the 1980s appear somewhat more ready to mobilise resources to try to solve—or perhaps absorb—family problems; perhaps because there is not as comprehensive a welfare state to draw on to solve those problems and perhaps because the US military has so expanded its global mission (taking over from the British military in areas like East Africa and the Indian Ocean) that it needs to do more to guarantee that it retains its soldiers beyond their first or second voluntary tours. The US Department of Defense has long stood out among NATO military establishments for its use of—even co-option of—social scientists and social workers when coping with military morale problems. The Defense Department awards literally dozens of contracts to scores of social scientists every year to study everything from clothing design to race relations.

This difference between the Americans and the British military's current approaches to wives and children, however, should not be exaggerated. Senior officers in each generally wish they could enlist and re-enlist volunteers without having to contend with those volunteers' families. Both institutions see women married to soldiers and their children as 'problems'. Finally, both care about 'solving' those 'problems' only insofar as, left *un*solved, they could jeopardise, first, the military's political legitimacy in society at large and, second, the military's ability to recruit and *keep* the kinds of soldiers—in class, ethnic, education and sex terms—it thinks it needs.

Militarised social workers

The British military depends on the volunteers, nurses and social workers (mostly women) of the Soldiers, Sailors and Air Force Association (SSAFA), as well as on its own chaplains, psychiatrists, medical officers and family officers (mostly men), to cope with the problems posed by military families. Most of these social service personnel operate at the local base level and are subject to the base commander's authority, which limits their autonomy and influence. The British military today, unlike its American counterpart, directly employs few professional social workers. Some military welfare officers do take occasional special social work courses, but rarely with the goal of professional certification.[21]

At present, SSAFA fulfils many of the functions one might expect of a militarised social work agency. It concentrates its work on the army, since, once again, the navy seems to have its own distinct approach to military families. SSAFA (originally SSFA) was created in 1885 when two developments which affected the relationship of the military to British society converged: first, the ambitious expansion of the British empire by military force, which required the overseas posting of more and more British men at a time when more soldiers were allowed to marry; and second, the late-Victorian 'rediscovery' of the poor, among whom were most of the women married to rank and file soldiers.[22]

SSAFA was founded by Colonel James Gilder, in the wake of General 'China' Gordon's 10-month siege at Khartoum in the Sudan and on the eve of the departure of a large British task force to Egypt. From the start SSAFA was organised around the principle of unpaid women's labour. In the 1880s and 1890s local committees were set up around Britain—especially in towns hosting army garrisons. Local 'ladies' were urged to visit the homes of poor soldiers' wives. But SSAFA adopted a policy that caused some worry in the War Office: it refused to confine its charity services to the wives and children of soldiers who had married with official permission. Instead SSAFA's leaders saw *all* military families, even those furthest from official blessing—i.e. further 'off base'—as needing care. Only such a comprehensive approach, they reasoned, could ensure that British imperialism did not compromise the emergent Victorian social ethic. Nor did SSAFA volunteers focus, as the military establishment wished they would, on the moral failings of soldiers' wives. Rather, they took into account the inadequacies of the British military system itself, and the poor relief system, which left so many women desperately poor.

Among the 'ladies' recruited to do SSAFA's work were the wives of military officers. Officers' wives were thought to be especially well equipped to provide these services because they were women, because they were middle class and because they were uniquely familiar with the problems posed by military life. This sort of unpaid work also kept an officer's wife attached to her husband's regiment while he was abroad, thus perpetuating the notion of the regiment as a 'community'. Today, it is still typical for the SSAFA garrison committee to be headed by the wife of the base commanding officer.[23]

In 1892 SSAFA created a nursing branch, from which descended the SSAFA sister, so familiar to Connie and other contemporary British military wives. In the 1960s, SSAFA created a small cadre of social workers. By 1979, SSAFA had 21 social workers; most of them were women. Sixteen of SSAFA's social workers were posted overseas, most of them to West Germany.[24] Currently they see their role as coping with marital problems, especially the loneliness of young women, often 18 or 19 years old, married to young rank and file soldiers. By 1979, 64 per cent of the army's soldiers were married, a jump up from 50 per cent in the mid-sixties. The greatest increase in marriage has been among the youngest and lowest-ranking soldiers.[25] SSAFA now has a child abuse register, but since SSAFA sisters and social workers have no powers and are subject to military rule and law, the ultimate decision on any child abuse case remains in the hands of the base commander.[26]

The British military establishment, especially the army, has been wary of social workers and has generally kept the services that deal with military wives as peripheral as they have the wives themselves. But in the 1980s there may be gradual steps towards militarising social work more directly. The ultimate goal of military officials is to ensure that neither readiness nor re-enlistment is jeopardised by family—i.e. women—problems. In the early 1980s the army, for instance, was moving toward establishing a new 'marriage guidance programme'. Like SSAFA, however, the army would rely on volunteer workers.[27] The military may seem to resist, give in, waffle, then retrench on the question of whether the military itself should provide social service to military families; but what remains constant is the criterion against which any given scheme is tested: the military's *own* effectiveness and the maximisation of its *own* capacity for mobility, discipline and strategic force.

The US military is far less reluctant to use social scientists and social workers in its efforts to devise formulas to socialise women in being military wives and thereby reduce 'family problems' which might undermine readiness and re-enlistment. By the 1980s every branch of the armed forces had an elaborate family services unit which worked with the medical services and the chaplaincy.

An American television special in January 1982 reported on the country's new 'nine-to-five soldiers', men who joined the military at a time of high unemployment, attracted by technical training allegedly guaranteed to be transferrable to the civilian job market and living conditions of the sort they were used to in the civilian world.[28] These are the soldiers with whose families the US military social service establishment is being expanded to cope.

By 1982, *half* of the US army's personnel were married. The television cameras zoomed in on young male soldiers climbing into their Chevrolets and Fords in the late afternoon, driving home as if they had just finished work at a local factory. For the youngest and lowest-ranking men, 'home' was often an hour's drive from the base, a rundown apartment or a rented mobile home. At the end of the day, a pale young woman stood beside her khaki-clad husband outside their drab trailer home. In a listless voice, she told the TV reporter how hard it is to sustain their marriage when her husband is expected to work 14 hours a day, on unpredictable, irregular shifts, with moves every year.

Nowadays, 80 per cent of US army personnel move every year. Only about one-third of army families can obtain housing on base; the rest must compete in the local housing market, which may already be tight. For a military wife a transfer order means taking the children out of school, surrendering a hard-to-get, even if low-paid, job. Once transferred, she must again try to make shabby housing liveable, help the children readjust, make new friends, find a new job. Being told by their own social workers and by outside social science consultants that these strains are hurting their soldiers' morale and cutting into re-enlistments, Pentagon officials have begun experimenting with alternative transfer schemes. One such scheme is a deliberate borrowing from their British allies: the regimental system, which allegedly sustains morale and cohesiveness among soldiers (though not necessarily among wives) by transferring men in whole units instead of individually.

Aside from this example, however, it does not seem that the kind of extensive sharing of information and 'lessons' that goes on in the areas of technology, training and strategy also takes place within NATO on matters of military wives and military families. It may be that notions about what is the proper way to deal with wives and families are more culture-bound and that this makes each military establishment more confident in its own home-grown analyses and prescriptions.[29]

As in Britain, the American military tries to cultivate the ethos of being a 'family'. The military-as-family myth encourages men to feel emotional bonds to a collectivity beyond their own wives and children. It is also meant to bind soldiers' wives and children to the larger institution in which their husbands and fathers serve.

Chaplains in the US military currently act as family officers, although they identify most closely with the soldiers themselves. The Vietnam war prompted many army chaplains to question the idea that they were an instrument in the hands of commanders designed to keep up the troops' morale. Since chaplains are inside the regular military structure and depend on a commander's evaluation for their own promotion, they have been understandably reluctant to act on their own scepticism.[30] Whether their post-Vietnam questioning wins out over their investment in the military hierarchy will shape how much effective assistance they can and will provide to women on base, since providing that assistance—say, to a woman being battered by her officer husband—could rouse the irritation of the chaplain's military superior.

The American military hires its own social workers and contracts civilian schools of social work to put on special courses for their family service personnel. For instance, in the mid-1970s Boston University School of Social Work was paid by the Department of Defense to train military school workers for work with troops stationed in West Germany, a posting where young enlisted men's wives suffer both social isolation and miserable off-base living conditions. The Boston University course was intended to develop military social workers' 'community organising' skills, skills to persuade military wives—especially officers' wives—to participate in on-base programmes aimed at alleviating the difficulties of *rank and file* soldiers' wives.

Many of the military social workers were frustrated at the hierarchy they confronted at every turn. Not only were they expected to be sensitive to their particular commander's priorities, not only were they expected to reinforce the already existing chasm between officers' wives and ordinary soldiers' wives. The social workers were also, they felt, not fully used by many women on base who feared that they and their children would be labelled 'problem families' in some bureaucratic evaluation file and that this could hurt their husbands' chances for promotion or for an attractive transfer.[31]

Some of these dilemmas and contradictions faced by military social workers are identical to those experienced by civilian social workers employed by state welfare bureaucracies: they may be motivated by the desire to help individuals, but they depend on the authority of a state which is suspicious of or hostile to those individuals.[32] But the military social worker is part of an even tighter chain of command and has less access to those civilian political support groups—feminists or a progressive party organisation—trying to monitor and transform the welfare system in which the social worker plays so instrumental a role. The military social worker works within an establishment which sees women as not just potentially a financial drain (a theme certainly familiar to civilian social workers) but as a threat to its mobility and fighting capacity. It uses psychiatrists to keep its soldiers psychologically fit to fight and chaplains and social workers to keep soldiers' wives supportive of their husbands' combat readiness.[33] The American military establishment contracts out many of its social service functions commercially. Scores of academically affiliated sociologists conduct research for the Department of Defense—on housing, spouse employment, recreation, child abuse, and 'dual career families'. In the 1980s, as funds for social science research from civilian agencies become scarcer and as the Defense Department becomes more worried about fashioning a policy on military wives that will serve its re-enlistment and readiness needs, American academics and their university administrations are likely to be more tempted to compete for DOD research contracts. The convergence of these two trends could make civilian social science a tool increasingly available to the American military, regardless of the intent of the civilian researcher.

On the Virginia side of the Potomac River, where so many sprawling American government agencies and contracted consultants are vying for office space, the Military Family Resource Center has been established. A sub-unit of the YMCA, the Center receives Defense Department funding. It serves as a co-ordinator for the mountains of information generated nowadays by contracted social scientists, civilian social agencies and the Defense Department itself on all aspects of the military family. Its computerised archives testify to the military's worried uncertainty over what to do with the military wife. A recent issue of the Center's newsletter, *Military Family*, reveals the range of activities in what might be termed the 'military family industry': a report on wife abuse in the military; an upcoming conference on child abuse; a national 'hot line' for recruiting officers dealing with family questions; an FBI training programme on family violence prevention which will include military trainees; a study of stress experienced by the US Asian-born military wives; the creation of a new 'Brides' School' in South Korea for new wives of American soldiers; an announcement of a new association for young children of European-based American soldiers; a review of a new resource book *Temporary Military Lodging Around the World*; a report on the 'Week-end Husband, Week-end Dad' for the navy's family service officers.[34]

Promoting 'readiness' and servicing the military family

> The US Army, along with the other branches, realises that strong healthy families play a highly important role in on-the-job performance of the uniformed (male) members, which eventually equates to improved operational readiness. The services also recognise the impact that the family career decision process... Measures that address family issues in the military reflect an understanding that the military's family's well-being and the welfare of the military are parallel.[35]

These 'family issues'—violence against women, child abuse, mental health, decent housing, spouse job placement remain salient only when male officers believe that, by tackling them, they will serve *military* objectives:

> The primary aim of the QOL (Quality of Life) program is to promote the development of military and civilian group commitment essential to combat readiness... Effective quality of life programs help soldiers *to concentrate on mission performance...* as well as helping *to foster loyalty and dedication to the Army* [emphasis mine].[36]

One American general's wife observes that under the Reagan Administration 'readiness' has become *the* criterion for evaluating virtually every US military practice because the military's capacity for 'rapid deployment' (to Central Europe, to the Persian Gulf) is believed by Reagan strategists to be the key to

US national security.[37] In other words, the more a government's basic national security formula lays stress on its military capacity for rapid deployment, the more likely are soldiers' wives to be seen as needing attention not for their own sake but so they will not *jeopardise* military mobility.

The ideological beauty of 'readiness' is that it can be used to refer to *everything*—from the state of truck repair to the quality of troops' training. 'Readiness' requires that a wife's depression or impoverishment not make a soldier reluctant to board ship. 'Readiness' requires that a male soldier be sure enough of his wife's sexual fidelity 'back home' that he can give his primary attention to following orders in battle. Paradoxically, that is, wives are being aided today in order to ensure that a soldier's *first* loyalty is to the military.

'Readiness' is closely tied to 'retention'. An armed force is presumed not to be in a state of readiness if it can't fill its ranks or if it can't retain its seasoned soldiers. A 1981 US Department of Defense study concludes that the two variables having the most significant impact on a married military man's or woman's decision to re-enlist for another tour are, first, spouse attitudes toward the military, second, the family members' commitment to the particular branch of the service.[38]

So we come full circle: wives and children must be kept happy enough so that male soldiers can give their primary loyalty to the military. And the soldier is most likely to re-enlist if his wife and children are also committed to his service.

Britain's Ministry of Defence puts out recruiting brochures portraying the military as an ideal setting for happy family life. A full-colour pamphlet shows a 'modern' apartment complete with male soldier, wife, toddler, and two young girls drawing contentedly at the Danish-style dining table. Encircling this scene of military domestic tranquillity are photos of men in khaki fatigues deployed on field manoeuvres, rolling through a quaint German town in an armoured vehicle, or taking an electronics course. The brochures don't reveal how the soldier's wife fills her days while he's carrying out the military's mission.

Soldier, the slick magazine of the British army, carries features aimed at the military wife. In its wives' complaints column there are reports on special seminars organised for army wives. The patroness of one such seminar, Lady Elizabeth Kitson, assured soldiers' wives that they were valued by the male hierarchy. According to Lady Elizabeth, wives provide the unpaid support that ensures British military readiness:

> I believe that wives have a great part to play in the future, not only supporting their husbands (*the more demanding his job, the more support he will need*) but also in their contribution to the Army and life in general [emphasis mine].[39]

Working wives as military wives

Historically, a soldier's pay has rarely been adequate to support two adults and their children, while military mobility and sexism in society at large has made it impossible for a soldier's wife to get and keep a waged job. Until recently, pay scales have assumed soldiers to be bachelors. The resulting economic hardship this has caused women and children has been put to the military's own use. Base commanders have hired wives of rank and file men to do such 'unskilled' military jobs as sewing, nursing, cooking and cleaning. Other wives, especially women married to officers, have provided labour for bases' social services without pay. This two-layered system has provided the military with cheap female labour while relieving it of the responsibility for paying a family wage to its soldiers. In periods when the military has promoted the notion of itself as a 'family', this system has also reinforced institutional ties and intensified the militarisation of soldiers' wives and children:

> In keeping with the notion of the regiment as a family, wives [in the mid-Victorian British Army] worked for the regiment instead of just for their own husband and children. Thus, the dependency ties between individual husbands and wives were loosened and the commonalty of regimental life was stressed.[40]

Usually, however, the labour of military wives is used not as a subtle scheme to build 'regimental familialism' but simply to avoid paying male soldiers a decent wage as well as to take advantage of easily available cheap women's labour.

Susie King Taylor was a black woman born a slave in the American South in 1848. During the civil war her husband joined one of the Union army's black regiments. Susie King Taylor 'followed' her husband, earning no pay, but surviving by doing soldiers' laundry in exchange for rations. Later she also provided the Union army with her services as a nurse and teacher to the largely illiterate soldiers. But in the military command's eyes she remained just a soldier's wife. Writing after the war, she recalled,

> The first coloured troops did not receive any pay for eighteen months and the men had to depend wholly on what they received from the commissionary... A great many of these men had large families and as they had no money to give them their wives were obliged to support themselves and the children by washing for the [white] officers of the gun boats and the [black] soldiers, and making cakes and pies, which they sold to the boys in camp...[41]
>
> I taught a great many of the comrades in Company E to read and write when they were off duty, nearly all of them anxious to learn... I gave my services willingly for four years and three months without receiving a dollar. I was glad, however, to be allowed to go with the regiment, to care for the sick and afflicted comrades.
>
> I learned to handle a musket very well... I assisted in cleaning the guns and used to fire them off, to see if the cartridges were dry... I thought this was great fun. I was also able to take a gun apart and put it together again.[42]

Both military labour cost cutting and military familialism is served when some wives work for other wives on a military base. In his memoir of a childhood spent on a 1930s peacetime US army base in Missouri, the poet William Jay Smith describes the ordinary daily life of a woman, his mother, married to a career enlisted man. His father played the clarinet in the base band, gambled away his pay and tried to earn some extra money by producing home brew. His wife's life at the Jefferson Barracks was defined by her husband's rank (which sometimes rose and other times tumbled) and by the ranks of the other women's husbands:

> Some of the officers, not content with the way the Post Laundry did their khaki trousers, took them to the wives of enlisted men so that they might get special attention...
>
> My mother's sewing prowess became well known, and she soon found herself employed by friends and neighbours, and finally, of course, by the officers' wives...
>
> My mother also began to serve at officers' tea parties and luncheons, mainly in the quarters of lieutenants and captains. The officers of higher rank usually had help in the house—often Filipino [male] servants whom they had brought back from the Orient.[43]

However, when soldiers' wives go 'off base' for waged jobs, they pose a dilemma for army officialdom. On the one hand, military wives who are able to get decently paid civilian jobs on their own reduce the demoralising poverty of soldiers' families and lessen the pressure for pay raises. On the other hand, in the process military commanders lose some of their control over those more independent women. The soldier husband also becomes harder for the military to move because his wife now has an economic stake in staying where she has found employment. Furthermore, as more officers' wives as well as those of rank and file soldiers get off-base jobs, the myth of the single-minded devoted 'military family' cracks. The military family has to be recognised as the household of women and men and children with differing powers and needs that in fact it has always been.

The US military, with its current penchant for contracting social science investigations into all new issues, is already producing scores of studies of the 'problems' posed by this new generation of working wives in the military.[44] The US air force, the service that prides itself on being in the vanguard of services recognising and responding to new social problems, has established a Military Spouse Skills and Resource Center near Washington, DC, to provide job information for the thousands of military wives who move in and out of the Washington area every year.

What is new in the military is *not* that there are working wives, but that they are working for *pay*, off base, in jobs to which they are developing some commitment of their own. Military policy-makers do not feel threatened by women's labour, but by women's commitment to that labour and its rewards.

Women who are military wives often find that they gain more than simply added financial security when they get a job off base. As Connie found, a soldier's wife can break out of depressing isolation and can acquire friends who do not relate to her merely as a sergeant's wife or a captain's wife.

But a military wife working off base may also find that she is subject to military suspicion. Is she neglecting her duties as a loyal military wife? Is she becoming a liability to her husband's upwardly mobile career? Is she going off base in order to have relations with other men?

Such suspicion is rooted not only in the idea that the wife of a soldier has loyalty to her husband and his military mission as her first priority. It is rooted also in the assumption that the military life is a *good* life, and it is life lived *on* base. With all the perquisites and securities offered by the military to members of its 'family', why would any reasonable, *respectable* women want to go off base?

An American woman who grew up in the 1970s as the daughter of an officer recalls that she and her friends and their mothers were constantly told that civilians envied military families because of all the benefits they enjoyed. And while the base was a secure haven, society outside the gates, they were told, was full of uncertainties and potential disorder. All of these on-base, off-base distinctions, of course, were intensified when the base was located in a foreign country and the people outside the gates were poorer or spoke a different language.[45]

In a recent issue of *Soldier*, the British army sounded a similar alarm to its soldiers and their wives and children:

> [For] wives and children... left behind by soldiers of today's highly mobile, go-anywhere army, there is a more sinister trend in society which only personal security can really combat. Military families are probably less at risk than

> the public from the mugger, the rapist and the burglar. But the risk is still there and the military and civilian police cannot hope to be in the spot every time.[46]

For a woman married to an enlisted man—just out of school, forced to move every one or two years—there is little chance to acquire skills or seniority in an off-base job. She takes whatever job she can find—on an assembly line in a nearby factory, behind the counter at a Wimpy bar or a McDonald's. Such a job may relieve some of the financial strain in her marriage to a lowly paid soldier and may loosen the military's grip on her daily life, but she is scarcely setting out on a rewarding, liberating 'career'.

Most military bases rely on the *unpaid* labour of officers' wives. An officer's wife is supposed to be the quintessential civic volunteer. The base is a 'community' and, like so many middle-class suburbs, it is made liveable by the unpaid services provided by women-as-wives. Even more than in an affluent civilian suburb, however, the volunteer work of officers' wives is tied to their husbands' upward career mobility because, more than most suburban communities, the base 'community' and the husband's employer are tightly integrated. Maybe the closest analogy is the set of expectations imposed on executives' wives in a company town.

An officer's wife is expected to aid her husband in winning promotion. She is expected to be the gracious hostess, to donate her time and labour to the service organisations that make a base a 'home'. A wife who refuses to perform this duty is told—by her husband, by his superiors, and by other military wives—that she is jeopardising her husband's career. He will be evaluated on how well he controls his troops and keeps his tanks and planes in repair but also partly on how well his wife helps to keep the military's social gears turning smoothly. Many of the unpaid volunteer jobs done by officers' wives are in organisations meant to benevolently service the wives of enlisted men. This, of course, reinforces the stratified structure in which military wives are supposed to relate to each other. It also allows the male military officialdom to use the unpaid labour of some women to plaster over the problems of other women. Today not all officers' wives are compliant.[47] A general's wife tells this story of her own rebellion and she tells it with an undisguised pride:

> I was stationed with my husband in Germany. There was a new unit opening up north. The job was to serve as 'city manager' for the military community. It would have been a good move for him.
>
> My husband and I talked it over and decided to accept the post offer. So he went to the officer in charge of his transfer and told him of his decision, adding that 'My wife is teaching school and has already worked out a transfer, too.'
>
> But the superior quickly retorted, 'Oh no, your wife would be expected to set up the community services there.' For free, he meant.
>
> So my husband turned down the job. But naturally, the post didn't go unfilled. Some other general's wife did it.[48]

Military wives mothering the military

> 'Vous travaillez pour l'armée, madame?' [Are you working for the army?] a Frenchwoman said to me early in the Vietnam war, on hearing I had three sons.[49]

Adrienne Rich recalled this experience in the 1960s as she sought to understand the purposes to which society—and its military force—puts women's capacity to mother.

Social policy on abortion, sterilisation, homosexuality and family allowances can *potentially* be incorporated into government schemes to enhance militarism. Even before Hitler came to power for instance, powerful political forces in Weimar Germany were promoting state regulations directed at women which would help the government re-militarise. Bertolt Brecht and the composer Hans Eisler collaborated in the late 1920s to write the song, 'Abortion Is Illegai', to protest at the militarist intent that lay behind the paragraph 218 of the Weimar Republic's constitution:

> 'Well, doctor, it's my period.'

'Why, you should just be glad. The population figures are getting a little boost.'
'But, doctor, we have no place to live.'
'But you've a bed, I'm sure, so chin up, little lady! Don't overwork for a spell. You're going to be a lovely little mother, you're going to make a hunk of cannon fodder...'
'But doctor...'
'Please, Mrs Renner, I can't quite follow you now. Our country, you know, needs people to man the big machines! You're going to be a lovely little mother, you're going to make a hunk of cannon fodder. It's what your belly's for. And that's no news to you and what else can you do? And now do not squall. You're having the baby, that's all...'[50]

It is never easy for the armed forces to acquire the manpower they claim they need. Male conscription helps, but it may be politically palatable only for a short time and it may fill only the ranks of the army. High population growth, rising male unemployment, development of capital intensive weaponry, wartime fervour—all can help bolster voluntary enlistment. Still, even in the nuclear age, military planners constantly worry about acquiring the quality and the quantity of soldiers they consider adequate to guarantee military effectiveness.

Military commanders and civilian security officials have tried to fill their particular manpower needs by convincing women in the country to think of themselves as reproducers not just of 'the nation', but of their government's soldiery. Campaigns celebrating 'patriotic motherhood' have been launched in virtually every country whose government has set about to build or rebuild a powerful military organisation.

These campaigns seem to occur most commonly during the '*post-war era*'. A post-war era is not simply the years that happen to follow a war; it is a time when society is being reorganised to relieve whatever tensions developed as a result of the extraordinary level of militarisation that characterised wartime. Governments thus see the post-war era as a time to demobilise many women recruited into 'men's jobs' during the war. It is a time when any relaxation of sexual mores permitted for the sake of male soldiers' 'morale' is likely to be reversed. And it is a time when the relative moratorium on having children because of wartime separations of husbands and wives must, in government's eyes, be ended.[51]

Men killed in the war must be replaced. Women, who during wartime were urged to define themselves chiefly as defence workers, will now have to be encouraged to think of themselves once again as mothers. If they do work for wages after the war—and many women who lose their high-paying industrial jobs are still in demand at lower wage rates in service jobs—women will still have to be urged to see mothering, replenishing the nation, as their principal vocation.

Yet such campaigns to militarise motherhood do not usually deal with all women in society in the same way. Precisely because they are at best partially informed by official ideas about the requisites for 'national security', these campaigns make distinctions among women according to class, race and ethnicity ('ethnicity' means a division that is not strictly racial, i.e. between WASPS and Italians, or between Welsh and Scots). So in the 1980s Soviet planners are urging their racially Russian women, not their racially Asian women, to have more children. South Africa's white elite is encouraging white women to have more children so as to fill the already white-male-deprived military, while it grows anxious over large families in the African community. Likewise, the US, Israeli, Guyanese, and Malaysian governments are all building up their military and this is matched by growing attention to different birth rates among their politically unequal ethnic and racial groups. Militarising regimes may share the idea that all women are potential mothers, but they usually do not look upon the mothers of all ethnic groups as equally beneficial for 'national security'.

Soviet, German, Italian, American, Canadian, British, and Israeli post-war eras all reveal this governmental preoccupation with women as mothers. As the experiences of women in all these countries suggest, mothering the military isn't defined simply as producing a new generation of men. It also implies that women should *nurture* and *socialise* their sons to become strong and soldier-like and their *daughter* to develop penchants for loyalty, mothering, low-paid and unpaid labour.[52]

Some post-war periods in fact extend so long that they become *pre*-war periods. That is, some campaigns to rebuild the nation and replenish the military after the *last* war help to create social structures and ideological expectations that themselves make the next war a foregone conclusion. Should Britain's 1930s be thought of as the post-war era of the first world war? Or is it more accurate to think of that decade as the pre-war era leading to the second world war? The answer may lie in analysing how Britain's post-first world war ideologies and policies served to create its pre-second world war era. The motherhood campaigns of the 1920s and 1930s were planks in the bridge between 'post-war' and 'pre-war' eras.

For centuries armies have relied on the *sons of soldiers* to replenish their ranks. While these offspring could never completely fill commanders' manpower needs, they could supply a steady, predictable flow of pre-conditioned, loyal soldiers and officers.

> Sons whose fathers made a career of military service... [are] an important source of high-quality recruitment of both officers and enlisted personnel...
>
> Without such occupational inheritance, the all-volunteer force would have an ever greater difficulty in obtaining personnel.[53]

It was the military wife who was counted on to produce the next generation of the military's most loyal soldiers; it was the military wife within the military family who was expected to socialise the children so as to save later drill sergeants the bother.[54]

Both British and American forces see the children of military personnel as forming a valuable pool of potential recruits. A combination of circumstances is currently prompting British and American military recruiters to devote more time and energy to military children: both forces now depend on volunteers; both face national birth rates in sharp decline; neither can count on the current economic recession to keep unemployment rates so high that jobless youths will continue to look favourably on military enlistment; both have become so strategically and technologically sophisticated that training costs have skyrocketed, making it economically imperative that the recruits who come into the military have the commitment to *stay* in.[55]

When the military wife is a man

All military strategy on soldiers' spouses has been rooted in the assumption that a soldier—or sailor or pilot—is a man and, if a soldier is allowed to marry, the soldier's spouse is a woman.

The benefits as well as dangers allegedly flowing from the military spouse are defined by military officials in terms of gender, not mere spousehood. The military spouse is presumed to be an effective morale booster or a comforter of the wounded partner because the spouse is a woman doing what a woman 'naturally' does so well. Likewise, commanders try to reduce any danger the military spouse poses to military 'readiness' by reinforcing the gender ideology which claims that men decide where a family will reside and how it will make a livelihood. It follows also from gender, not just spousehood, that the military spouse can nonetheless jeopardise military readiness because she is a woman and as a woman she puts emotional attachments and loyalty to her children ahead of her husband's occupation or abstract patriotism.

There have been women *soldiers* in armies for centuries. But they have not upset this set of assumptions. Many of those women soldiers entered the military disguised as men or boys. Or they were mobilised only when the government was desperate and then only temporarily. Or strict military regulations prohibited women soldiers from marrying while in the service. Or those women soldiers were lesbians and did not want to marry.

Since the early 1970s, the all-volunteer forces of Britain and the US have recruited women into their 'peacetime' regular forces in greater numbers than ever before. Their numbers are significant even if they remain a small minority—4 per cent of the British forces; 9 per cent of the US forces.

The need to cut down on 'wastage', the drop-out of expensively trained and skilled manpower, combined with the general

—if often superficial—social acceptance of more equal treatment for working married women, has made it harder to discharge married women soldiers. The result: male military spouses.[56]

It is less their numbers than their ideological awkwardness that makes 'military husbands' politically significant. The military husband is not expected to play the same helpmate, nurturing, soothing role for the military as his female counterpart. He is not expected to quit his job and move every time his soldier wife is transferred. He is not expected to be as deferential either to the general's wife or to the general as his female counterpart. And he cannot be expected to provide unpaid or cheap labour to make the base 'a community'.

Some of the ideological hazards produced by the emergence of the military husband are diluted, however, because so many of these military husbands are themselves soldiers. As of 1981, there were 55,293 'dual career' families in the American forces. As many as 25 per cent of all women in the US military are married to men who are in the military. If they are not kept happy, the military risks losing not one, but two trained soldiers.[57]

Military wives coping with racism

> I think the women generally of that class in England look more to the future and hesitate to marry a soldier, whereas in Ireland, and indeed in Scotland, they do not think about it, they marry them at once without reflecting. I think that the young women in England are more careful about marrying a soldier.[58]

This member of a nineteenth-century British government commission was investigating the impact of marriage regulations and other conditions on the Victorian army's ability to fill its recruiting quotas. In doing so, he made an assumption as common today as it was in the mid-nineteenth century—that these are ethnic divisions, as in this case between the English and Scots or Irish, in military forces, and that the relationships of women to any military force will reflect that ethnic design.

Soldiers themselves are typically recruited by security-conscious regimes from particular ethnic groups in order to ensure that recruitment quotas can be met but also that the forces will remain loyal to the government. These two objectives are not always compatible, since the men most often accessible to recruiters are from the ethnic or racial groups lowest on the economic-political ladder and least able to get jobs in the civilian sector. In such a situation the ranks and officer corps are likely to look strikingly different ethnically—e.g. Irish and Scottish men filling the ranks, while the English, Anglo-Irish and Anglo-Scottish dominate the officer corps. Thus the women who marry ordinary soldiers, not surprisingly, have different ethnic attachments than those women who marry officers, so that ethnic/racial stereotypes reinforce ranking stratifications. The popular belief in 1870s Britain, for instance, was that a large proportion of soldiers' wives were Irish and that Irish and Scottish women 'were the backbone of the slatternly class of soldiers' wives'.[59]

Although information isn't readily available on the ethnic composition of British military wives in the 1980s, women married to British soldiers and sailors still reflect the internal stratification of the military as well as its foreign basing strategies. Maltese women who married British soldiers while they were stationed in Malta stick together as a distinct group on some bases today.[60] The number of Irish women who have married British soldiers posted in Ulster is now large enough to be cited by SSAFA social workers as a potential 'problem group' on bases in West Germany.[61]

Black women have been American military wives since the civil war. But it has been in the 1970s and 1980s, especially with the end of the draft and the rise in black males as a proportion of all male volunteers, that black military wives have grown in number. The US military's long history of institutionalised racism suggests that black women married to American soldiers have to cope with the problems confronting white military wives but in an exacerbated form. This is borne out by black observers. One black woman who spent four years as a military wife came away from that experience with the impression, for instance, that the white women she knew were more likely to come from backgrounds that stressed traditional women's roles, whereas she and other black women married to soldiers expected to have jobs and thus were especially frustrated at having to make continual moves that meant giving up off-base jobs.[62] In addition, a race relations officer recalls that in the early 1970s on a base in Florida any black woman in civilian clothes seen in the vicinity of the base was presumed to be a prostitute: 'This was embarrassing when it turned out to be a colonel's wife.'[63]

As the British forces have been pulling back from their global policing role, their American allies have been reaching out. Each expansion—to Panama, Cuba, Japan, South Korea, the Philippines, Thailand, Vietnam, West Germany and Britain itself—has produced large numbers of marriages of local women to American soldiers and US military wives are therefore increasingly culturally and racially diverse.

Between 1945 and 1980, nearly 250,000 Asian and Pacific Island women married American soldiers overseas. Most of these women immigrated back to the United States after their husbands' tours of duty were completed.[64] US military men at both the command level and the 'buddy' level worry when an American soldier becomes seriously involved with an Asian woman. Friends try to introduce him to their American girl friends on the base; commanders urge him to have a good talk with the chaplain; the US Consulate conducts a security check and physical examination before permission to marry and to take his Asian wife back to the US is granted. There seems to be a widespread fear that Asian women are likely to be little more than prostitutes latching on to a naive American soldier in order to gain access to an immigration visa and economic security. Indeed, according to Bok-Lim Kim, an Asian woman who is a social worker servicing Asian wives of soldiers, many American men do transfer their simplistic racial and sexual notions on to the Asian women they meet while stationed overseas:

> Many of these men discovered that in their relationships to Oriental women, their feelings, comfort and welfare were given precedence. Thus for the first time they felt accepted by solicitous, unquestioning women who respected them... Handicapped by a language barrier, by an ignorance of

American culture, and by limited social experiences, these women failed to view the men in realistic terms; they considered them masculine and potential security-giving mates.[65]

Many American male soldiers see Asian women as an appealing contrast to what they perceive as the 'bossy, domineering and castrating' American women back home. Needing to find a validation of their own beliefs about natural femininity, these men imagine Asian women to be docile and subservient, part innocent, part 'Susie-Wong', eager to please their men.[66]

This sort of male fantasy may be especially harmful for Asian women in the 1980s, a time when the American women's movement is pushing toward its demands *and* when American military strategists are reasserting US dominance of the Indian-Ocean-to-China-Sea region by expanding the ring of US overseas bases.

Many Asian women who marry American soldiers meet them while working in service jobs on base or in nearly off-base 'R&R' businesses in Asia. They have sought out these jobs, often with their parents' encouragement, in order to earn money to send home to impoverished families. After they have married and followed their husbands away, they still carry responsibility for their family's economic subsistence back home even though they now are thousands of miles away.

Asian-American women social workers have reported that the Asian wives of American soldiers face awesome problems, magnifying the isolation, marginalisation and violence that so many military wives experience. In 1976, a coalition of women's groups, the military Chaplain's Office and the American Red Cross came together to form the National Committee Concerned with Asian Wives of US Servicemen.[67] Their principal concern is the high incidence of physical abuse suffered by Asian military wives.

One Korean woman's experience shows up the complex threads of militarism, sexism, and racism that are woven together in the lives of Asian military wives. Misook was an infant when her father died. She left school to earn money to assist her mother, a peddler, and to support her six brothers and sisters. She taught herself English and mathematics so that she could get a job as a cashier on one of the several bases the US military occupies in South Korea. There she met Marvin, a young American man who had dropped out of college, had had several brief jobs and joined the army in order to escape a smothering home environment:

> Until the birth of her first child, Susan, Misook continued her work (on the base in Korea) and Marvin was agreeable to their financial support of Misook's family. Misook was extremely happy with Susan, but Marvin began to stay out with his drinking buddies...
>
> At that point she discovered Marvin's heavy drinking and heroin addiction... She managed to get to see the military doctor, a Korean herbal doctor, his commanding officer, and the chaplain, a rabbi. When each of these measures failed to cure him of his addiction, she asked his commanding officer to transfer him to the United States...
>
> Marvin's violent behaviour began when Misook took a strong stand against his drinking and pill taking... She was determined that Marvin must either quit his bad habits or she would divorce him and go to work. She was no longer nurturing or subservient toward him, and he started hitting her when she disagreed with him... The pattern of violence escalated to the point of knife wielding and that was when Misook took the positive step of seeking help from the neighbour.[68]

Military wives militant

As the contradictions in the military's attitudes and policies towards military spouses have become more acute in the 1980s, space has opened up for some military wives to assert their autonomy and to begin to organise politically.

Not surprisingly, perhaps, the military wives who have led the way in political organising are those enjoying the greatest cultural and bureaucratic distance from the military—the widows of servicemen and the divorced wives of servicemen.

These still nascent efforts do not challenge the fundamental myths of the 'military family'. Rather, they *use* them to legitimise their claims. These women make their claims *as* military wives.

Military widowhood can be both an ideological boon to militarism, but also a liability to the military itself. Widows can be used to symbolise the 'supreme sacrifice'. Encouraging *all* women in the country to identify with each military widow or grieving mother, a government can try to turn the government's soldiers into 'our boys', deserving of *all* women's support. Mussolini's Italian regime elevated the widows and mothers of dead soldiers to a special status. Israel's government has bestowed special state pensions on women who have lost either husbands or sons in its wars.

At the same time military widows are expensive and often politically awkward. The Argentinian military regime is embarrassed by its Falkland war widows. It wishes they and the surviving veterans would stay discreetly out of public view.[69] In the aftermath of their Falklands victory Britons set up a private South Atlantic Fund for the widows of 247 servicemen and merchant seamen killed in the conflict. The Fund was testimony not only to British militarist pride but to the inadequacy of the current military pension scheme. It also raised questions about inadequacy and inequities of compensation for widows of British soldiers killed in Ulster.[70] Are the women widowed in some wars less worthy than women widowed in other wars?

In 1981, the Reagan White House, intent upon reducing social programme budgets in order to pay for larger defence outlays, cut social security benefits to soldiers' widows once their children reached the age of 16 and to the children themselves once they reached 18. Widows began to organise opposition through groups such as 'Survivors of Sacrifice' (SOS).

> Our husbands made a contract with the government that if anything happened to them, their widows and children would be taken care of... Our husbands kept their part of the bargain. Now we want the government to keep its part...

> It's broken promises. I'm suppose to be the widow of a hero, and I have to be down on the ground.[71]

Another group of angry American military wives is composed of *ex*-wives. EXPOSE—Ex-spouses of Servicemen (women) for Equality—was formed in May 1980 to 'alert members of congress to the need for laws to correct injustices to ex-military spouses caused by the loss of military benefits in event of divorce —especially of long marriages'—and to educate 'past, present, and future military spouses to what happens to spouse benefits in event of divorce from a member of the Uniformed Services'.[72]

The women spearheading EXPOSE's mobilising and lobbying efforts are heartened by their group's growth from a dozen women in 1980 to over 3,000 women in mid-1982. One ex-wife of a general explained that the catalyst was the US Supreme Court's 1980 'McCarty' decision. The Court declared that a man with military retirement benefits (pensions, PX privileges, health care) had total control over those benefits and did not have to share them with his ex-wife in any divorce settlement. Since retirement benefits constitute the chief property of a military careerist, this decision left military ex-wives essentially with no alimony.[73]

The women most enraged were those who had been married to their husbands during most of their 20 years of pre-retirement service. They had worked to promote their husbands' careers; they had staffed on-base volunteer services; they had 'kept the home fires burning' while their husbands were off fighting the government's wars.

To Winnie Cowan, Vice-President of EXPOSE, the Pentagon seems concerned solely about the military man. It protects its soldiers and designs programmes that give him incentives to stay in the military. Were the Pentagon to accept the military ex-wives' claim, it would undermine the male careerist incentive to serve his full 20 years. After all, she explains, his retirement benefits would no longer be his to control, withdraw or bestow on a new wife.[74]

EXPOSE has tried to reach out to wives of officers, NCOs and enlisted men. The ex-wives' principal organising criterion has been the length of service and thus benefits at risk in case of divorce after retirement. One woman explained her activism:

> I'd always been shy, keeping the home going when we moved, did the entertaining required of an officer's wife. My husband retired as a Brigadier General. I was never active, I was a helper. Then after 31 years of service, my husband divorced me and married a younger woman he'd known for two months. Now she gets all his benefits. I resented it and so I'll fight to the grave for this. Other women, too, who've felt all alone, divorced, stripped of benefits we deserved—now we feel part of a group.[75]

In the past, divorce was frowned on by the American military establishment. Ex-wives tell of then General Dwight D. Eisenhower in the 1940s wanting to divorce Mamie. His superior, General George Marshall, told Ike in no uncertain terms that he would stay married to Mamie or else ruin his military career. Now, however, 'all the top brass are divorcing—even three and four star generals'. The 'military family', that structure designed to maintain military cohesiveness, is becoming a base for the rebellion of the most militarised of military wives.

While most of these newly militant military ex-wives and widows are not yet questioning the role of the military in society, they are at least challenging the idea that women deserve attention, protection, counselling or pensions only insofar as they enhance male soldiers' military effectiveness. In challenging this idea they are coming to realise that if there is ever a choice posed between the military's own needs and military wives' needs, there is no question that the latter will be treated as expendable—not only expendable, but as a threat to the male soldiers' performance and ultimately to the mission of the entire military establishment. They are exposing the myth of the 'military family' that has structured their own lives.

Militarising the movement for women's shelters and refuges?

> There was always violence just below the surface of military life, a violence that led many men to blow their

tops, get busted and sent to the guardhouse.[76]

According to the 1979 US Inspector General's report on domestic violence, 'social workers and other persons working with battered women in [American] military families agree that military service is probably more conducive to violence at home than at any other occupation' because of the military's authoritarianism, its use of physical force in training and the stress produced by perpetual moves and separations. In addition, those men in the civilian population most likely to physically abuse the women with whom they live are men who have had prior military service.[77]

It does not take war to generate that 'violence just below the surface' that so many observers have seen running through military life. In her novel, *Reflections in a Golden Eye*, Carson McCullers draws a portrait of the sexual tensions and ultimate violence permeating the dreams, waking thoughts and frequently actions of enlisted men and officers.[78] The story is especially haunting because it is set in a stagnant backwater army base in the peacetime American South of the 1930s. There are no gun-shots to be heard, no mangled bodies being brought into the base hospital, no enemies on whom to focus hatred, no battle decorations to be won. There are only the daily routines—drills, classes, officers' bridge parties and horseback rides, enlisted men's chores and boredom. Carson McCullers makes us feel the boredom, the routine of an isolated community infused with rank consciousness, frustrated ambitions, preoccupation with discipline and sexual (denied homosexual and acknowledged heterosexual) desire and fatigue. It is in such a militarised peacetime, as well as under the strains of war, that many military wives suffer physical abuse from their soldier husbands.

Until recently, however, military officials refused to admit that widespread wife battering occurred under their commands or to take any responsibility for the 'exceptional' incidents that did get reported. Military social workers, chaplains, police, psychiatrists and doctors joined with base commanders to weave a curtain of silence around military wife battering.

The silence is being broken in the 1980s by a convergence of civilian women's shelter movements in the US and Britain and military manpower officials' need to be more candid about the factors which are frustrating their efforts to persuade higher percentages of their soldiers to stay in the military.

The American military seems more affected by this convergence, perhaps because it has been more eager to enlist the services of social workers and social scientists and because, even more than the British military, it needs to find ways to retain large numbers of soldiers if it is going to maintain and extend its global mission.

The relatively greater acknowledgement of military wife battering in America may also be due to the tendency of many (not all) American battered women's shelters to see themselves as social agencies rather than political campaigns against male violence, a tendency which leads them to be accessible to troubled Pentagon policy-makers and to feel less ambivalent politically in seeking contacts with the military in order to expand their services to meet the needs of military wives. Britain's shelter movement, by contrast, may be more wary of the social agency approach and also less dependent on direct public funding. Both of the factors may insulate British refuges from military penetration, but it also may mean British refuges are less able to provide protection to British women married to soldiers and living in military housing.[79]

But one should not overstate the eagerness of American officers to tackle the issue of wife battering. Lillian Tetzlaff, a trained psychological counsellor and wife of an American air force officer, tells of the reception she received from the 'powers-that-be' on a US air force base in England when she sought to find out simply whether there was a sufficiently high incidence of wife battering to justify a shelter on the base:

> I had hoped to present the problems, then get some sort of figures so far as the numbers of women [the chaplain] might be seeing each month, compile them with those figures of other organisations on base, such as medical, OSI, Security Police, etc. I was hoping to present these figures along with other emerging evidence, to the Wing

Commander, thereby convincing him of the base's need for a shelter...

A Chief Master Sargeant informed me most emphatically that if the military wanted the men to have a wife, it would issue them one. In the meantime, the military was an instrument for fighting wars, and a wife's role—if any—was incidental only...

I think that the most ignorant and unenlightened person I have encountered has been the Fundamentalist military chaplain. He was one of the first persons I approached about setting up a shelter, and I think that he hit me the hardest... He pointed out that, 'after all, this is the way that some couples communicate with each other. They simply batter as a sign of affection...'

...The women's group that I spoke with were unusually warm and responsive, often coming forward and offering their help and support.

Mainly, the argument against having a shelter at Mildenhall (the USAF base) is that there *is* one at Lakenheath (five miles from base)... but the one at Lakenheath is very small... and therefore often filled, especially on weekends... Also when a woman is running for her life... dragging small children along with her, five miles is a long way to run, especially in the middle of the night...

I am about to give up.[80]

In 1981 there were 1.1 million spouses (mostly women) and 1.6 million children who were legal dependents of American military personnel.[81] Policies on wife battering and child abuse are rather vaguely worked out at senior central government levels and then left to field officers to specify and implement. Thus the US Department of Defense has issued directions that both wife battering and child abuse be taken seriously by today's readiness-and-attrition-conscious forces; but just how much sympathy, support and protection any given woman has available to her depends on where her husband is stationed.[82] Thus for instance, while Lillian Tetzlaff was running into official resistance on the

US air force base in England, some women married to sailors stationed at the submarine base in Groton, Connecticut, were being given at least temporary relief from battering from navy commanders ordering known wife batterers to attend the 'men's anger control group'. The group is run by women who organised the battered women's shelters in the next town to Groton and has an official sanction as an on-base organisation. Sailors are being *ordered* to attend. But other women active in the nationwide shelter movement worry that this new direction—and money—devoted to programmes for violent men could be at the expense of the already hard-pressed shelters for the women who are the victims of male violence.[83]

Shelters around the US were surveyed to find out just how much contact they were having with nearby military installations. The responses revealed an uneven pattern. They were neither uniformly co-opted or co-operative with the military, nor uniformly wary of such contact. The Director of the Family Services Center in Gulport, Mississippi, reported that 15 per cent of crisis calls came from 'military related women', and that 'it has been easier to provide services to military related spouses than to civilians'.[84] On the other hand, the YWCA in Jersey City, New Jersey, which runs a battered women's programme reported that a military wife who sought their help 'felt that her husband's superiors were aware of the marital problems but chose not to interfere. She viewed the military as being protective of her husband.'[85] A report perhaps somewhere in between these two, and suggesting the pitfalls of relying on the military to provide genuine protection to the wives of officers and enlisted men, was submitted by the YWCA in Omaha, Nebraska:

> for the most part, abused wives relay similar information as do women in non-military environments. The distinction bears out when the abused military wives experience an 'extra' obstacle dealing with the base operations. These women are discouraged from seeking
> help on the outside and are 'comforted' by military chaplains...
>
> ...we have achieved limited success with the social

actions officer. The mental health workers within the [base] offices have received our counsellor training. Yet, women are reluctant [to seek help] as their husbands' rank would be jeopardised.[86]

4. Nursing the Military

Probably all of us have some childhood image of Florence Nightingale. The picture that comes to my mind must be from a painting I once saw. Florence Nightingale in the Crimea, ladylike in her long Victorian dress, moving competently and calmly from one wounded soldier to another. You can almost hear the artillery guns echoing in the distance. Some of the young men are up and about, unshaven, wearing torn uniforms, talking with their mates. They have fresh bandages around their foreheads or newly folded slings holding up their wounded arms. Other soldiers seem in more desperate condition, lying on cots or on the floor, or leaning up against the walls of this makeshift hospital. The childhood image that so many of us carry in our heads is of a woman who is daring but proper, a pioneer woman among men, a Victorian lady, not a feminist warrior.

Camp followers as medics

This romanticised image of military nurses as daring but devoted, disciplined and ladylike omits the thousands of women who nursed soldiers long before the 1850s. We know little about Florence Nightingale's foremothers because military commanders were often embarrassed by their presence and by having to depend on them.

Medical care has always been a part of military planning and wartime operations since it would be intolerably expensive for commanders and military politicians to discharge every wounded soldier or to let men trained and fed at military expense die on the battlefield for lack of care. But before the mid-nineteenth century nurses remained invisible both because they came from a low social level, and were lumped together with the 'masses' swooped up in any wartime, and because nursing was not yet a job done by specially designated individuals, let alone individuals organised and trained into a profession. Throughout the seventeenth and eighteenth centuries, army women nursed thousands of soldiers, but not as a distinct vocation. Ironically, while this may have made women's contribution to warfare invisible and unrewarded, it also meant that women's provision of health care was much more independent of military organisation and authority than it is today.

A woman who had become dependent on the military for her subsistence employed a variety of skills in order to earn minimal rations from the military store. Mother Ross was an army woman described by Daniel Defoe in his 1740 book, *The Life and Adventures of Mrs Christian Davis*. At one time or another, Mother Ross worked as a military housekeeper, sutler, prostitute, nurse, laundress, cook, and even soldier. Her nursing was necessary to the massive armies of her day. As a woman who performed nursing functions, Mother Ross was just a notch up the military social ladder from a laundress or a prostitute; but many times she was performing all three functions simultaneously. Among the soldiers she nursed was probably her husband. The distinction between nursing and performing the duties of a military wife was not at all clear in the eighteenth century. She did the washing as part of maintaining a minimum of cleanliness and thus sanitation for the troops. If her husband died, she lost her already tenuous claim to army rations and so she might be compelled to work as a military prostitute. If she remarried another soldier, she would most likely once again nurse and do laundry to earn a share of the military rations.

In the seventeenth century, women on naval war ships were 'tolerated' but not officially recognised by the British Admiralty. In the early eighteenth century, as part of the cyclical efforts of military commanders to increase their control over their military forces by separating them from the general society, the Admiralty imposed a ban on women acting as nurses aboard navy ships. But the ban did not end the ships' need for nursing, so even afterwards women could be found tending the wounded in Lord

Nelson's navy. Many of the women who served as nurses aboard ships in the early nineteenth century were sailors' wives.[1]

On the one hand, commanders needed nursing of a sort they thought could only be done by women, given women's 'natural inclination' to provide comfort and cleanliness. On the other hand, these same commanders were convinced that women's presence in camp or aboard ship compromised their male authority, blurred lines of command and narrowed the gap between military and civilian society.

One British soldier, noting the unkempt colonial soldiery he faced during the American Revolution, attributed the rebels' uncleanliness to the fact that they didn't have their women with them:

> When at home, their female relations put them upon washing their hands and faces, and keeping themselves neat and clean; but being absent from such monitors, through an indolent, heedless turn of mind, they have neglected the means of health, have grown filthy, and poisoned their constitution by nastiness.[2]

General Robert Venables, commanding the British forces in the West Indies campaign of 1656, concurred. Soldiers' wives had to be brought along.

> [There was the] necessity of having that sex with an army to attend upon and help the sick and wounded, which men are unfit for. Had more women gone, I suppose that many had not perished as they did for want of care and attendance.[3]

Women in the Crimea

The Crimean War was a turning point in Western military men's thinking about how to organise their forces. The frustrations and failures on all sides—widely publicised in the contemporary press—of the Crimean War prompted many European armies to design new regulations concerning VD, prostitution, marriage and careers. It also produced a marked change in the class composition and bureaucratic status of women military nurses. For military officials, one of the lessons of the Crimean War was that medical care was so critical to military effectiveness that it had to be brought under tight military control; it could no longer be left to camp followers. This 'lesson' was not learnt easily by many military officers. It was taught to them in part by a crusading Florence Nightingale, who aimed her criticisms not only at what she saw as an unprogressive, aristocratic male military elite but at the 'socially disreputable' women without formal credentials who performed so much medical care in nineteenth-century Europe.

Although she met resistance from British army officialdom, Nightingale was not challenging the military's hierarchical structure, its imperial mission or its basic sexual division of labour. Just as in the hospitals which were developing as part of the new political economy of health care in the civilian sector, Nightingale and other women reformers argued, women nurses in the military, too, should be trained, employed and treated as professionals, worthy of respect. Still, in the military as in the civilian medical system, they were to remain subordinate to male physicians. What my romanticised childhood painting of Florence Nightingale in the Crimea omitted was the male military surgeons who wielded ultimate authority over both the wounded male soldiers and those competent, energetic nurses.[4]

In the 1850s, no women were taken seriously in military operations. Consequently, we need to acknowledge Nightingale's ideological breakthrough at the same time as we weigh the long-range implications of that breakthrough for the militarisation of women's services:

> Two days after my arrival, Miss Nightingale sent for me to go with her round the hospital... it seemed an endless walk, and it was not easily forgotten... Miss Nightingale carried her lantern, which she would set down before she bent down over any of the patients. I much admired Miss Nightingale's manner to the men; it was so tender and kind... The hospital was crowded to its fullest extent... The building, which has since been reckoned to hold with comfort seventeen hundred men, then held between three and four thousand...

> Whether in the strain of overwork, or the steady fulfilment of our arduous duty, there was one bright ray ever shed over it—one thing that made labour light and sweet; and this was the respect, affection and gratitude of the men... Familiar as we were to become to them, though we were in and out of the wards day and night, they never forgot the respect due to our sex and position... where stood groups of soldiers smoking and idling, the moment we approached all coarseness was hushed.[5]

The Crimean War provided more public access for Russian middle-class women as well, again by presenting them with the chance to serve the military not as destitute and despised camp followers but as professionalised, formally integrated military nurses. Together, Nikolai Pirogov, a noted Russian surgeon and educator, and Elana Pavlovna, sister-in-law of the Czar, persuaded the Russian government to solve its increasingly acute manpower shortages in the Crimea by sending female nurses to the front. Elana Pavlovna, as a court liberal and a friend of Russian social reformers, was convinced that creating even an 'auxiliary' nursing corps would not only save men but would allow women to play a larger role in Russian public life. She didn't believe that such a unit could be commanded by a woman, however, so she urged her ally, Nikolai Pirogov, to supervise the new nurses' corps. Pirogov agreed with her that Russian society was backward partly due to its wasteful treatment of women. It was the state that ultimately suffered from such wastefulness. Thus women should be educated, and no longer 'treated in an archaic and inane way... women must take a role in society more nearly corresponding to their human worth and mental capacities'.[6]

The resultant Russian nurses' corps, the Sisters of Mercy of the Society of the Exultation of the Cross, mobilised 163 women volunteers. Of the total, 110 were from ethnic Russian (i.e. Russian-speaking) privileged orders—wives, widows and daughters of officials and landowners. Another 24 came from the Russian petty bourgeoisie; and about 5 came from the families of clergy. Five were nuns, two were domestics, and one entered the auxiliary after already having worked as a nurse. In his *Sevastopol Tales*, Tolstoy describes the Russian military nurses on the Crimea as 'sisters with peaceful faces and with the expression not of futile female lachrymose pity, but of active useful participation, stepping here and there among the wounded'.[7]

They served the Czarist military at the Crimean front, not at base hospitals such as at Scutari where Florence Nightingale directed her nurses. But, at the front or in the rear, despite their greater integration into the military organisation, the nurses still had to be coped with by the military mind as *women*. As in the burgeoning industrial factories of this same era, 'modernisation' did not make gender ideologies and sexual divisions of labour obsolete, but put those divisions to new uses.

The French forces also introduced women into formal military roles in order to carry on their Crimean operations. Every French regiment had its 'Mademoiselle Courage', its *cantiniere*. Many of the *cantinieres* were wives of NCOs.[8] Unlike earlier camp followers, these *cantinieres* were sufficiently 'on base' to be assigned specially designed, feminised military uniforms: brass buttoned, tight-fitting military tunics and baggy zouave trousers beneath voluminous skirts. They carried little barrels of brandy, from which they sold drink to the French troops, and were considered important to the health and morale of French troops serving in the disease-infested Crimea. But it wasn't until 1886 that the French army's health services explicitly relied on women as health professionals, in the form of private agency, the Societé Secours aux Blessés Militaires. This later became the Red Cross. In France's war with Russia during the 1870s and its 1907 war in Morocco, French women served in military hospitals and in the evacuation of the wounded from the front lines. Gertrude Stein and Alice B. Toklas serving as ambulance drivers for the French military in the first world war, joined a line of women that could be traced back to 'Madamoiselle Courage' in the Crimea.[9]

Florence Nightingale exposed the terrible neglect of the British wounded in the Crimea. She introduced far-reaching administrative reforms in military battlefield medicine and demonstrated that trained, disciplined, ladylike middle-class women could be of great practical value to the male military establishment *without* radically altering the sexual division of labour in military operations. In Europe and North America the role of both military and civilian nurses was shaped by the Victorian ideas of class and gender articulated by Nightingale: deference of women to men; the superiority of bourgeois educated women over either poor or aristocratic women; women's natural inclination to self-sacrifice and nurturing.[10]

Not until 1884, 30 years after the Crimean War, were British women used in large numbers in army hospitals. During those decades, War Office officials claimed that such widespread employment of women nurses to tend wounded or diseased men violated society's sense of propriety, especially perhaps since many of the ill soldiers were suffering from sexually related diseases.[11]

American officials have always kept an eye on British military practice. Exchange of information and 'lessons'—about how best to use women as well as about the latest fighter jet technology—between governments is one of the chief functions of NATO today. Even without benefit of such an elaborate alliance structure, nineteenth-century American officers were watching Britain's medical innovations in the Crimea. When the Civil War broke out in the 1860s they had a chance to put some of those innovations into military practice. Like the Crimean War, the American civil war produced male manpower shortages that demanded the expansion of medical services and the more calculated military use of women.

As in Britain, this change in military needs came at a time when middle-class white women were beginning to assert that they had a public role to play. In the eyes of the young Louisa May Alcott, a 30-year-old white middle-class spinster who wanted to '*do* something' in 1862 had only unsatisfactory choices before her. Her friends and family in Concord, Massachusetts, suggested that she: 'Write a book'; 'Try teaching again'; 'Take a husband... and fulfill your mission'; 'Turn actress, and immortalise your name'. But then one relative added, 'go nurse the soldiers'. Without a moment's hesitation Louisa May declared, 'I will.'[12] She was responding to a deliberate Union recruiting campaign aimed at young women. In all, an estimated 3,200 women provided nursing services to both the Union and Confederate armies. Most received no pay.[13]

It is always a difficult moment in the evolution of a women's movement when women's desire to break out of the airless domestic sphere crystallises *at the same time* as their government's military commanders decide they can make use of at least a select, limited and controlled number of women in military roles formerly closed to women. At times like these —1852, 1862, 1914, 1982—it is easy to mistake women's militarisation for women's liberation.

During the civil war, Union and Confederate officials temporarily modified American gender ideology in order to make use of women for military purposes. There were many, however, who remained unconvinced. A male military surgeon wrote to the *American Medical Times* in 1861, at the start of the civil war, when casualties on both sides were beginning to mount:

> Our women appear to have become almost wild on the subject of hospital nursing. We honor them for their sympathy and humanity. Nevertheless, a man who has had experience with women nurses among male surgical cases cannot shut his eyes to the fact that they, with the best intentions in the world, are frequently a useless annoyance...
>
> Imagine a delicate refined woman assisting a rough soldier to the close-stool, or supplying him with a bed-pan, or adjusting the knots in a T-bandage employed in retaining a catheter in position, or a dozen offices of a like character which one would hesitate long before asking a female nurse to perform, but which are frequently and continually necessary in a military hospital...
>
> Women, in our humble opinion, are utterly and decidedly unfit for such service. They can be used, however, as the regular administrators of the prescribed medicines, and in delicate soothing attentions which are always so grateful to the sick...

> A (male) surgeon on duty with troops, by showing proper interest in the men, without allowing himself to be humbugged by them, will gain their affection as well as respect.
>
> S.G.[14]

One of the paradoxes of the situation is that overcoming such male resistance is one of the experiences that can persuade a progressive woman that she *is* taking a step toward liberation when she presses for inclusion in the military.

The feminisation of military nursing

The worries of 'S.G.' echo down through generations of military officials when they think about medical services and about nursing. The more they made medical care an object of military strategy, the less they were willing to leave it to casual labour—camp followers or the wives of non-commissioned officers. But while they disparaged the 'amateurish' nursing of women camp followers, they saw advantages in keeping the more integrated military nursing corps feminised. If military manpower strategists could keep women nurses ideologically peripheral to the combat-masculinity core of the military, they could expand their medical services without diverting scarce male combat or technical manpower to medical units.

Military officials have seen the value of recruiting morale-boosting, caring persons to provide comfort as well as pills and injections for wounded men, yet have hesitated to introduce any change that would dilute the man-to-man bonding between troops and their officers on which so much military discipline depends. They have felt most threatened when that male bonding is compromised in the most exclusively 'masculine' realm of military life, combat. But at the same time, the armed forces have been developing transportation and medical technology precisely to ensure that medical care could be as close as possible to the front lines, providing *immediate* treatment of wounded soldiers.

Nursing's femininisation did not begin in the military. Women nurses have long struggled against the constraints of the sexual division of labour and the hierarchy of power in civilian as well as military medical establishments. But the military's dependency on a masculine image, man-to-man bonding and the uniquely male experience of 'combat' have combined to make the military high command even more reluctant than the senior staff of most civilian hospitals to acknowledge how crucial women nurses are to the organisation's effective operation.[15]

Britain's Army Nursing Service was founded in 1881; for the next 20 years British army nurses served in a succession of colonial wars in South Africa, Sudan, and Egypt. In the Boer War alone, 1,400 British women served as army nurses. Women were nursing British imperialism. Their units were given names of royal patronesses in order to raise the social status of military nursing and attract more middle-class women: Princess Christian's Army Nursing Service Reserve, Queen Alexandra's Imperial Military Nursing Service, and later Princess Mary's Royal Air Force Nursing Service.[16]

The naming strategy which was intended to make nursing military men respectable for British women explicitly feminised the nursing corps. It made them organisationally semi-autonomous from the branches which they served, an autonomy which today British military nursing officers guard jealously in the face of current ministerial proposals for tighter organisational integration.[17]

Race and military nursing

The 1981 recruiting brochure from the Queen Alexandra's Royal Army Nursing Corps shows a photograph of eight 'QA' nurses. Seven of the eight smiling British women are white, each dressed in the uniform of a different nursing rank. But the Ministry of Defence's advertising specialists added an eighth woman: an Asian British nurse. She represents a lower-ranking nurse. Nowhere else in the brochure, which entices potential women enlistees with pictures of the varied duties of today's military nurse, is another Asian or black nurse (or soldier) shown. British military recruiters seem to be picking up from their American counterparts the sort of public relations 'photographic pluralism' that calls for at least one non-white person in every ad.

Official resistance to recruiting black and Asian women into the military nursing corps is the result not only of the racism that has structured both the British and American armed forces for generations, but also of the peculiar gender strategy that has shaped the military nursing corps. Male military recruiters, and Florence Nightingale herself, believed that the desirable sorts of women could be persuaded to join such a male-defined institution only if they could be made immune from charges of promiscuity. Thus military nurses would have to be strictly trained and disciplined and recruited from society's 'respectable' middle-class families. Furthermore, until 1950, British nurses were cut off from the presumably lower-class enlisted men by being assigned to the officer ranks. Such personnel strategies not only made the nursing corps class exclusive, they also made them virtually race exclusive, since the entrance of non-white women was also presumed to jeopardise the military nurse's safe social status.

Despite the nods toward a multi-racial image by military recruitment advertisers, Britain's military nursing corps and the government civilian nursing sector look quite different in racial mix in the 1980s. National Health Service nurses and hospital workers are drawn heavily from Asian and West Indian immigrants and from the growing population of black and Asian women born in Britain. The same does not hold for military nursing.

It was only during the second world war that black nurses were formally integrated into the US armed forces. They were finally allowed to serve officially *not* because of self-initiated desegregation by the government, but because of concerted political lobbying by black civilian nurses themselves.

Black women had nursed the US military long before they were officially recognised members of the regular forces. After emancipation, black women ex-slaves, many of them wives of black men who had enlisted in Union regiments, served unofficially as nurses, laundresses and cooks (as well as spies and scouts) for civil war troops. Two of the most famous black women political leaders of the civil war era, Harriet Tubman and Sojourner Truth, nursed Union soldiers.

During the first world war the Red Cross agreed to admit

black nurses, but the US Surgeon General vetoed the plan. It was only in July 1918, on the verge of peace, after an epidemic had caused a huge demand for nurses, that the government finally allowed 18 black nurses to be appointed to the Army Nurse Corps. But, by the outbreak of the second world war, the Army Nurse Corps had been restored to its previous whiteness.[18]

At the outset of black nurses' integration into the US military, they were permitted to attend only black male soldiers. It was only at the very end of the second world war that they won the right to nurse all American personnel. This reflects a broader pattern of racial and ethnic manipulation in the military. Military commanders often run out of their '*preferred* manpower' late in the war. Thus it is usually late in wars that a government begins to compromise its ethnic and racial and sex recruiting preferences.[19]

So it was in the second world war. By 1944-45, American military policy-makers were confronted by a worsening nursing 'manpower' shortage. President Roosevelt feared that Congress would pass a bill instituting compulsory conscription of women nurses (most of whom, of course, would be white). Roosevelt feared that such a bill would alienate a large proportion of the American public, who still had grave reservations about women serving in the military. It was this fear of offending white Americans' notions about the proper roles for *white* women, combined with the political efforts of black nurses, which led to full integration of black military nurses late in the war.

But in 1941, before wartime racial/gender politics had reached this point, Army General George Marshall could reply to a black official in the War Department who had been urging that quotas and segregation be abolished:

> the War Department cannot ignore the social relationships between negro and white which have been established by the American people through custom and habit... Either through lack of opportunity or other causes, the level of intelligence and occupational skill of the negro population is considerably below that of whites... ⅜such a social experiment½ would only bring a danger of efficiency, discipline and morale.[20]

If the US army was racist and reluctant, the US navy presented an even stronger bastion of white male exclusiveness: it simply deemed black women ineligible and undesirable for service in the Navy Nurse Corps. The white woman who was superintendent of the US Navy Nurse Corps tried to rationalise this by saying that navy nurses were *special nurses*; they combined the responsibilities of teacher, counsellor, dietician, laboratory technician, X-ray operator, bookkeeper, and confidante of the sick. In sum, she said, a navy nurse had to be a 'tactful, clear-minded administrator and teacher'.[21] Black women, by inference, were judged by commanders to be incapable of such things. Furthermore, since there were very few black sailors in the US navy in the 1940s, and since it was presumed that if black nurses were to be allowed to serve at all they would nurse only black sailors, it was officially reasoned that there would be no jobs for them to perform.

As late as January 1945, the US Surgeon General told a meeting of politicians and private citizens regarding the advisability of drafting nurses who would nurse only black soldiers: 'I believe that the average share of coloured nurses in the army is equal to the total number of negro troops.'

Just weeks later, however, to avoid drafting white women nurses, President Roosevelt adopted the plan put to him by Eleanor Roosevelt, who in turn had been persuaded by the persistent lobbying of black nurses: nurses would be accepted into the Army and Navy Nurse Corps without regard to race.[22]

White nurses, at least in their national organisation, had not given much support to the black nurses in their push to be integrated into the regular military. The American Nurses Association was not racially integrated until 1948, three years after the end of the second world war.

Romance in the burn ward

One strategy for papering over the contradictions in the military use of women nurses has required the active complicity of the civilian media. The idea of women as military nurses can be coped with—by civilian and military officials alike—if such women can be convincingly portrayed as experiencing not warfare, the preserve of men, but romance, the natural arena of women. So, for example, Vera Brittain's powerful autobiography in which she tells of her experiences as a British army nurse during the first world war, first on Malta and then amid the horrors of the French front, is heralded by her present-day American publisher as, 'A heartbreaking record of the holocaust. But, most of all, a love story'.[23]

Similarly, Patricia L. Walsh has written an autobiographical novel based on her 14 months nursing Vietnamese and American war casualties, exposing in uncompromising detail the burns from napalm, the cynicism of US military personnel who called the victims 'crispy critters', and the black- and grey-market deals in medical supplies. Her publishers, however, decided that the novel should be packaged as a romantic tale to get it on to grocery store and news stand racks. Thus they have given it a suitably romantic paperback cover and teased the reader with the question, 'She was fighting to save lives, but at what cost to her own?' Inside, the novel is subtitled: 'Their War-Torn Love'.[24]

Current military advertising reinforces this media-constructed image of the de-militarised, romanticised military nurse. Advertisements in both the US and Britain offer a mixture of upward mobility via paid training on the one hand, and social life and adventure on the other. Queen Alexandra's Army Nursing Corps' 1981 glossy brochure, for example, describes the nurse as a woman whose job and social life reflect some of the new as well as the old gender conditions of the British military:

> *On Duty:* You'll work in up-to-date hospitals with modern equipment nursing servicewomen as well as soldiers, their wives and children, and civilians.
>
> Your career in the QAs will normally bring fresh posting every two years, perhaps to Hong Kong, Nepal, West Germany, Cyprus, Northern Ireland... wherever you go, you may have the opportunity to use any specialist qualifications you may possess, and plenty of time to be a good nurse. And except in the rare emergency, you will never find yourself with too many patients.

> *Off Duty:* Comfortable accommodation is provided for everybody... you are well looked after in the modern army...
>
> You can join in with other serving men and women in dramatic and folksinging clubs. Your social life—in effect—can be as active and varied as you like.

Such advertising strategies have to balance on an ideological knife-edge because of the uncertain sexual meaning associated with military nursing. The legacy of the camp follower myth puts women who nurse 'rough and ready' men in constant danger of being labelled whores. Consequently, military nurses must be portrayed as proper, professional and well protected. On the other hand, simultaneously, military recruiters feel they have to portray military nursing as at least socially up to date, and even socially (romantically) advantageous so that young women will find it worth all the discipline, transience and possible danger.

Nurses under fire

During the Spanish American War, the Chief Surgeon of the US volunteers wrote:

> During the four trips I made on the hospital ship relief, to and from Cuba and Puerto Rico, I had ample opportunity to compare the work of the male and female nurses and I have no hesitation in speaking in decided terms in favour of the latter. Nursing is women's special sphere... She is endowed with all the qualifications, mentally and physically, to take care of the sick. Her sweet smile and gentle touch are often of more benefit to the patient than the medicine she administers... Her sense of duty and devotion to those placed under her care seldom is equalled by men.[25]

Nurses serve in combat regardless of official prohibitions. They serve in combat not because of unusual individual bravery—the stuff of nursing romances—but because they are part of a military structure that needs their skills *near* combat. Though military planners and their civilian superiors are not opposed to using nurses in combat, they have resisted the *image* of women nurses as regular troops with regular military rank:

> Trained female nurses have been used in dangerous wartime locales... yet the combat experiences—even the existence—of US military nurses have been ignored by those concerned with the potential of women in combat situations.[26]

To close the gap between myth and reality, however, would require that military officials resolve their own ideological gender contradictions, something they are loath to do. Instead, they prefer to leave the public naive and military nurses themselves coping privately with the psychological strains of such a gap.

Thus, for instance, when British army nurse Leslie Rutherford was photographed by a London paper boarding a ship joining the huge naval task force headed for combat in the Falklands, she was shown smiling, waving and 'clutching her teddy'.[27] Stuffed animals seemed to be the British civilian and military press's device for 'feminising' women on their way to the South Atlantic front. *Navy News* also carried a story of army nurses on their way to board the Falklands-bound hospital ship, *Uganda*. Six women in uniform were pictured smiling and showing off their stuffed penguins.[28] While all the nurses were portrayed as non-combatants, in reality hospital ships such as the *Uganda* were subjected to Argentinian bombing attacks. Their smiles and stuffed penguins and teddies notwithstanding, British military nurses were in combat.

Rapid changes in military medical technology since the second world war have made the myth that nurses work far from combat less and less tenable. In 1942, the US army created its first Mobile Army Surgical Hospital Unit. Out of this experiment came the famous MASH units, now popularly known through the American television comedy series, 'MASH' which is set in a medical unit in the South Korea war during the 1950s.

MASH units were designed to follow troops into battle so soldiers could get rapid medical support; they were to include a surgeon (male), doctors (male), medical corpsmen and nurses. The MASH units were to be able to break camp and move on at a moment's notice, instantly responsive to changes in battle deployment. As in so much of military technological and organisational innovation, rapid mobility was a key objective.

The first nurse in the US army to be wounded in Italy was part of a MASH team. Because of their success in Europe during the second world war, MASH units became popular with other allied commands during the rest of the war and for NATO forces in later wars. In 1982, the British army held 'Exercise Maxi Mash' in West Germany, designed to test the British military hospital's ability to move and deploy to a wartime location and to perform its role as a forward surgical complex. Women nurses were among the 800 army participants in this battlefield simulation. One report concluded that a time when some army medical bands are being considered for reorganisation, 'it is worth remembering that the medical bandsman's [sic] speed and skill on the battlefield will initially decide who lives and who dies'.[29]

Helicopters were introduced to enable military commanders to evacuate soldiers quickly direct from the battlefield. Helicopters have nurses among their crews, and those nurses have acquired an elite status among nursing corps partly *because* they are so close to combat and at the frontier of the military's medical technology.

The development of MASH medical units and the increasing use of helicopters sharpened the contradiction between the ideologically acceptable image of women nurses, safely away from combat, and the reality of their being directly subject to mortar and artillery fire.

However, as is so common when militarised women try to address the way they are ignored or marginalised by the very armies that rely on their labour, if military nurses insist that they be recognised as the soldiers they indeed are, they seem to be calling for *further militarisation*. The only alternatives available to these women appear to be, on the one hand, passive acceptance of 'feminised' roles in exchange for the supposed security and benefits offered by the military or, on the other hand, active challenge of the male military commands' gender ideology for the sake of being more totally integrated into the military machine.

Forgotten veterans of the Vietnam war

Nurses who have served on or near the front of men's wars have suffered from their invisibility. They have been pushed to the back of the bureaucratic filing cabinet. For example, when it uses the term 'Vietnam Veterans', the US Veterans' Administration usually means *male* veterans. Many men who served in Vietnam for the American military have protested at the way they have been treated by the VA, as well as by the neighbours and potential employers, when they returned from that unpopular war. But the men have been visible, if not well served. By contrast, American women who served in the US military in Vietnam are scarcely acknowledged to exist.

Only 2.3 per cent of American Vietnam veterans are women. But of all the American women who served in the US military in the Vietnam war, 80 per cent were nurses. Many nurses contend that they saw the worst of the Vietnam war, an endless procession of mangled bodies across the operating table.

Adding to their invisibility is yet another perpetuation of the myth of the sexually promiscuous camp follower. A long article appearing in the *Washington Post* reported that America nurses who had served in Vietnam,

> lived in a world of wartime romances that often ended abruptly and painfully. They returned home to not only a hostile nation, but to frequent questions of why a decent woman would want to be stationed way around the world with so many men.[30]

American Vietnam war nurses blamed themselves for the problems they endured after the war, whereas their male counterparts seemed better able to blame the US government or the war itself. One therapist who has counselled more than 200 US women Vietnam veterans concludes that,

> Women had to be warm fuzzies. They had to be a wounded soldier's mother, wife, and girlfriend. They saw these beautiful young bodies, 18- and 19-year-old kids, coming in every day with second degree chest wounds and ripped off flesh and they had to hold their hands and tell them

> everything was OK.[31]

How were these nurses, enduring this daily awfulness, able to express their anger and frustration? Because they were women, they were not allowed to shoot back. Because they were women and because military nursing was defined in feminised terms, they were not allowed even to show their anger with their military compatriots, the men they served with. They were supposed to soothe and comfort, not display anger and certainly not go crazy with fury as did so many male soldiers who shot each other on base or in brothels or picked off harmless water buffalo from their helicopter gunships. Because women are brought up to nurture and protect others, many nurses felt like failures because, no matter what they did, the GIs kept dying.

Lynda Van Devanter is one of the American nurses who now, eight years after the American troops were forced to pull out of Vietnam, is finding her voice. She is organising women nurses so that they can become visible, stop depending on private coping and make the American military establishment accountable. Lynda Van Devanter was in her mid-twenties when she went to Vietnam. She was posted in Pleiku from June 1969 to June 1970.

> Every Vietnam vet was told he was a fool, a real sucker, for going over there, but for women it's been even worse... people figure you were either a hooker or a lesbian if you were a woman in the [US] army in Vietnam. Why else would a woman want to be with 500,000 men unless she was servicing them?[32]

This was not 1850. It was 1969. But the contradictions were strikingly familiar. The military establishment depended on women in order to carry out their military operations, but were fighting to defend a social order that presumes that 'respectable' women are not appropriate to or capable of wartime roles. Thus women have to be ignored or so ideologically degraded and marginalised that they do not pose a threat to that carefully protected social order.

Lynda Van Devanter and other nurses have formed a

women's veterans project within the Washington-based Vietnam Veterans of American (VVA). Their potential membership is the 7,500 American women who served in the military in Vietnam in the 1960s and 1970s. They are pressing the US government bureaucracy to acknowledge that women veterans exist and ensure they get the educational, health and financial benefits due to them. They are arguing that the psychological and social legacy of Vietnam which women vets must cope with is not identical to that of male vets. Lynda Van Devanter took several years to realise that many of the problems she was having in civilian life were not due to her own maladjustment but to the consequences of serving in the army in a peculiar kind of war. She would feel guilty, suffer constant headaches, explode at her husband and friends for no reason; she couldn't concentrate or remember what people had said; she wanted to be alone, yet she was lonely and afraid. She consulted a therapist, but never even told him about Vietnam, never described her recurring nightmares about the war:

> We talked about marital problems and other pressures, but I kept telling myself that Vietnam was five, six, seven, years ago... I was afraid my therapist would think I was crazy if I told him about Vietnam. I was ashamed of Vietnam.

It was only when she went to a counsellor who had already counselled many Vietnam war military nurses, and had begun to recognise a common pattern, that Lynda Van Devanter began to talk about what the war had been like to her. She learned that her story was the story of dozens of other American women Vietnam veterans. Only then, years after the war, did she finally muster the courage to reveal her recurring nightmare. She tells it now in a monotone:

> It is 3.00 a.m. in Pleiku, South Vietnam. I had been sleeping under my cot because I was afraid of the rocket attack outside. It is only a few days until my hump point, when I will pass the halfway point of my tour. They send me to the Neuro-Emergency Room. The longest trail of blood I have ever seen leads the way.

> He is there. His entire face was blown away when the flare he was handling exploded. A perfect set of straight, even white teeth is swinging from a jaw that dangles loose. The anaesthetist calls me and a wall goes up. I become a robot, doing my job.

She then describes the eight hours that this medical team worked on the young wounded soldier, pumping 120 units of blood through needles in his leg, neck, and both arms:

> I always believed that you could stop bleeding. The lesson I learned that night was that we have developed the ability to destroy something beyond repair.

While changing one of the bloody bandages, her foot kicked the soldier's clothes lying on the floor and a photograph fell out:

> It's a picture of him and a girl. He is gazing sweetly at her. Straight, blond, and tall, he looks proud in his tuxedo. She, too, is tall with shiny black hair and a pastel gown. Suddenly, he is real again and the wall falls down. I gaze at the mass of blood vessels and burned skin in front of me, and I feel sick.

Somebody on the medical team yells at her; again she becomes a robot working with the team. Finally the team gives up on the young soldier.

> We wrapped his face with layers of pressure dressings and send him [to post-op intensive care] to die. I keep telling myself that a miracle could happen. He could stop bleeding. He'd be all right. Picking up the bloody linens and putting them into the hamper, I see the photograph again and stare at it. This boy was real. He was a person who could love and think and plan and dream and now he is nothing, there is nothing left.
>
> I must see him again. I take his hand. Already the blood is coming through the bandages. I ask him if he is in pain. He squeezes my hand. I ask him if he wants pain medicine. He squeezes again. I call a nurse and tell her to give him some. I know it will cause him to go faster.

> That's what I want to do, for him to go easy. I stand with him, 20-30 minutes. I want to say something, to tell him it is OK, that he will be fine and that I care.
> He stops breathing. He is dead. I am crying. I want my mother and father. I want to go home and forget everything that is around me, the death, the destruction, that I am a part of, but they are calling me, saying more wounded are coming and I must put the wall up again, always the wall.

Lynda Van Devanter is not telling a nightmare. She is telling what happened in real life to a woman nurse in wartime. She is telling us what we are not supposed to know about women in wartime.

The armed forces may get nervous when nurses start telling their stories because they reveal so much about the nature of war itself. Not only the military gender structure is being protected by military nurses' silence; the basic legitimacy of the military as a pillar of civilised society is being protected by their silence. A nurse who *talks* of war as seen from a military hospital or a MASH unit is a dangerous woman.

Gayle Smith, now 34, was a post-op nurse in a MASH unit in Vietnam from November 1970, to November 1971. Though a skilled military professional, she says that she knew she was too exhausted to return to a hospital environment when she got back to the US. Today she is a nurse with a ski patrol in Stow, Vermont. She spent ten years trying to forget the war, trying to bury the horrors under layers of silence. Then one day while on ski patrol, she fell and hurt her thumb and began to cry. She recalls it was a 'ridiculous little injury' but it was the first time she had allowed herself to feel any emotion since she had returned from Vietnam.

After leaving the military, Gayle Smith married and had a child. She seemed to be living a 'normal American family life'. Still she found it difficult to answer doors: 'I was afraid that somebody was going to throw a grenade in or kill me.'[33]

Many American nurses quit nursing after serving in Vietnam because they could no longer bear the sight of suffering and death.

Nursing in the nuclear era

The North Atlantic Treaty Organisation (NATO) has provided a vehicle for military policy-makers to exchange lessons about how best to use women in both medical and other 'support' operations. However, it has also provided a space for women military officers (less so women in the enlisted ranks) to build a network of information and support.

Senior officers from the various nursing corps were among the leaders in creating what has become institutionalised as the Brussels-based Senior Women Officers Committee within NATO. At the time of its formation in the early 1970s nursing officers were the highest-ranking women throughout the North American and Western European forces. They and women officers in other branches—who now exist in greater numbers—pressed the military to make greater *use* of women, to open up more promotion opportunities. Initially, they argued this by pointing to the growing strategic importance of medical care in all NATO planning.

These senior women officers are arguing for increasing militarisation as the means of increasing the acceptance in society generally of women as professionals and 'first-class citizens'. Again, because they meet resistance from male commanders in the various NATO forces, the women nursing officers are apt to feel confirmed in their belief that they are challenging the base of sexism in the various societies they come from.

Male officers in NATO are evidently becoming anxious over precisely this trend and the increased military dependence on women that it implies. A US Defense Department report in 1982 noted that in that year, of all US army medical personnel stationed in Europe, 40 per cent were women (as versus 9 per cent in the US army as a whole). The report—available throughout NATO's bureaucracy—warned that as a result of this apparently rampant feminisation, US army medical units' 'readiness' was endangered. The reason: women weren't strong enough to carry a patient on a litter. In the wake of this report, the Pentagon set an official 35 per cent limit on the proportion of all US army medical unit personnel assigned to Europe who could be women.[34]

The picture of women—or men—picking up patients on

litters on a European battlefield doesn't seem to fit with the scenarios of nuclear warfare that we currently hear in official justifications of the build-up of missile-launched nuclear weapons in NATO countries in the 1980s. But in fact, the idea that there will be 'patients', 'litters', and 'medical corpsmen' out on a 'battlefield' is indeed integral to the nuclear military strategy. For the governments of both Britain and the US have been trying to portray a nuclear war as survivable.

The nuclear politics of civil defence depend not only on the use of military nurses but on the militarising of 'civilian' nurses. The militarisation of civilian nursing began with the latest government campaigns to convince citizens that a nuclear war is survivable.

The militarisation process has taken the form of encouraging women to go through nursing school on military scholarships. Because nurses' training is so expensive and sources of funds are so limited in the US, this becomes a genuine temptation. In return for tuition support, a graduate nurse serves time in the military. In the process the civilian nursing school itself is militarised insofar as it depends on the Defense Department for its tuition revenues. Thus nursing school administrators may be tempted to suggest to prospective nursing students that they accept military tuition subsidies. In Britain nurses trained in the QA acquire credentials that are now recognised in the civilian sector, thus giving the military a persuasive argument for enlistment. The ways in which the military uses the civilian health systems shortage of resources to fulfil its own needs reflect the basic connection between militarising processes and the overall political economy of a country's system of medical care.

Civilian nurses, however, who may never have considered military enlistment, and who may never have protested at the fact that their schools and hospitals routinely trained military-subsidised nursing students, are today starting to question their own political militarisation at the hands of *civil defence* bureaucrats.

In 1981, the US Department of Defense contacted 900 hospitals in order to guarantee that 50,000 beds be reserved in case of war. Allegedly, these beds would be used for European casualties from a future *conventional* war waged in Europe. While 433 hospitals agreed, 20 have refused. Medical staff, doctors and nurses, at the University of California Medical School and the Massachusetts General Hospital, among others, have told the Defense Department that they view such a plan as one more step toward making *nuclear* war acceptable, a step they refuse to take.[35] In Britain, similarly, the Home Office has pressured Regional Health Authorities, the Red Cross, and the St John's Ambulance Brigade to co-ordinate plans for the evacuation of Greater London, to fit with the Thatcher government's civil defence strategy.[36] All of these organisations, on which the military and civilian defence strategists depend, in their turn rely on women's labour and skills. Any civil defence strategy for making nuclear war palatable will need the co-operation of many women. While nurses are a crucial part of any hospitals' capacity to serve government's civil defence needs, it is not clear whether nurses have the decision-making power in most large hospitals to take a decisive role. Thus to fight militarisation nurses may have to first demand far more power in the overall hospital political process.[37]

Using women on the battlefront has been considered ideologically unacceptable, but it is, in the case of nurses, common in practice. Women nurses have been left to cope with the consequence of the military's ideological contradiction: the pretence that they weren't there. Now, in the 1980s, the contradictions are sharpening further still: medical care is becoming so central to military planning that commanders are worrying about their dependence on military nurses; at the same time nuclear technology and strategy is making the notion of 'front' and 'rear' meaningless. The nuclear battlefield would be our own cities, where more and more nurses and other women health care workers are being called on to serve military planning purposes.

5. 'Some of the Best Soldiers Wear Lipstick'

The word 'Amazon' is thought to be derived from the ancient Greek words *a mazon*—'breastless'.[1] According to legend, each Amazon seared off her right breast so it would not interfere with her use of the bow. Over the centuries Amazons came to represent a nation of women warriors. Their home territory moved from place to place depending on the teller, but always Amazons were portrayed as inhabiting a region just beyond the borders of the known world, and in this sense, their story is a variant of the familiar tale about a distant land where everything is done the wrong way round.

What is 'wrong' about the Amazons is not only that they are women who fight using military equipment and tactics, but that they live without men. They govern themselves and require heterosexual sex only periodically for the functional purposes of procreation. Male warriors have imagined Amazon women as a military challenge *and* a sexual challenge—or better, as a sexual challenge *because* they dare to present a military challenge. Amazons have been portrayed simultaneously as sexless and promiscuous. In myth, victory over the Amazons therefore entailed their defeat in battle followed either by rape or seduction.[2]

Tales of the Amazons re-emerged in the twelfth, sixteenth, and eighteenth centuries, periods of revolutionary imagination. These warrior women, these 'unnatural' creatures, capture the imagination of societies that are struggling to redefine social and political relationships. Always, they are surrounded by ambiguity, disguise and confusion. In sixteenth-century Italian literature, for instance, there was the popular cautionary tale of the man who bragged too much of his sexual prowess, until finally he was confronted and humbled by a woman warrior.[3] Amazons emerged again in the 1970s, but this time in the hands of radical feminists like Mary Daly and Monique Wittig, who used the Amazon myth to suggest new possibilities for women and for entire societies.[4]

Today one can visit the British Museum's Bassae Room to see Amazon warriors perpetually waging a fierce battle against Greek male soldiers. Now housed in a strangely intimate, dimly lit room, the Bassae frieze captures the strength and beauty of these mythical women as they boldly challenge the enemy and protect injured sisters with raised shields. But the Greek sculptors who created the Bassae frieze have frozen, along with the Amazon women's boldness, their defeat. For, ultimately, the lesson the sculptors have urged on the viewer is that Amazon women are a threat to men, that they must be defeated—to preserve masculine self-confidence, and *thereby* to ensure the survival of 'civilisation'.[5]

Like the Amazons, Joan of Arc has become as significant ideologically as historically in shaping our images of women and soldiering. Unlike the Amazons, Joan of Arc travelled with male soldiers. She joined the fifteenth-century male-dominated military campaign against Britain in the service of a male monarch, who in turn represented French nationalism. But though she was in the military, according to Vita Sackville West, one of her many biographers, Joan 'had no respect for military strategy or obligations'.[6]

It was this illiterate peasant girl's clothes more than her soldiering *per se* that symbolised her defiance of patriarchal, ecclesiastical authority. To dare to dress as a man—this was an act that shook the foundations of the French social order. According to the trial records, Joan had

> Given up and rejected female dress, had her hair cut round... wore a shirt, breeches, a doublet with hose attached by twenty laces, leggings laced on the outside, a short robe, to the knees, a cap, tight boots, long spurs, a sword, a dagger, a coat of mail, a lance and other arms...[7]

Joan's judges declared that such attire was 'in violation of canon law, abominable to God and men, and prohibited by the actions of the Church under the penalty of anathema'.[8]

For her part, Joan of Arc expressed bemusement. She explained—not to her judges' satisfaction—that she had been told by God to dress in this manner and that she simply ran less danger of rape—on the battlefield and in the English prison—if she dressed as a man than if she dressed as a woman.[9]

The question of attire crops up repeatedly over the years as male officials have tried to figure out how to use women in armies without altering what it means to be a *soldier*, a *man* and a *woman*. If women are called upon to soldier, should the government issue them uniforms that declare their 'femininity', at the risk of emphasising their sexual otherness in an essentially masculine institution? Or should women soldiers wear uniforms designed to *hide* their sexual identity, to make them blend in with men, thus sacrificing whatever privilege males get from being soldiers and whatever protection women are supposed to get from their 'vulnerability'?

During the first world war British officials had a hard time deciding where to put the breast pocket on the uniforms of their newly mobilised women soldiers. Wouldn't a breast pocket dangerously accentuate the female anatomy, and so fuel the already widespread popular assumption that the WACs were promiscuous? The uniforms were issued without breast pockets.[10]

Ambivalence about the meaning of women-as-soldiers continues to plague military uniform and cosmetic designers. A woman in the present-day American army is instructed to keep her hair short enough so that it just reaches the collar of her uniform but *not* so short that it looks 'unfeminine'. Women in the US marines must tweeze their eyebrows in a regulation arch. An American army recruiting brochure reveals the military's ambivalence and institutional nervousness: below a colour photo of a pretty woman smiling out from under a camouflaged combat helmet is the caption, 'Some of the best soldiers wear lipstick'.

Many women have disguised themselves as men in order to be soldiers, but women have always assigned their own meanings to soldiering. Soldiers' songs of the eighteenth and nineteenth centuries, for instance, tell of women who donned male uniforms as sweethearts and wives, in order to travel with and care for their husbands or lovers. But sometimes there was a twist to the tale:

Young men and maidens and bachelors sweet,
I'll sing you a song that is new and complete,
Concerning a damsel that followed the drum
For the sake of her true love for a soldier she's gone.

She listed volunteer in a regiment of foot
By beating the drum great honour she got;
Twice as much more she does undertake,
For she beats on the drum for her true lover's sake.

Her waist it was slender it was slender,
Her fingers long and small,
For beating the drum she exceeded them all;
Now she's drum major and carries the sword,
And appears like a hero, as fierce as a lord.[11]

A woman who masquerades as a soldier, even a mere drummer boy, violates social expectations. It is all well and good that she joined in order to follow her male lover, but when she rises to drum major, the social order is strained too far. The ballad writer moves swiftly, therefore, to put things right. One day, so the subsequent verses tell, a fellow soldier spies the drum major bathing. Her deception is uncovered. But since she joined the ranks only to follow her man, young Shelton, she wins forgiveness from the male soldiers. And so,

The drummers, the corporals and ensigns, also
Took this maid by the hand and to church they did go;
Sergeants, corporals and fife,
And rejoice and was merry with Young Shelton and his
wife.[12]

The world is put right when a woman drum major is transformed into a wife. Although the ballad ends here, it is easy to imagine the ex-drummer thereafter following the troops as a military wife, cooking, nursing and doing their laundry. In a year or so she will become indistinguishable from the other camp followers.

Another British army ballad traces one woman's migration from orphan to mistress to soldier to sailor to actress. Mary Anne Talbot, inspiration for the ballad 'The Female Drummer', was born an orphan in London in 1778. A Captain Bowen, into whose guardianship the young Mary Anne had been entrusted, made the girl his mistress. When his regiment was sent to the West Indies, he forced her to accompany him, dressed as a foot soldier and taking the name John Taylor. From the West Indies, Bowen was ordered to Flanders where he enrolled Mary Anne as a drummer boy. When she objected, Bowen threatened to sell her as a slave.

Mary Anne Taylor, disguised as a drummer boy, fought at the battle of Valenciennes and suffered two wounds. Bowen, however, was killed; Mary Anne Talbot seized the opportunity to desert. This time she masqueraded as a sailor. Only later was she discovered by a navy surgeon treating her wounds. She left the navy, went on the stage, and wrote her autobiography, *The Life and Surprising Adventures of Mary Anne Talbot in the Name of John Taylor, Related by Herself*. She died in 1807 at the age of 30.[13]

Lillian Faderman tells of numerous women who joined military forces disguised as men. Henrica Schuria served as a soldier under Frederic Henry, Prince of Orange, and fought in the Seige of Boisleduc. When she returned home she lived as a woman, but had sexual relationships with other women. When one of her liaisons was discovered she was subjected to a public whipping.[14] Similarly, in early eighteenth-century Germany, Catherine Margaretha Linck disguised herself as a man and fought as a soldier with four different armies—the Hanoverian, Prussian, Polish and Hessian. She ended her military service in 1717, but kept her disguise as a man so that, as a man, she could work as a cotton dyer. In this guise she also was able to marry another woman. Later, however, she was discovered, imprisoned and, in 1721, executed.[15]

One of the most celebrated women to disguise herself as a man in order to soldier was an American, Deborah Sampson.

She fought with the rebels in the American Revolution. When found out, she was discharged but not punished, perhaps because her masquerade was taken to be a sign of patriotism. She was later treated as a popular heroine, though by that time she had married a neighbouring farmer and become a mother.[16]

One of the best-known folk heroes of the American Revolution was a woman who has come down to us in patriotic lore as 'Molly Pitcher'. Molly Pitcher is the heroic version of a camp follower. She is never portrayed in a man's uniform. She is always clearly identifiable as a woman and a civilian. According to legend, Molly Pitcher loaded and aimed or fired field artillery after her gunner husband collapsed from wounds.

However, historian Linda Grant DePaw's research has uncovered quite a different 'Molly Pitcher'.[17] She was not one woman—she was hundreds. They did not stand in the wings until their husbands collapsed. They were deliberately organised by General George Washington to serve as members of Continental Army gun crews. Their collective *nom de guerre* was derived from their relationship to the technology of eighteenth-century warfare. Artillery pieces of this era became too hot to fire if they weren't watered down between shots. It was the task of the Continental Army's 'Molly Pitchers' to carry water to the male gun crews in pitchers, or jugs. Using women to carry water to the guns, reasoned the manpower-short generals, would 'free men to fight'.

The Molly Pitchers were in combat. They were at the front. But the ideological construction of soldiering was so tightly bound to *masculinity* and to *combat*, that the Molly Pitchers' biographers presumed a woman couldn't be in combat and was at the front only by singular accident. The Molly Pitchers after all were ordinary women; it was only a mythical Amazon across some distant frontier or a Catherine Linck in deceptive masquerade who could be soldiering like male soldiers. The experience of the Molly Pitchers at the hands of male historians suggests that women will be used deliberately by manpower-short commanders, but only within an ideological framework that preserves for men the privileges that derive from soldiering.

During the second world war Winston Churchill encouraged

anti-aircraft commander General Frederick Pile to form British anti-aircraft batteries composed of men and women. The general was advised by a woman engineer, Caroline Hazlett, that women could operate the guns' fire control instruments and so 'free' male soldiers to actually fire the guns.[18] Thus, in the new mixed artillery crews women were assigned to fire control, searchlight operations, targeting and hit confirmation. An ideologically nervous British government defined these artillery women as 'non-combat' personnel. Men standing next to them, but assigned to *firing* the guns, were designated as 'combat' personnel.[19]

Women were used in the first and second world wars only reluctantly. Furthermore, women were recruited into the military force only when recruitment of men from usually marginalised ethnic or racial groups wouldn't satisfy the generals' and admirals' manpower needs. As always, sexual ideologies and racial/ethnic ideologies operated simultaneously to determine who the government would use in its armed forces.

Once the war was over, women were demobilised as quickly as possible. Any Amazons were pushed back across the frontier of social imagination. The world was put right once more. War and peace were portrayed as distinct—war abnormal, peace normal. In 'normal' times women do not soldier.

Manpower politics in a nuclear peacetime

Separating history into distinct wartimes and peacetimes permits the convenient notion that any mobilisation of women soldiers is short term and basically anomalous. But such an idea is becoming harder and harder to sustain. In these latter decades of the twentieth century militarisation is proceeding at a breath-taking pace, though we are allegedly in 'peacetime'. In reality, this 'peacetime' is thought of by national security officials as an era of global threat. Consequently, 'peacetime' has come to be defined today in terms of national insecurity and an obsession with defence. It is during this sort of 'peacetime' that military forces are calling for more soldiers than their male populations can supply without seriously weakening their civilian economy.

For both the US and Britain, the early 1970s marked the

beginning of the first 'peacetime' military recruiting campaigns aimed at women. These campaigns won the support of some women activists pressing for equal rights.[20] But they remained under the control of male military manpower officials whose concern was *not* with women's liberation, but with maintaining large military forces suited to East-West confrontations without the aide of male conscription.

At first sight this development seems puzzling. In the 1980s women are still recruited into the armed forces at the very time when *any* human beings—male or female—seem irrelevant to warfare between the 'great powers' and their allies in the Warsaw and NATO pacts. Three decades after the atomic bomb attacks on Hiroshima and Nagasaki, aren't ordinary soldiers overshadowed by the real wielders of modern military force—physicists, weapons technicians, strategic theorists and a handful of nuclear submarine captains, bomber pilots and subterranean missile crewmen? Aren't 'manpower' worries redundant?

When a new generation of destructive missiles is being readied for placement in Europe it is easy to slip into the assumption that flesh and blood soldiers have become obsolete, that 'conventional' warfare has been relegated to the military dustbin. In an age shaped by peacetime nuclear weaponry, one might think that British and American commanders could get all the white male educated youths they needed.

The reality is rather different. Military commanders and government officials do not stop worrying about how they are going to fill the ranks when nuclear missiles are introduced into the strategic calculus. First of all, the nuclear strategies of both the Warsaw and NATO alliances are predicated on the notion that nuclear weapons will be of greatest political value as a *threat*, and that actual military engagements will be fought at the 'conventional'—i.e. 'non-nuclear'—level. Consequently, by mid-1982, 1.7 million Warsaw Pact troops faced two million NATO troops in Europe. Each alliance's commanders were keeping a careful watch on the other, making sure that these conventional forces remained in what military strategists misleadingly refer to as 'balance'.[21] The Reagan administration made it clear that it saw the build-up of conventional forces *and* nuclear forces as simply two sides of the same Cold War coin. Thus in 1982 while Reagan and his advisers were pushing Britain, Italy and West Germany to accept Pershing and cruise nuclear warhead missiles, they were *also* calling for an additional 200,000 soldiers in American's conventional forces.[22]

Second, conflicts in Vietnam, El Salvador, Angola, the Falklands, Oman, Ethiopia, Iran, Afghanistan, and the Lebanon have shown that most of the military competition between the two major alliances is being conducted today on Third World territories by local armies, most of whom do not (yet) possess nuclear weapons. Many anti-nuclear weapons activists insist that attention to conflicts in the Third World must be an integral part of any political movement to bring about serious nuclear disarmament.

Third, many observers believe that the entire dichotomy between 'conventional' and 'nuclear' warfare has lost its meaning. The evolution of weapons technology and 'strategic science' (as taught in military academies and staff colleges) is making the nuclear warheads *part* of regular field equipment. The result: boundaries between conventional and nuclear war will be more easily crossed in the course of any great-power military engagement.

Fourth, there are people in and out of government who see the expansion of conventional forces as the prime alternative to the current reliance on nuclear strategies. Some peace movement activists even seem willing to look favourably on the reinstatement of conscription as a way to bolster the 'conventional' alternative. As one US anti-draft commentator wrote, some anti-nuclear, pro-weapons-freeze activists appear ready to 'trade the freeze for the draft'.[23]

But it is military manpower planners who, like baby food company executives, keep their eyes on census charts. Marked drops in birth rates have been occurring during the 1970s and 1980s in most of the countries of the NATO pact, as well as in the Soviet Union among the ethnic group the Soviet military elite trusts most, ethnic Russians (now barely half of the Soviet population). In other words, women making decisions about their own reproductive capacities are sending waves of anxiety down defence establishment corridors. Military planners recognise that in times of falling birth rates, the ranks can be filled only by deliberate recruitment strategies. Manpower officials in Britain, the US and Canada have jobs twice as hard because their legislators have abolished male conscription (at least for the time being). But even those NATO and Warsaw governments enjoying the convenience of male conscription are seeing hard times ahead.

Even with male conscription, West Germany's military, for instance, relies on volunteers for 40 per cent of the Bundeswehr's troops. By 1990, the number of conscriptable West German young men is expected to fall to 200,000, and by 1995 it will have plummeted to 150,000. Such demographic crystal ball gazing prompted German military elites and senior politicians to start speculating out loud about conscription of women. West German feminists protested, tracing conscription of women back to Nazi militarism rather than forward to an era of liberation. In 1982, when the Social Democratic regime of Helmut Schmidt fell and was replaced by the conservative Christian Democrat regime of Helmut Kohl, Germany's gender politics of conscription became more contradictory. The CDU may be even more militarily minded than its SDP predecessors and thus even more determined to maintain German manpower strength; however, the CDU's male leadership is also more devoted to a gender ideology which frowns on women serving in such public and 'masculine' roles as soldiering. This sort of regime is more likely to resist liberalisation of the still restrictive German abortion law and offer incentives to women to celebrate motherhood than it is to conscript women. Consequently, if, as the 1990s demographic crunch approaches, the West German government shies away from the expanded voluntary recruitment or the conscription of women, it may be less a testimony to German feminists' political influence than to a conservative regime's inability to resolve its own gender/manpower dilemma.[24]

Military officials in all the countries belonging to the NATO and Warsaw pacts are worrying about the quality and quantity of their manpower—how to get what they need and how to keep it. And it is that elite-level worrying, far more than women's liberation movements, which has set the stage for the current push to find ways to increase the military uses of women *without* upsetting either the military's own masculine ethos or society's expectations about men's and women's proper roles.[25]

The 15 national armed forces of NATO vary in the degrees and ways they use women. These variations reflect, firstly, the degree of ideological conservatism of the current regime; second, the ambitiousness of the given military's regional or global mission; third, the country's birth rate; fourth, the level and quality of civilian unemployment; fifth, the social status of soldiering; and lastly, the country's ethnic or racial groups' 'trustworthiness' and 'competence' in the eyes of military officials.

NATO has a 'Committee on Women in the NATO Forces' which reports annually on the status of women in the alliance. These reports were in part a response to pressures from NATO's Conference of Senior Service Women Officers, which has become an in-house lobby for 'greater understanding and recognition of the ever-increasing contribution women can make to the Allied Services'.[26]

NATO's 1982 report on women in uniform reveals considerable differences within the alliance:[27]

Belgium (1981)
- women are 5.8 per cent of the total armed forces
- of the total 3,547 women, 116 are officers
- women are enlisted only as volunteers, beginning at the age of 16
- women soldiers have rights to maternity leave
- there are no legal prohibitions against women serving in any military posts including combat

Canada (1981)
- women are 7.9 per cent of the regular force; 20.2 per cent of the reserves
- women and men enlist as volunteers
- women soldiers have rights to maternity leave
- of 6,275 women in the regular forces, 830 are officers (including 319 nurses)
- government policy prohibits the employment of women in

combat and duty at sea, though women *are* being used in 'near-combat units'

Denmark (1980)

— there are 498 women in the Danish forces
— 12,000 women serve in the Danish Home Guard
— women are enlisted on a voluntary basis
— women are not allowed to serve in combat roles
— women have rights to maternity leave

France (1981)

— its forces are not formally integrated into NATO, but it has 15,000 women serving in all three branches comprising just under 3 per cent of the total force; men are conscripted, women serve voluntarily[28]

Federal Republic of Germany (1981)

— as of May 1981 there were a mere 60 uniformed women in the three services; all were medical officers
— many clerical and administrative posts filled by uniformed women in other forces, are filled by 'civilian' women in the West German defence establishment
— all women are volunteers
— the post-second world war constitution limits compulsory service to men, but states that on no account may women volunteers serve with weapons (radar, electronic weapons, supply and logistics—all have been defined as 'weapons' under the law)

Greece (1981)

— there are 142 women serving as 'volunteer conscripts' and 822 serving as 'volunteer NCOs', as well as 11 women 'potential reserve officers'
— women must be high school graduates and unmarried
— women are excluded from combat

Italy

— male conscription; no women reported[29]

Luxembourg

— military service voluntary; no women reported[30]

The Netherlands (1981)

— the total of 1,229 women represents 1 per cent of the total armed forces
— 222 women are officers
— women serve on a voluntary basis
— though by law women are not excluded from any military roles, in practice women are excluded on grounds of physical strength and 'privacy' from certain posts

Norway (1980)

— women comprise 0.5 per cent of the armed forces, with a future goal set at 5 per cent
— women serve on a voluntary basis
— women are excluded from combat units, but receive weapons training and may serve in administrative positions in anti-aircraft missile units
— women have rights to maternity leave

Portugal (1981)

— women serve as military nurses
— at the end of Portugal's colonial wars in Africa the number of military nurses was reduced

Turkey (1981)

— no figures given
— women serve only as officers, on a voluntary basis
— women serve in pilot support services, administration, medical care and engineering

United Kingdom (1981)

— women comprise approximately 4.8 per cent of the total armed forces
— most women are members of distinct women's units, though they may be assigned to jobs in largely male units
— *Queen Alexandra's Royal Nursing Service* is all women; it includes 170 nursing officers and 450 naval nurses
— *Queen Alexandra's Royal Army Nursing Corps* is all women (male nurses are assigned to the Royal Army Medical Corps) with an average strength of over 500 nursing officers and approximately 1,000 servicewomen

— *Queen Alexandra's Royal Air Force Nursing Service* is no longer an all women's service, but includes 908 women nurses
— All nursing corps are 'non-combatant', though during hostilities nurses are permitted to serve 'at the forward edge of the battle area'.
— *Women's Royal Naval Service* consists of 3,300 women, 5 per cent of the Royal Navy; they are excluded from sea duty and combat
— *Women's Royal Army Corps* consists of 5,075 women, comprising 3.1 per cent of the Regular Army (and 4.8 per cent of the Territorial Army); only certain posts are open to women; combat posts are not open to women, though some servicewomen can be trained in the use of small arms for the sake of self defence
— *Women's Royal Air Force*—women comprise 6.15 per cent of total RAF and RAF auxiliary personnel; one flying and 12 ground jobs are open to women. Women may volunteer to be trained with weapons, but may not be employed on 'front line' combat aircraft
— all British women serve on a volunteer basis

United States (1980)
— women comprise 8.2 per cent of the total armed forces active duty personnel and 6.8 per of the reserves
— women range from 10.8 per cent of the air force to 3.6 per cent of the marines
— women are integrated with men in each service
— specific jobs are closed to women
— women are excluded from combat
— women have the right to maternity leave
— women serve on a voluntary basis

NATO is an alliance of unequals, as is the Warsaw Pact. We know all too little about the internal workings of NATO—how decisions are made, where compromises are hammered out, what items never get on to the agenda, how public and private arms manufacturers make their wishes felt, how civilian politicians and military professionals get on together. What we do know is that, with the small but interesting exception of the Senior Women Officers Commission, the NATO elite is an all-male club. Secondly, we know that over the last two decades NATO has become an elaborate multi-national bureaucracy whose interests extend far beyond simply co-ordinating battlefield manoeuvres.

From its Brussels headquarters NATO extends its complex web of communications reaching out to each of the 15 member capitals. NATO thereby acts as a vehicle for interpreting economic, social and political change, for assigning meaning to trends and choices current in North America, Western Europe and the whole world. It is in their interpreting role that NATO strategists weigh each member government's capacity to deliver the quality and quantity of military manpower deemed necessary for NATO in the 1980s. Such manpower calculations generate NATO concern about each member country's birth rate, educational standards, labour supply, youth alienation and availability of women. To the extent that NATO planners are worried about members' capacity to deliver sufficient manpower, women in those countries are being scrutinised.[31]

NATO is partly a teaching machine. In 1981 when the Dutch navy first allowed women sailors on its combat ships, all of its military allies watched to see what would happen. A year later when the American army reduced the number of jobs its women could fill, the rest of the alliances watched. NATO is a structure for experimentation in gender just as it is a structure for weapons experimentation. What 'works' or 'fails' in one member force is likely to have repercussions in the others.

The recruiter's game: 'skirts, travel and opportunity'

Mary Lee Settle, an American woman who volunteered in 1940 to serve with Britain's Women's Air Force during the second world war, describes the transformation of her young English working-class comrades in the military:

> They looked 17, in what seemed to me a life without joy which was imposed on most of them without their choice; they were beginning to thrive. The days that had stripped

> me of weight, well-being and habits so soon, were acting on them in the opposite way. Air, exercise, regular meals, and the very act for some of them of sleeping above ground for the first time in years, were making the blood run better through their bodies... I saw all this without conversation, only with horror that such a life, such indifferent regimentation, such ciphering, was better than they had known before. It presented a terrible social excuse.[32]

Forty years later the glossy brochure of the Women's Royal Army Corps assures potential recruits that they will enjoy food that is 'first class, imaginatively prepared by army cooks who take great pride in their work'. And if that isn't sufficient, 'as well as usual team games, you can swim, play tennis or squash, learn to ride. You could even take up gliding, canoeing or sailing'. Some of the smiling, attractive white women are pictured working as stewardesses, switchboard operators and electronics technicians; others are shown serving as postal operators, clerks, supply specialists and military policewomen. Furthermore, according to the brochure, as a woman you will be protected:

> One thing is certain—wherever you serve and whatever job you do, the WRAC will look after your personal welfare. You will receive the finest medical and dental care in the world, and if you have personal problems, you will always find someone ready and willing to listen and help.

Beyond the crucial day-to-day necessities, 'the WRAC means new friends, new activities, and the chance to see new places'. One woman soldier pictured in the ad says, 'On 48 hours leave, I got bored. I missed my friends back at camp.'

The armed forces are offering today's women, then, not simply the chance to learn military skills or demonstrate patriotism. They are holding out to women a chance to leave stifling families, dead-end jobs and home towns, without sacrificing the security those institutions are presumed to give women.

Some women, in fact, join the military, that epitome of patriarchy, to avoid or delay entrance into that other patriarchal institution, marriage.

Helen is an ex-nun. Recently she has been trying to figure out why she joined a Catholic order at the age of 17. She has talked it over with a woman friend who enlisted in the army at about the same time. Helen says that she and her ex-army friend have discovered that their reasons were strikingly similar: 'To get away from home'; 'To find a safe place'; 'To be with other women'; 'To put off marriage and yet do something parents couldn't oppose'.[33]

To a woman walking past a recruiter's window, the choice may appear to be between a part-time job at the local Wimpy bar and getting married or enlisting as an army driver, travelling to Cyprus or Germany. British women soldiers are paid 2.5 per cent *less* than their male soldier counterparts, but that is far less than the gap in pay in the British civilian job market, in which women earn an average of only 69 per cent of men's weekly pay-cheques.

The thousands of women who are joining the military may be part of a deliberate government manpower strategy to expand the recruitment pool in a time of declining birth rates, but it would be a mistake to think of them as mere puppets on the ends of military strings. Women are trying to make individual choices in societies that are structured to limit those choices. Military recruitment strategies exploit those limitations by playing on women's desire to be independent and economically secure and to live and work closely with other women.

Linda Haymes went through a tour of duty as a US army enlistee. Once out, she tried to understand just how at 18 she had been appealed to by the army's recruiter:

> The recruiter is a trained manipulator. Once he is able to assess a woman's needs, he glamorises a response based on them. If she is unstable financially, he will concentrate on saying that the military will take care of her by providing free shelter and food, a good paying job, free medical care, and will assist with college tuition. He will emphasise that the military will continue to provide medical and educational benefits after her term is completed. If she expresses boredom or unhappiness with her present living situation, he will feed her promises of travel, romance and adventure.[34]

To a young woman, a poor woman, all of the recruiter's offers and reassurances struck a positive note:

> At 17, I had survived a childhood that clashed early with society. As a chronic runaway, to avoid an unhealthy family environment, I experienced juvenile court, a home for girls, and then was juggled around the country between different relatives. Upon graduating from high school, I was frustrated with the educational system and society.
>
> I wanted an alternative; a place where I could be independent. I saw a recruiter's poster and found myself at the recruiting office of the United States army. I was 18 years old, angry, and defiant, with no one to direct me.[35]

Not all women respond to the 'economic draft'. Brenda, an American black woman from Long Island, just outside New York City, wasn't young or unemployed or stifled by life in a small town when she was attracted by the military recruiter's message. She was a woman in her early twenties who had been a black student activist at her university but had decided to leave her studies for a while to take a job with one of the urban development corporations that started up in the early 1970s. One day as she was making her daily morning trip to work on the Long Island railroad, she spied an army recruiting poster. The opportunities being offered seemed an appealing change from what was becoming a less than stimulating job. Without telling any of her friends, who she was sure would try to talk her out of it, she went straight to the nearest army recruiter's office and signed up as an enlisted woman. The recruiter didn't tell her about the possibilities for officer training for someone with a university education. So, during the next six years, Brenda served as a clerk, nutritionist, and finally as race relations officer with the US forces in West Germany at a base with 17 women and 70,000 men.[36]

The appeals offered by military recruiters are most likely to connect with the private aspirations and needs of those women who have the fewest alternatives for education, income, and autonomy. In France, it is from regions where the textile industry—a major employer of women—is failing, that the French military has recruited the most women.[37] Similarly, in the US, black women in the military far exceed their proportion in American society as a whole.

This was not always so. Black women served in the American military before the 1970s, but in numbers far *below* their proportion in the civilian population because of official policies of exclusion and segregation. For instance, during the second world war the navy's and coast guard's women's corps, the WAVES and SPARS, refused to accept black women until 1944, late in the war; the US Marine Corps Women's Reserve excluded black women altogether. The Women's Army Corps enlisted 4,000 black women, but relegated most of them to jobs as cooks, bakers, laundry workers, hospital orderlies and waitresses. Only one black WACs unit, the 6888th Central Postal Battalion, was allowed to serve overseas.[38] Why the reversal in the 1970s and 1980s?

This reversal is dramatic. While black women are approximately only 11 per cent of all American women, by June 1982 they comprised 25.7 per cent of all women in the armed forces combined and *42.5 per cent of all enlisted women in the US army*:

—Women were 9 per cent of all US armed forces personnel
—Black men and women were 19.7 per cent of all US armed forces personnel
—Black women were 25.7 per cent of all US armed forces women

—Women were 9.5 per cent of all US *army* personnel
—Black men and women were 29.5 per cent of all US army personnel.
—Black women were 25.7 per cent of all US army women

—Women were 7.9 per cent of all US *navy* personnel
—Black men and women were 11.1 per cent of all navy personnel
—Black women were 14.8 per cent of all US navy women

—Women were 4.3 per cent of all US *marines* personnel
—Black men and women were 19.7 per cent of all marines personnel

—Black women were 22.1 per cent of all US marines women

—Women were 11.1 per cent of all US *air force* personnel
—Black men and women were 14.7 per cent of all US air force personnel
—Black women were 17.9 per cent of all US air force women.[39]

Virtually all of the political discussion of the racial composition of, and racism in, the US military has concentrated on black men. Black women have been filed under the problem heading: 'women in the military'. Institutional racism as it affects black women soldiers has been treated as a non-issue. This is emphasised by the recent book title chosen by American black feminists: *All the Women Are White, All the Blacks Are Men, But Some of Us Are Brave.*[40]

The disproportionate numbers of black women voluntarily enlisting in the military in the 1980s as well as their political invisibility needs to be explained in order to make sense of how the current military recruitment strategies exploit women's frustrations and hopes. Black women—especially young black women —suffer some of the highest unemployment and underemployment rates in the American labour force. They, even more than white women, live in conditions which offer few options. When a black woman does find a waged job, her pay is likely to be even lower than a white woman's or a black man's pay. Education beyond secondary school is hard to afford. Perhaps this also explains why black women soldiers have *re*-enlisted at higher rates than their white women counterparts. Still, as the 1982 documentary film *Soldier Girls* revealed, black as well as white women have not endured the male-defined military discipline without resistance. Slowing down the forced march, or smiling into the face of an angry drill sergeant can serve as forms of resistance to a male-defined, white-controlled institution.

But the US military has not been as afraid of taking in 'too many' black women as it has been of taking in 'too many' black men. In the early 1970s many white Pentagon officials and conservative pro-military white congressmen feared that the end of the draft and reliance on an all-volunteer military force would produce an armed forces heavily dependent on black males. The black male leadership itself was divided over the volunteer army issue. Some black spokesmen predicted that the volunteer army would relieve middle-class white men of the duty of risking their lives and transform black young men, unable to find jobs, into modern mercenaries. Others saw the all-volunteer force as a potential jobs programme for young, disaffected black men.

Women *were* discussed, but as if the racial divisions, which so preoccupied policy-makers considering male volunteers, simply didn't exist among women volunteers. In the 1970s women were seen by many Pentagon manpower strategists and their congressional allies as the means to *dilute* black males' potential dominance of the rank and file in the post-Vietnam volunteer army. If women could be recruited in greater numbers than ever before, so this reasoning went, they could forestall the 'blackening' of the US military.

So, black women soldiers have been treated by military officials as *women*, and in political circles 'black soldiers' has meant black *male* soldiers. *They* were the soldiers whose allegedly low educational attainment, or high drug use or political disaffection posed a 'problem', a threat to the US military and, it was implied, to US national security. No black woman in uniform made security-conscious congressmen or Pentagon officials nervous in the way that a black man in uniform—with a gun—made them nervous.[41]

Thus, the percentage of black men in the all-volunteer army —and navy and air force—was closely monitored in the years after 1972, with the unspoken official understanding that they should not become over 30 per cent of any service. Meanwhile black women, along with white women, were being deliberately recruited and scarcely counted in this racial panic. With the economic recession of the late 1970s and early 1980s, and with the growing frequency of military enlistment throughout the black community, the numbers of black women in the American military spiralled, especially in the enlisted ranks.

In September 1982, when the US army announced it was going to restrict the jobs that women could fill, it was not a reaction to the high proportion of black women in the service; it was a reaction to military commanders' anxieties about *all* women in uniform.

The anxious scrutiny of sexual difference

In both world wars the contradiction between the need to mobilise women as soldiers and the need to prevent women's presence from undermining the military's legitimising image of manhood was softened somewhat by the very notion that the time was peculiar and finite: female recruitment was only 'for the duration'. In contrast, current recruitment is less time-bounded and thus more acutely contradictory. It is being carried out in order to compensate for long-term demographic changes in society and because of the long-term need of the armed forces to acquire soldiers with educational standards that match their ever more esoteric weaponry.

Lacking the finiteness and ideological peculiarity of wartime, a peacetime military force relying on women soldiers seems to have an exaggerated need to pursue more and more refined measures of sexual difference in order to keep women in their place. Western armed forces now conduct official studies of pregnancy, menstruation and 'upper body strength' in an almost desperate search for some fundamental, intrinsic (i.e. not open to political debate) difference between male and female soldiers. They search for a difference which can justify women's continued exclusion from the military's ideological core—combat. If they can find this difference, they can also exclude women from the senior command promotions that are open only to officers who have seen combat.

Women soldiers, not men soldiers, get pregnant. A pregnant soldier is likely to suffer morning sickness, her performance will not be up to standard; her comrades have to do extra work to compensate. A pregnant soldier who gives birth and takes time off, even if the law (as in most NATO countries) allows her to stay in the military, is the soldier/mother who, it is alleged, is likely to quit so she can devote her primary attention to child care. Thus, many military officials argue, it is not surprising that women recruits have a high 'attrition rate', that is, a high incidence of leaving the military rather than finishing their tours or re-enlisting.

Military pregnancy studies omit the fact that in the US military it is *male* soldiers who proportionately lose the most days of active duty—because of drug abuse, going AWOL (absent without leave), and as a consequence of disciplinary actions. Despite all their supposed 'frailties', women soldiers lose fewer days.[42] Furthermore, some American black women believe that one reason that black women soldiers have lower attrition rates in the US military than their white sisters is that black women soldiers are likely to have children for whom they are the sole source of support, and thus are less able to have the luxury of giving up a secure military salary than are those white women with no children or with a second income in their families.[43]

Military commanders hostile to having women in their units argue that a soldier who menstruates is likely to jeopardise her unit's mobility and thus its 'readiness'.[44] Military establishments commission studies of the consequences of menstruation. Such studies, of course, can draw on a whole mythology surrounding women's bleeding. But these studies are conducted with special enthusiasm by the US military in the 1980s, perhaps because it is the US military that is under the greatest pressure to expand its manpower in an era when the American government is increasingly involved in global conflict and when it faces declining birth rates in the societies of all its Western allies. The American studies—conducted by in-house Pentagon officials and, increasingly, by civilian social scientists under contract—are readily shared throughout NATO alliance.

Pregnancy and menstruation studies are ideological sandbags piled up to construct a essentialist barricade that many senior military policy-makers hope will protect their institution against the onslaught of 'feminisation'. Their goal is to create an ideological/political climate which allows them to *use* women as soldiers without being *threatened* by them. One half-step above these studies are those which measure men's and women's 'upper body strength'. This is such a frequently used term in American military bureaucratic lingo that it has been reduced to the shorthand, UBS.

Upper body strength differences may be a weak defence against women's feared intrusion into the military's inner sanctum, however. As women who have broken into American all-male fire-fighting departments have demonstrated, upper body strength can be developed; equipment and team procedures can be redesigned. Thus the question of UBS is not quite as impenetrable a defence against feminisation as menstruation or pregnancy. For the time being, though, it will do as a patriarchal military stop-gap.[45]

The reasoning goes like this: soldiers assigned to 'combat' must *lift* and *carry* heavy things and *pull* themselves over formidable obstacles. Therefore, every soldier assigned to a role that the military commander chooses to define as a 'combat' must have a certain minimal body strength. Moreover, presumably, it is too taxing on a military organisation to test every individual soldier's UBS; it has to use gross categories to sustain its division of labour. So, if it can be determined officially that women as a class have less UBS than men as a class, women soldiers can be excluded from any role that military officialdom places under the rubric of 'combat'.[46]

As these biological arguments are circulated among NATO governments and picked up by the media, they help to reproduce patriarchal sexist ideas in the society as a whole. If a menstruating woman soldier is imagined to jeopardise national security, what are the chances of any woman escaping the confines of biological determinism?

'You're either a whore or a lesbian'

> The WAACS at one time had a bad name for morals... I knew intimately about twenty of the fifty-two girl residents there [in a camp in France]—girls drawn from North of England factories, post offices, and domestic service... I never witnessed conduct which struck my unsophisticated eyes as unseemly.[47]

British feminist Winifred Holtby was writing in 1935, when the loose morals of the 'modern woman' were being widely deplored. The supposed lessons flowing from the mobilisation of women as soldiers in the first world war shaped the discourse. The post-first world war debate in turn influenced how, and with what justifications governments recruited women again in 1940 and later in the 1970s.

The young American woman smiling out from under a camouflaged combat helmet in the advertisement is headlined, 'Some of the best soldiers wear lipstick'. On the one hand, the military has internal and external needs for its women soldiers not to seem to violate conventional gender norms; they must be 'feminine', that is, smiling, pretty and heterosexual, even while being loyal and competent. Such women soldiers will not generate politically embarrassing controversy in the society at large. On the other hand, lesbians aren't new to the armed forces. After the second world war, when the women corps were sharply cut back and persisted as small self-contained communities marginalised by their senior commands, many lesbian women were able to use the WACs to develop comfortable women-identified worlds.[48]

What is new today is not just the numbers of women—heterosexual and lesbian—in the military, but the sharpening of commanders' ambivalences. Is it safer to have women who will 'fraternise' with, 'use their charms on' men, get pregnant, and taint the masculine force with their traces of lipstick? Or is it better to have women who will pursue military careers out of self-generated enthusiasm but who will also use the military as a place to develop emotional attachments among themselves, threaten their male soldiers' sense of masculine sexual self-confidence and offend civilian society?

In 1981 only 5 per cent of the British armed forces were female. Yet, during the 1978-82 period, over *one-third* (3,160 women or a total of 41 per cent) of all soldiers dismissed from the British armed forces for homosexuality were women. Furthermore, British women soldiers—straight and lesbian—were 10 times more likely than men to have their private lives officially investigated.[49]

Why, in the 1980s, should women soldiers (and sailors) be so disproportionately the targets of military homophobia? Maybe there are a lot of lesbians in the various women's corps. Or perhaps the notion of a 'woman soldier' is fraught with contradictions that do not equally confuse the notion of a 'male soldier'.[50]

Britain's 1967 Sexual Offences Act decriminalised male homosexuality, but exempted the armed forces. Still, in early 1982, the British Ministry of Defence leaked news that officers were being told to be 'flexible' in handling discharges in keeping with society's more liberal attitudes towards lesbians and gay men.[51] Groups which had been formed to press for lesbian and gay rights in the military (with help from a Dutch group, *Werkgroep Homosexualiteit en Krygsmacht*, Homosexuality in the Military Working Group) warned, however, that such news might be premature and there was no cause for relaxing pressure.[52]

Anne, Barbara, and Carol (not their real names) were 'administratively discharged' in 1982 from the British Women's Royal Army Corps for being lesbians. Anne joined when she was 20; Barbara and Carol when they were just 17. Each of them hoped to escape dead-end jobs. Though recruiters' career promises didn't materialise, each woman enjoyed being away from home, having the chance to play sports, and 'the idea of 20 girls going out on a big binge is marvellous'.[53]

Then, in the early 1980s, the British army started to follow the American lead, integrating WRAC women into mostly male units. Simultaneously, the pressures for heterosexist conformity increased. Still, it seemed to Anne, Barbara and Carol, the official attitude toward lesbianism was ambivalent: formally condemn it, but act as though lesbianism in the ranks simply couldn't and didn't exist. This strategy on the part of the middle level officers left it to male squaddies to perform the sexual policing duties:

> *Barbara:* The blokes don't like the women being so close-knit and together so much!
> *Anne:* Men soldiers don't respect WRACs at all. If you're in it, you're a lesbian or a slut. And there's a real pressure to sleep with men. In the men's quarters at one of my driving units, they had a list of all the WRACs pinned up and a tick system on whether they thought you were gay or straight —on the basis of who *they'd* slept with, of course... Going to a new unit as a lesbian, well, you have to pretend a lot. If anyone asks, you've a boyfriend on the other side of the world.[54]

But Northern Ireland seems to be constructed ideologically by the British military as a 'special case'. Ulster is such an unpopular posting and soldiers there are subject to such stringent security regulations, that it seems the army relaxes its sexual restrictions somewhat.

> *Cathy:* Because they're so tight on general security they lay off the petty discipline. There's no bed-checks or anything like that. They know it's rough job wise so they lay off other things and you can get away with more.[55]

When Cathy, Barbara and Anne were eventually reported, it was by other women, women who had been encouraged by WRAC officers to fear lesbians in their ranks. All three women fought to stay in the army. They endured searches and interrogations by the Army Special Investigation Branch. But their appeals ran out and they were discharged. Now out on 'Civvie Street', they are bitter; they think that WRAC officers who are lesbians are not subject to the same oppression, that lesbians should be able to serve, and that in fact hundreds of lesbians *are* still in the British army—and navy and air force.[56]

The American patterns of control are very similar. According to a 1981 study, women were discharged from the US navy on the grounds of homosexual conduct at a rate two and a half times higher than men. Figures from the air force show similar disparities.[57]

US army records show that in 1979, 104 women and 198 men were discharged 'for reasons of homosexuality'. Given the fact that in that year there were a mere 60,912 women (as opposed to 697,940 men) in the US army, women were six times more likely than men to be discharged from the army on the grounds of homosexuality.[58]

The US Defense Department says it bars all known homosexuals, male and female, from the military because their presence in the ranks hurts morale and discipline: 'It's not a matter of morality, simply of practicality.'[59]

According to the US army judge advocate general:

> Soldiers are required to live and work under entirely

> different conditions than civilians... Civilians generally need only associate with their co-workers during business hours. Soldiers, on the other hand, must often sleep, eat and perform personal hygiene under conditions affording minimal privacy.
>
> The presence of homosexuals in such an environment tends to impair unit morale and cohesion as well as infringing upon the right of privacy of those service members who have more traditional sexual preferences.[60]

Ironically, though, in this era of non-conscription, the need to reduce attrition and prevent soldiers from leaving after they've been expensively trained has compelled the Pentagon to warn base commanders to be on the alert for 'false gays', soldiers claiming to be homosexuals just to get out of the military before their tours are over. Thus at the same time as it is investigating and discharging scores of women and men accused of being homosexuals, the American military is refusing to believe other soldiers who say they are gay or lesbian, insisting that they 'prove' that they are indeed practising homosexuals.[61]

> I just got tired of having to bounce back and forth all the time.[62]

Susan (not her real name) sat on the couch surrounded by four other American navy enlisted women ranging from early twenties to early thirties, all dressed casually in faded jeans and T-shirts. Each woman thought of herself as a lesbian. Two wore gold wedding bands. All of them wished they could stay in the navy but had come together out of outrage, overcoming the fear produced by a 'lesbian witch hunt' then being waged aboard their ship.

Susan had gone to the ship's 'Ex-O' (executive officer, one rung below the ship's captain) to confess she was a lesbian. She said she simply wanted to stop the 'bouncing back and forth' between faked heterosexuality and clandestine lesbianism that she felt was imposed on her by the navy's social conventions and its criminal code. 'When a gay guy is found out they get him off the ship pronto. It's all fast and hush-hush. But when one of us confesses, they make a big deal about it.' Susan thought she would be discharged quickly once she had told her Ex-O she was a lesbian. But, instead, he demanded that she endure a formal hearing—'captain's mast'—where she would have to present evidence and witnesses. The hearing turned into the launch pad for an investigation which touched the lives of virtually every woman aboard the ship. Within a month, two women sailors had been issued discharges. The Naval Intelligence Service had spied on on-shore apartments and gay bars; private mail had been opened; women thought by the NIS to be straight were urged to tell 'anything you know' about women suspected of being lesbians; women being investigated tried to stay away from friends in order to protect them; lesbians persuaded male friends to act as boyfriends—one arrived at dockside with a big bouquet of roses.

> There are black and white women on our ships but there are good race relations. It's as *women* that we have hassles...
>
> We used to have a really good spirit. Now everyone is suspicious of everyone else.

Was it simply homophobia that was motivating the captain, the Ex-O, and the NIS? It seemed more basic than that. The lesbian sailors broadened their off-ship discussions to include supportive straight women sailors. Together they tried to sort out the patterns that caused all of them to feel so torn and cheated:

> If I go out with more than one guy on the ship, I'm called a slut. If I don't go out or won't 'put out' for guys, then the rumour mill labels me a lesbian. You can't win.

It was not just women suspected of being lesbians who bore the brunt of official navy hostility. It seemed to be all women:

> When a guy sees a woman out there on the decks sand-blasting, he thinks, 'That's not right. She should be at home being protected, waiting for me when I come home.'

The more the women sailors talked about what had happened since Susan had gone to the Ex-O, the closer they moved towards concluding that the lesbian purge was a campaign against *all* women on this ship and on all navy ships. They all knew that most middle level officers (those in command of troops) hated the Pentagon's 'women at sea' programme, which had been begun at the end of the 1970s to overcome the manpower shortage. Officers' hostility came out in the way they made women the butt of sexist jokes and shunted women with technical training into secretarial jobs. But such strategies weren't entirely successful aboard their ship. There were over 100 women in a total crew of 600. Some women, especially if they persisted, would get into technical jobs and would earn promotions. When directed against women sailors, the navy officers' homophobia seemed to be intended to demoralise all women, to get them off the ships.

The top American strategists' plan to expand the navy to confront the Soviet Union in a period of non-conscription demands that women be recruited. But at least women could be purged from the *ships*. The ship is the ideological core of the navy, the place where combat is experienced and where men are confined in such physically close quarters. The mixed ship could be seen as a sexual time bomb in the ideological heartland.

Sexual harassment as a military issue

Those women not purged as lesbians often leave the military because of sexual harassment. The higher attrition rates that women display may have little to do with pregnancy and a lot to do with frustration at being the targets of sexually harassing jokes, innuendos and retaliations on the job. Out of its concern with high attrition rates, the US Department of Defense contracted a study of sexual harassment and issued orders to commanders to take steps to prevent and punish sexual harassment.[63] *Attrition*, not women's liberation, has motivated any military efforts to curtail the sexual harassment that pervades so much of any woman's life in the military. It is only when officers think their chances for promotion are affected by the number of soldiers under their command who drop out of the military and when they become convinced that sexual harassment is a major reason for women soldiers' departure, that sexual harassment is likely to be taken seriously on any military base.

In other words, sexual harassment only becomes an issue in

the eyes of military officials when it is seen to jeopardise the 'attrition-morale-readiness' trinity that modern military officers so hallow.

Sexual harassment has intensified, first, as the numbers of women in the military have increased; second, as the practice of integrating women into once all-male units has become more common and, third, as women have gradually moved into those technical jobs once considered securely 'masculine'. Not surprisingly, these are the same trends that have transformed lesbianism into a burning 'issue' for many male officers.

> It's a verbal cesspool. We get hassled by male soldiers constantly. They hang around the barracks entrances at night, in the parking lots, hassle every woman who walks by. At first you try to ignore it, or laugh it off, but eventually it wears you down...
>
> I can handle that, but I can't handle it when they block my way as I walk, run after me, ask me to perform sexual acts or won't let me into my barracks.[64]

This young woman at Fort Benning, Georgia, was discussing a process of escalation that women soldiers believe to be woven into the very hierarchical ranking structure that is the hallmark of a military organisation. A woman sailor who says she is regularly propositioned by her male officer supervisor but has learned to suppress her anger and 'just laugh it off' tells what happened when another enlisted woman on her ship decided to file a formal complaint:

> She was being harassed on her watch, so she filed a written complaint as a means of requesting a transfer to another job. Of course it had to go through channels. The first officer OK'd it (he's a good guy); the second officer OK'd it. But when it got to the third guy, he denied her request and wrote on the form, 'If she'd do her job right, maybe she'd find she wouldn't be harassed.' So, see? What does it get you to complain? You're just put down as not doing your job.[65]

The military organisation's response is especially likely to produce feelings of isolation and alienation because of the explicitness and rigidity of its hierarchical ranking system, its bureaucratic formality and its underlying male-bonding. Mary Lee Settle remembers how the British air force looked to her as a young WRAF enlisted woman:

> I saw the hierarchy as like peeling an onion, skin after skin, with no end except the military mind itself, seeking its master at whatever rank. Like the onion, when it was peeled away, nothing was left but an abstraction—a 'they'...
>
> The awareness of being at the mercy of such caprice was boglike in its uncertain threat. Authority, the anonymous, had long arms but no discernible respected head. What strength I found, I found in surviving underground among my friends.[66]

The formal, up-through-proper-channels complaints procedure leaves a soldier feeling exposed and isolated. But if women were to try to organise collectively they could be charged with 'mutiny'.

Furthermore, there is always the fear of peer reprisal. After the woman at Fort Benning did eventually file a complaint, she began to find threatening notes on her car, and the verbal and physical harassment from her male workmates worsened:

> I moved off post for three months, but ran out of money and had to come back... I'll never go through the legal process again unless I am really scared for my life.[67]

One year later, in March 1980, a US army court handed down the first conviction for sexual harassment in its European command.[68] Despite such gestures, many observers believe that women's high attrition rates may be due to a very significant degree to the continuing demoralising effects of sexual harassment despite such publicised official sanctions. In fact, the pregnancy rates that some male commanders are so quick to cite as an irrefutable reason for marginalising military women may be more related to sexual harassment than to women soldiers' alleged sexual promiscuity. According to Retired Air Force General Jeanne Holm, one of the US military's most outspoken advocates of women soldiers' rights,

> Where morale is low, you have higher pregnancy rates... Whereas men go out and get hung up on drugs, women go out and get pregnant.[69]

Senior officers wield attrition as an issue while playing down the issue of sexual harassment as part of their strategy to use and control women. At the same time, enlisted men use sexual harassment to control women who dare to invade a realm that has always been defined as masculine. Sexual harassment will be treated by officials as a serious issue only insofar as, by acknowledging it and preventing it, they will not erode male soldiers' morale and, in turn, male officers' bonding with male soldiers.

In 1982, the US army command announced it was distributing a film on sexual harassment; base commanders were instructed to show the film and to curtail such behaviour because it was hurting combat readiness.[70] Simultaneously, however, the army announced that integrated male-female training units weren't working and also that women would be excluded from a great number of jobs. It may not be surprising that in this atmosphere 40 women at a navy and marine base in Millington, Tennessee were investigated on grounds of lesbianism after a number of women had rejected sexually harassing advances from their male instructors. The local chapter of the National Organisation for Women, which mobilised support for the women, criticised the Naval Intelligence Service's investigation, concluding that it was part of a

> discriminatory persecution of women in the military and a serious abridgement of the civil rights of lesbians and gay men... Such activities evidence a 'witch hunt' mentality which has at its core a deep-seated hostility toward women in the military.[71]

'Tooth to tail'

Most of the public discussion of the role of women in the military has revolved around the concept of 'equal opportunity', rather than the concepts of militarisation and exploitation. This liberal interpretation of the issue has been generated by women's understandable anger in the face of exclusion from certain jobs and thus from the skills and social status they can bestow. Such an equal opportunity preoccupation, however, implies that the military is 'just one more employer', an employer that happens to measure success in terms of kill ratios rather than miles-per-gallon or rates of profit.

Yet even women who believe that armies are qualititively different from Ford or IBM can gain valuable insight into militarism by exposing how the military creates and rationalise its internal sexual divisions of labour. First, such classification systems don't merely reflect the larger society's sexism, they help to perpetuate sexism in civilian society by backing it up with the State's authority. Second, the military periodically adjusts its sexual divisions of labour to meet current material and political challenges. These adjustments do not occur without setting up internal tensions and contradictions. By examining these contradictions, women opposed to militarism can gain a greater sense of their own power. They know they are confronting not an omniscient monolith but, instead, an often divided and confused institution.

In military lingo, the ratio between 'combat' personnel and 'support' personnel is the 'tooth to tail ratio'. The thousands of women who travelled with pre-industrial armies as camp followers showed how weighty the 'tail' of any military manoeuvre can be. In the latter half of the twentieth century there are trends that are making the tail an even more significant factor in military calculations. Military manpower strategists draw more and more on the modern camp followers, whether as uniformed decoders or as 'civilian' secretaries, computer programmers and social workers.

Between 1945 and 1977, the proportion of the total enlisted personnel to be found in the American army's combat arms (infantry, artillery, armoured and related trades) decreased from 39 per cent to 29 per cent. Similarly, in Canada's entire armed forces less than 20 per cent of non-officer personnel are in combat jobs.[72] The US military's much heralded Rapid Deployment

Force (designed especially for use in the Persian Gulf) is an ideal example of this 1980s model of a streamlined combat force dependent on a large and complex support establishment. Today's 'New Model Army' will deploy front line units that will be 'lean'—tightly *integrated*, *flexible*, *mobile*, and capable of *mobilisation* at a moment's notice.

As one American army document explained:

> No longer will the outcome of battle be decided by attrition between lines drawn up as in a football game. Picture a soccer game as opposed to football—each element manoeuvring in what appears to be an independent uncoordinated way. In reality, it is a highly co-ordinated plan.[73]

Just when 'combat', that centuries-old site for testing masculinity, seemed to be fading into oblivion to be replaced by high tech software and white collar technicians, it was suddenly revived—not so much in numbers of troops as in military prestige. Combat troop effectiveness is now being spoken of with a new sense of urgency and celebration just at the time when many military jobs are being made accessible to women. A new exclusiveness is being created around 'combat'. The so-called 'airland' military model is being idealised in Western Europe as well as in the US. It is praised as mobile, flexible, integrated and technologically sophisticated (e.g. using helicopters, gunships, backpacked 'smart' weapons, faster than ever armoured vehicles).

Implicitly, these attributes are seen to require a no-hassle, men-only organisation. The entrenched military notion of women and femininity is really a *package* of assumptions: women are distractions, women lack physical stamina, women are unaccustomed to complex technology, women require special facilities. Whether as wives, prostitutes or soldiers, women 'slow down the march'. No such drag will be tolerated in the go-anywhere combat units of the 1980s and 1990s.

Yet such wishful thinking on the part of military officials does not mean that women won't be needed. In fact, if combat can be ideologically protected against the onslaught of women, then women can be *more* usefully exploited than ever, in the military's expanding 'tail' section. For instance, the French military has cautiously begun recruiting women. Thus far its elite feels every confidence in the survival of the institution's masculine ethos and exclusively male combat core. But since its defeat in Algeria in the 1960s, the French military has stressed its nuclear, high tech development. This in turn has required a build-up of its 'tail' section. By 1981, only 2.7 per cent of the French military were women. But *50 per cent* of its computer operators were women.[74] Similarly, of all the four branches of the US military, the air force has the highest proportion of women. In large part this derives directly from the air force being the most technologically oriented of the services.[75]

A woman walked into the British army recruiting office on one of Brighton's busy shopping streets in the summer of 1981. The male recruiting officer was pleasant and happy to describe the opportunities open to women in the army, though he warned that, with civilian jobs now so hard to get and more British young people looking to the military for employment, there would be a two-year wait for any woman wanting to enlist. Still, he said, the opportunities for training were attractive once a woman got accepted, and, he added reassuringly, while women serving in Ulster were issued hand guns for self protection, women didn't have to serve in any combat jobs.[76] The army advertising pamphlet listed an assortment of jobs for which a woman in the WRAC could apply: intelligence analyst, military accountant, data telegraphist, electronic technician, driver, administrative assistant, stewardess, hairdresser, cook, switchboard operator and 'kennel maid'. The list itself reveals the character of the tail-heavy modern army, despite its new image of battlefront speed and flexibility.

Between 1977 and 1981 the number of women in the regular British forces had only grown from 14,500 to 15,800. By the latter date, 6,200 of the total were in the army, comprising just less than 4 per cent of the army's total personnel. Of the total air force, 6 per cent were women; the navy was just under 6 per cent female; the marines reported no women.[77]

Many vacancies in the British armed forces are officially closed to women e.g. any posting on a ship at sea. In addition, some postings are closed to men: e.g. naval transport driver, telephonist, kennel maid and welfare assistant. Recently the British air force opened the jobs of helicopter pilot (non-combat) and air traffic controller to women.[78] But every time a redefinition occurs it requires a delicate ideological adjustment. For the military's sexual division of labour is rooted ultimately in two rather tenuous notions: first, that there is a clear line between 'combat' and 'non-combat' and, second, that there is a geographically real place called 'the rear'. It requires considerable semantic and symbolic agility to sustain the credibility of either notion. But the stakes are high. If the 'front' is not where 'combat' exclusively occurs, then there is no way to ensure the survival of the essential masculinity of the military as an institution and the gendered basis of the militarist ideas which legitimise it.

The Pentagon relied heavily on the US Congress' prohibition of women from combat roles when it argued before the Supreme Court in 1981 that the new military registration law (and thus, potentially, conscription) should apply solely to men. The military's argument was: being legally excluded from combat made women too difficult to administer as conscripts, thus only those Americans eligible for any military posting—combat or non-combat—should be covered by the 1980 military registration law. A majority of the Supreme Court justices (six to three) accepted the Pentagon's reasoning.[79]

As Commandant of the US marines, General Robert H. Barrow oversees the lowest percentage of women of all the four US services. But women marines are being trained with guns in boot camp alongside male recruits because, after all, the introduction of even a few women must not be allowed to dilute the marines' overall image as the 'toughest' soldiers. Thus it is important to General Barrow to draw the boundaries between 'front' and 'rear' sharply. There must be no confusion:

> War is man's work. Biological convergence on the battlefield would not only be dissatisfying in terms of what women could do, but it would be an enormous psychological distraction for the male who wants to think that he's fighting for that woman somewhere behind, not up there in

> the same fox hole with him. It tramples the male ego. When you get right down to it, you've got to protect the manliness of war.[80]

This helps to explain the seemingly disproportionate amount of political energy invested in debates over if, when, and why women soldiers should be trained in the use of guns.

In 1981, after two years of study, the British air force recommended that its women be issued guns. The British army reported that it too wanted to start training members of the WRAC in the use of hand guns. Did this mean women were to be finally acknowledged as on the 'front'? Did this suggest that wherever a gun-carrying woman was posted *was* 'the front'?

The military plans sparked a debate in the House of Commons. The Ministry of Defence's civilian spokesman moved quickly to reassure his fellow MPs (97 per cent of whom were men) that women would be trained to use guns 'for defence purposes only', so that in the case of war, a woman assigned, for instance, to an air traffic control post could defend herself. Furthermore, hand guns, not rifles, would be employed by women on the assumption that the former is defensive while the latter is offensive.[81] One MP objected to his colleague's ideological tightrope walking:

> [Women] should not be put in a position where they need to defend themselves. I believe in chivalry in war.[82]

The British army and air force have proceeded to offer women hand gun training, though only on a volunteer basis. The Royal Navy has stuck to its traditional position that women should not have weapons or weapons training since that would only inch them closer to 'combat'.[83] On the other hand, navy commanders sent women nurses to the South Atlantic as part of the Falklands task force.[84] Presumably their being classified as nurses and serving aboard hospital ships placed them in 'the rear' despite the possibility of Argentinian attack jets zooming overhead.

Two criteria are referred to when officials try to delineate 'combat'. The first is the social space in which it occurs: is it the 'front'? Is it a relationship of direct, physical ('eyeball to eyeball') conflict? Thus a woman who is serving in the underground crew of an intercontinental missile in Kansas can be categorised as 'non-combat' although she may some day set off a weapon which will do far more destruction than any 'combat' infantryman with his rifle on the 'front'. This sort of definition prompts military officials to perform intellectual acrobatics in their attempts to distinguish 'direct, physical conflict' from the more subtle sorts of conflict. It may come down to: if a woman—as a *soldier*—is close enough to an enemy male soldier to be raped and/or captured by him, she is in 'combat'—that is, where she shouldn't be for not only her sake, but for the sake of the men fighting at her side who will be distracted and demoralised by such a possibility.

Weaponry is the second, equally malleable criterion officials use when struggling to define and redefine 'combat'. A WRAF woman holding a hand gun is not equipped for 'combat'. An American woman marine or any woman trained in the use of rifle but not issued one as part of her post-boot camp job is not a 'combatant'. A woman sitting at the control panel of a nuclear warheaded missile, but who doesn't directly *control* or *physically* wield that missile in her hands, isn't in 'combat'.

Rollback: the elasticity of 'combat'

The Israeli army is commonly held up as an army which has broken down the classic combat/non-combat sexual division of labour. The khaki-clad, rugged Israeli woman confidentally wielding her Uzzi machine gun—it is an image familiar to many of us. But the image is obsolete. It belongs to an era when the Israeli state was weaker, when the Israeli military was less technologically sophisticated, and when its weaponry was less awesome and its tooth-to-tail ratio narrower.

By the 1980s more than two-thirds of all women in the Israeli Defence Force were clerical workers, typing endless memos and reports (the underpinning of any modern bureaucratised military) and bringing a steady stream of coffee cups to desk-bound male officers.[85]

Shuli Eshel, an Israeli feminist, has made a film, *To Be a Woman Soldier*, portraying the experiences of Jewish Israeli women going through basic training and later taking up their army assignments. In boot camp the women exude *esprit de corps*; they are helping to defend Israel. They are taught to fire guns. A photographer comes to camp at the end of training to take photo portraits of each woman holding her rifle, looking very much her country's defender. The photographs capture the women's inflated hopes, not the intention of the male bureaucracy.

On the last day of basic training, expectations run high. Women conscripts listen as an officer reads out their army assignments: secretary, clerk, secretary... as they learn of their assignments, one woman soldier after another spontaneously breaks into tears. Was this what she was trained for? To be a servant or a girl Friday?

Shuli Eshel called this occasion 'the crying ceremony'. It occurred at the conclusion of every basic training session, and yet none of the women were prepared for the disappointment. Somehow, not only foreigners, but Israeli women themselves had been persuaded to sustain the myth of the Israeli woman warrior. Not until this film was shown on Israeli television did women—and their mothers—realise that they had been duped, that whatever equality did exist in their country's armed forces had been shelved when the male senior command decided it no longer served their own military purposes.[86]

Since the male military command, not women, controls national security decision-making and military manpower planning, any steps towards 'equal opportunity' in the military can be unilaterally reversed.

By 1982, the US armed forces had gone much further than their British counterparts in integrating units, training women in the use of weapons, opening 'non-traditional' posts to women and placing women in 'near-combat' roles. In fact, the British Ministry of Defence seemed to look to the Pentagon to take the lead, to perform the trial runs while it held back. By 1980 the American military had equal opportunity officers in each service ('race relations' officers had been turned into EO officers). Senior officials were boasting that only 30 of a total 230 job categories in the army were closed to women, and most of those were in infantry, artillery and armoured units.[87]

In August 1982, the US Department of Defense announced that the army would be closing 23 occupational skill categories that formerly had been open to women. Already, the army had announced it was terminating male/female integrated basic training because training with women was lowering men's incentives to excel.[88]

Brigadier General Cecil Neely, deputy commander of the army's Fort Leonardwood in Texas, explained:

> If there was a total move in our society to do this—eat, live, sleep in the same quarters together, then you wouldn't have problems of separate hygiene conditions for them, security problems... but this still doesn't mean they would have the same upper body strength...
>
> The men are not taxed sufficiently... They think the women are pretty, they like to have them around...
>
> I've got to be very careful here. I think the women have done a very fine job in the Army, and it is pleasant to have them around...
>
> [But] in training, people will reach the level of the lowest people... we're trying to toughen the Army.[89]

Closing an additional 23 occupational categories in August 1982 was justified by the Defense Department on grounds of physical factors—women's inherent inability to lift heavy objects—and newly expanded definitions of 'combat' and 'battle area'. The Assistant Secretary of Defense for Manpower struggled to explain why jobs like carpenter, plumber, construction surveyor, heavy construction equipment operator and interior electrician were being redefined as 'combat' jobs and thereby placed off-limits for women:

> Basically what you're talking about is the main battle area in the front. This is where people engage in direct combat. The combat exclusion here is applied to keep people who ...are permanently in the main battle area, to apply that to women. In other words, to keep them out of that particular area. Up to now they've been kept out of it primarily

> because in the main battle area you have people primarily in the combat areas, but there are other people who are behind the main battle area in what we call the division near support or the corps area or the so-called EAC (echelons above corps) in which people are in units which are not combat but are permanently stationed in the main battle area.[90]

'Combat' may be conveniently elastic concept in the hands of military manpower officials but, as this official's effort at explanation clearly demonstrates, once one gets beyond the eyeball-to-eyeball, bayonet-to-bayonet image it can turn into an ideological quagmire.

There was a second part to the Defense Department's announcement: while women's access to army jobs would be curtailed, the number of women to be recruited would be *increased*. By 1987, the Assistant Secretary told reporters, women's proportion of all army personnel would rise from its current 9 per cent to 10.5 per cent.[91]

Is the Israeli pattern to be repeated? It would seem so. Women are to be used more and more as birth rates decline and tooth to tail ratios widen. But women can be used in these larger numbers only *if* they can be more tightly controlled.

In past wars British and American military commanders, and their civilian superiors, have controlled women both by placing them in jobs defined as 'non-combat' and by defining their service as 'for the duration'. *De*mobilisation was built into the programmes to mobilise women in both the first and second world wars. 'Combat' was an elastic concept sometimes expanded widely to keep women in the 'rear', sometimes squeezed tightly to legitimate the deployment of women in anti-aircraft crews.

Today, high male unemployment in both countries is helping to offset the declining number of 18-22-year-old men eligible for voluntary enlistment. In an economic recession recruiters can get the men they want for their now widely defined combat roles.[92] Their superiors can thus afford to take steps to reduce women's access to the military's inner sanctum. Nevertheless, demobilisation of women soldiers is a luxury even the most patriarchal general cannot enjoy in today's nuclearised, militarised international system. But women's desire for autonomy, skills and security will be realised only insofar as exploiting those aspirations can help male military officials solve their own problems.

Military officials' problems, furthermore, are never merely technical or logistical. More often than is acknowledged, these problems are to do with sexual management. British Minister of State Cranley Onslow was the first minister to inspect the Falklands after the defeat of the Argentinian force. He returned to London with a shopping list of problems and proposed solutions that would consolidate Britain's military hold over the distant island colony: improved housing, reformed administration, minefield clearing. One of the top five military problem areas cited by the returning minister was defined as follows:

> Sex imbalance: the three-months postings for male troops should be revised to bring out a fair proportion of married men with their wives on longer tours. The services should also seek to post reasonable numbers of women in uniform.[93]

Women militarised as soldiers are not exotic Amazonian warriors. They are women used by patriarchal military officials in ways that fit their presumed cultural roles as women. At the same time they are women feared by those military men as women.

Ian McEwan, a British novelist and playwright, has sensitively summarised the nagging fear behind men's verbal gymnastics over the question of women and combat. In his television play *The Imitation Game*, Cathy, a young woman who has joined up during the second world war, muses:

> You know, on the anti-aircraft units, the ATS girls are never allowed to fire the guns... If girls fired guns, and women general planned the battles... then men would feel there was no morality to war. They would have no one to fight for, nowhere to leave their consciences...
>
> The men want the women to stay out of the fighting so they can give it meaning. As long as we're on the outside, and give our support and don't kill, women just make the war possible... something the men can feel tough about.[94]

6. Women in Liberation Armies

To what extent does participation in insurgent anti-state military forces emancipate women? So much of what is distinctive about a liberation army arrives from its being a *non*-state structure confronting a state institution. As such it needs both a set of beliefs and an organisational practice that moves people to take considerable risks. It needs to be decentralised so it can use flexible response to compensate for its typical lack of heavy weaponry. Under such conditions, a liberation army is likely to be more sensitive to women's immediate needs and not to be insistent upon the gendered distinction between 'front' and 'rear'. Such circumstances seem to open up possibilities for reducing the stratified sexual divisions of labour and trivialisation of women's needs that so mark state military forces.

Still, the question necessarily arises: What happens to a liberation army or guerrilla force *after* the war, if it manages to topple the old state? Does the revolutionary 'post-war' era deal with gender any differently to conventional 'post-war' eras? Is the decentralised guerrilla movement transformed into a hierarchical, centralised state bureaucratic organisation? Is the demobilisation of women an integral part of a post-war transformation? In the state-building, state-defending process, do women lose the status they enjoyed during the war of liberation?

We are not talking simply about a post-revolution regression —though that, of course, may occur. Once in power some male revolutionaries have indeed acted depressingly like the male state elites they have just ousted. Rather, we have to ask about the consequences for the relations between women and men of different types of military organisation even under a seemingly committed revolutionary regime. Even though the liberation army may legitimise the new state army and provide it with most of its personnel, the latter is unlikely to be a replica of the former. It is more likely to mirror the *state*: hierarchical, formal, based on a concept of society that dichotomises 'public' and 'private' space.

So far, women's experiences in many different wars of liberation have left a record that is not especially encouraging. Many liberation armies were themselves built on sexual divisions of labour. Women were concentrated in support roles meant to 'free' men for fighting. Women performing those support roles were doing something they had never had allowed to do before, something recognised as politically important. Nonetheless, as such, they were placed in the posts most likely to be demobilised when the war ended. The American Revolution left white women second-class citizens and black women slaves.[1] The men who led the French Revolution used women's political energies and labour but deliberately demobilised women's clubs in the post-war period of Jacobin state-building.[2]

Wartime is thought of as extraordinary time, even in a revolutionary society. Paradoxically, in the eyes of new state leaders, the post-war process of building a new society requires a return to some degree of normality. The population must be replenished by new births and healthy children. The state is plagued by shortages not only of material resources and cash, but also of skilled bureaucrats and trained police officers. Thus the *family*, so many revolutionary state leaders argue, must be reconfirmed and made to serve as the cornerstone of public order in the post-war era. Unless women are politically self-conscious and organisationally vocal *as women* about what they want to gain from their participation in the revolution's military effort, they are likely to be demobilised as part of the process of creating both a new public order and a new state military organisation. Eventually, even their political leverage as liberation army veterans may dissolve.

Soviet women were active as soldiers in both the Russian Revolution and the subsequent civil war. But post-war Stalinist policies gave priority to central state stability, economic productivity and defence against foreign invasion. Women's emancipation had been a goal for which Alexandra Kollontai and other leading Bolshevik women had fought in their efforts to mobilise women in textile mills and in rural villages. But in the 1920s it was to be rewarded with state attention only insofar as it furthered Stalin's top three state priorities. Women were on the agenda to help solidify the family as a bastion of Soviet social stability, to replenish the country's military manpower by serving as exemplary mothers, and to contribute more of their own labour to industry. Military operations and military decision-making, under this state-building formula, were to be left to men. Sixty-five years after the Russian revolution, the military elite remains one of the most powerful actors in all areas of Soviet policy-making but women are scarcely visible at *any* rank.[3]

Yugoslav feminists born after the second world war's anti-Fascist partisan movement are frustrated with what they contend is women's inferior position within Yugoslav society. Male leaders' laudatory references to women's participation in the 1940s partisan guerrilla movement, they contend, have created merely superficial myths which legitimise the contemporary Yugoslav state, but do little to ensure that Yugoslav women have full lives and valued status in their country. Some Yugoslav women go even further. They question the myth itself, describing women's actual function in partisan military units as far more traditional than is portrayed in official histories. Pre-war conservative definitions of women as, first and last, family members resurfaced too quickly after the war in both popular attitudes and government policy, Yugoslav feminists conclude, to believe that the partisan movement's leadership had been serious in its efforts to break down old stereotypes and sexist structures.[4]

China's Communist Party and Red Army leaders seem to have made more conscious efforts to use wartime's dislocating circumstances to alter the existing gender ideology and restructure sex roles in public and private life. Still, within the military organisation that was developed during the 1930s and 1940s, women were mobilised primarily to play support roles rather than combat roles (though many of the latter were performed near or on 'the front'). According to Delia Davin, the Women's Association mobilised its members 'to sabotage and repair bridges and roads, to prepare food for the soldiers and carry it to them, to rescue and nurse the wounded, and to carry messages and gather intelligence under the cover of going to market or visiting relatives'.[5] Davin reminds us that the importance of such support activities in mobile guerrilla warfare 'can hardly be exaggerated'.[6] However, it was *wives* of soldiers or peasant women living in villages near the battle zones who did much of the nursing of the Red Army's wounded.[7] Given this sexual division of labour, perhaps it is not surprising that 40 years later, while women are active in the local militia, the Chinese regular armed forces include only a very small proportion of women.[8]

Guinea-Bissau's liberation army, which fought and defeated the Portuguese colonial army in 1974, systematically mobilised African women. Still, the revolutionary party, the PAIGC, which directed Guinea-Bissau's insurgent army, did not overturn sexual divisions of labour in its military campaigns. Using, rather than upsetting, existing sexual divisions of labour may have facilitated mobilisation during wartime, but it has evidently made post-revolution state efforts to alter women's role more difficult.

Women were taught to use weapons when they entered the PAIGC liberation army; but they were primarily deployed in support roles. This was rationalised as being dictated by wartime reality: even during a revolution, it was believed, women still had to carry on child bearing and nurturing tasks. A woman, consequently, could be asked to fight only 'when necessary'. Moreover, PAIGC's leadership made the expulsion of the Portuguese the first priority; no social change could be allowed to hold back this effort. Training women to use weapons, a technology new to them, and depending on them to serve in combat roles when they also had children to care for might have created just a delay, endangering the revolution militarily.[9]

By the late 1970s Guinea-Bissau women were occupying economic and government roles to which they had never had access before. But women still had primary responsibility for child care and home management, arduous and time-consuming tasks because of the country's poverty and scarcity of resources.[10]

Wars and revolutions

Wars and revolutions are not synonymous. To carry on a *war* is to mobilise human and material resources for the sake of optimising military effectiveness. To carry on a *revolution*, by contrast, is to mobilise human and material resources so as to bring about fundamental alterations in the socio-political order. There are contradictions between the revolutionary programmes for the emancipation of women and transformation of gender ideologies, on the one hand, and the policies (enacted by that same revolutionary leadership) to conduct military warfare most effectively, on the other hand. 'Revolutionary warfare' may be a phrase more tension-filled than is usually imagined.

In the midst of revolutionary warfare there are a variety of formulas that can be employed by insurgent military leaders in order to mobilise women in the name of basic social change while simultaneously maximising military efficiency. For instance, to the dual roles of mother/wife and agricultural producer can be added that of military participant. Hard-pressed liberation leaders can simply make women's *new* military role an extension of their *existing* dual roles. Now, however, those traditional 'feminine' roles will be assigned greater political value and be more explicitly integrated into male political strategies.

A second formula for conducting 'revolutionary warfare' is to organise married women to perform 'support' or 'home front' roles, while *un*married women are channelled into the more strictly military roles. A Zimbabwean woman looking back on her part in the liberation struggle against the white Rhodesian regime recalls that virtually all Zimbabwean women participated in their country's liberation, but most of the women who did actual fighting were not married. Some married women, she recalls, did follow male guerrilla fighters to staging zones in Mozambique, 'to wait in the camps'. In the camps these women performed militarised though still feminine tasks, serving as cooks, nurses, and laundresses for the guerrillas.[11]

In the three years since the end of the war of liberation Zimbabwe's military has been reorganised, retaining many white officers but incorporating large contingents of former guerrillas. Most of these guerrillas-turned-government-soldiers are men. Zimbabwean women who acted as spies, supply carriers, nurses and soldiers, have been demobilised. Many have returned to farming, where they still have less opportunity than men to get titles to redistributed lands, according to the government's Women's Bureau. In addition, of the 100 members of the new African-dominated parliament, only eight are women.[12] Women who fought in the revolution expected that the gender as well as racial order would be reorganised as a result of warfare and their part in it, but a kind of participation that perpetuated a sexual division of labour could delay such expectations being fulfilled by a new state now short on resources, under attack and reliant on its new state military.

The co-existence in 'revolutionary warfare' of the twin dimensions of political revolution and military operations is apt to be even harder to sustain when the revolution is followed almost immediately by a relatively conventional war. And, in fact, many revolutions do turn into state-to-state wars before social transformation can be firmly set in motion. When warfare follows on the heels of revolution there is even greater urgency to reorganise the guerrilla army into a conventional military force that can be directed by and protect the fledgling post-revolutionary state. The result? The centralisation of military command, an infusion of more technologically sophisticated weaponry, a clearer delineation between 'home front' and 'battlefield', and the demobilisation of most women from the regular active forces. Some women will, however, be organised into newly created 'reserve' and 'militia' units, which may be strategically important but which typically carry less social status and political influence for their members. The Soviet Union, China, Cuba, Mozambique, and Nicaragua all experienced a rapid transition from revolution to more conventional state-to-state war.

The myth of the Israeli woman guerrilla fighter lives on, but a succession of conventional wars that followed the creation of the new state of Israel systematically undermined the equal status of women in uniform. Today the Israeli armed forces formally exclude women from the 'front' once an 'emergency' has been declared and the country's first law on equal job opportunity specifically exempts all jobs classified as 'security related' from compliance with the law.[13] The militarised Israeli state uses women more as supportive, dutiful, patient wives and mothers than it does as military defenders of the state.[14] In a similar transition the Hanoi government wound down its 25-year-long revolution and mobilised for its current war in Cambodia by passing a law in 1981 which made only men eligible for military conscription. Vietnamese women may volunteer in peacetime and be conscripted during formally declared war only to perform 'appropriate duties'.[15]

Who's holding the rifle and the baby?

A popular symbol of the many liberation armies in Asia, Latin America, and Africa is the woman with a rifle over one confident shoulder and a baby cuddled in her protective arms. The picture conjures up images of the can-do-everything 'superwoman'. It also seems to imply that the very process of revolutionary warfare, on the one hand, can transform women's role and sense of self-worth, while, on the other hand, sustain the social order that in the past has ensured the reproduction and nurturing of the next generation. Jane Hawksley has argued that, before we praise the poster as a symbol of women's liberation, we must ask the question: *Who owns the camera?*[16] Who prints and distributes the poster, and what are they trying to encourage us to conclude about the organisation, aims and goals of the insurgents? Where is the picture of the *male* guerrilla holding the rifle and baby?

Nurturing children is part of any revolution, particularly one that extends over many years. But interweaving the images of woman as combatant and mother so tightly suggests that as soon as the immediate threat recedes, as soon as the 'war is over', the woman in the picture will put down the rifle and keep the baby.

Maxine Molyneaux has sought to understand why so many Third World revolutions have produced social change that has fallen far short of genuine emancipation for women. She too wonders at the prevalence of the symbolic representation of woman with gun in one hand and baby in the other—in Cuba, Vietnam and Africa.

> Even in countries with a history of guerrilla struggle in which women have taken an active role in the revolutionary army, sexual divisions in this area have not been eroded, a woman's 'special' relationship to children continues unchallenged.[17]

Women who see violence, particularly organised, militarised violence, as something to be employed only as a last resort and only under strict social control, may see putting down the rifle instead of the baby as the best choice. But after the revolution, will the newly organised state military have high political status in the new state system since it becomes defender of all of the revolution's gains? If this is to be so, then the military demobilisation of women may mean that *only* women will be expected to nurture the society's children, while the men keep their rifles and the public authority those rifles symbolise. After the revolution, who will be the protectors and who the protected?

In 1982, Algeria's socialist regime, founded on the legacy of a liberation army's struggle against French colonialism, was on the brink of instituting a new family code designed by orthodox Muslims. The code, if enacted, would have reduced an Algerian woman's status to that of a legal minor and placed her under the tutelage of a male relative.[18] The Algerian women most outraged and vocal in protests at the parliament were those who had fought in the liberation war against the French army. In large part because of women's petitions and demonstrations against the code, the bill was shelved.[19]

How could a revolution which relied for its success on women playing non-traditional military roles in the liberation force (the FLN) and which supposedly had women's emancipation as one of its programmatic goals, produce a regime that, within a generation, supported such a reactionary code? A French journalist interviewed an exiled former minister of the Ben Bella regime (1963-65), Mohamed Harbi. According to his account of the liberation war against the French, women were used by the FLN's male leadership almost exclusively in roles analogous to traditionally 'feminine' roles, while simultaneously FLN leaders offered up to eagerly receptive foreign journalists the image of the liberated FLN woman guerrilla fighter:

> If you look at the official documents the areas in which women could participate were enumerated: moral support for resistance fighters, information liaison, food suppliers, shelter, and aid to families and children of resistance fighers and prisoners.
>
> Women were not willingly accepted into the *maquis* [the resistance]. One young woman, for example, in the Guelma region, was sent home after being told that the resistance was not the place for a young girl from a good family. She kept trying, and they finally allowed her to stay, but she was arrested very quickly.
>
> For the most part, the women fighters were forced to leave the resistance at the end of 1957 and the beginning of 1958. Those who remained performed only traditional tasks. They taught them to march in parades, and they would show them off in documentatories. Then they dispersed them. Their political role and participation ended... women who had political aspirations or who wanted equality with men had a lot more difficulty. Their behaviour and their desire for equality were considered a sign of loose morals.[20]

Trying to make a liberation army into an instrument of liberation

As more Third World societies have engaged in wars of liberation, women have accumulated lessons on which to draw for the sake of ensuring that revolutionary militarisation does not co-opt women's labour and symbolic value while reinforcing the patriarchical social order. One such lesson might be that liberation armies are *not* automatically non-sexist merely because they are non-statist, decentralised and reliant on women. Second, the sexual divisions of labour employed in a liberation army—and the rationalisations used to justify those divisions—might be best resisted *during* the revolution because, if allowed to persist, they are likely to become a deceptive part of the revolutionary mythology and the basis for the new state's demobilisation of women. Third, that the demobilisation process may be especially dangerous for women when it is carried out in a post-war period marked by the creation of an even stronger new state military force, no matter how justified such a military force may be.

Algerian women's experience might be taken as a warning, for instance, by Palestinian women who are participating in their society's liberation movement. One Algerian woman who has been active in the Palestinian resistance since 1967 describes her experience and the lesson it holds:

> A girl who lives alone, who works and struggles on top of that is surrounded by comments: where is her family, where does she come from, what is she doing, etc... If one wants to struggle with the Palestinians, one has to be patient... For (the men) the only worthwhile issue is the Palestinian struggle against Israel and they are unwilling to put any effort into the liberation of Palestinian women... All the militants agree that women should be liberated, but if one asks a militant why his wife is at home, his wife is his wife, after all... Women have begun to struggle against this mentality, but how long will it take to change it? Without this struggle, Palestinian women could end up in the same conditions as Algerian women: today Algerian women are still in their homes, just like my mother, like my grandmother.[21]

Women will find their struggle to restrict the sexual division of labour (and the resulting consolidation of ideas about 'women's place') especially difficult if during the war of liberation the insurgent army acquires sophisticated heavy weaponry. Nowadays it is not uncommon for some liberation armies (e.g. the Palestine Liberation Organisation and the Western Sahara liberation army, Polisario) to be equipped with ground-to-air missiles. While this kind of heavy equipment may not be sufficient to defeat the opposing state forces or to achieve the insurgents' goals, it is likely to reinforce the distinctions between 'mechanically oriented' men and 'support oriented' women. Such weaponry also tends to sustain ideological distinctions between 'home front' and 'battlefield', even in the midst of a civil war.

Therefore, women's efforts to make the liberation war itself a site for revolutionary change in relations between women and men will be aided or undermined by the structural transformations that occur *during* the liberation war itself.

The harsh political repression meted out by the Nicaraguan National Guard under the command of President Somoza provided the impetus to military involvement for many Nicaraguan women in the 1970s. It was frequently as wives, daughters and mothers that Nicaraguan women decided to become insurgent military activists. But as the insurgency turned into a full-scale revolution, many of these same women began to see their military participation as a means for not only ending Somoza's repressive regime but for changing the relations between women and men in Nicaragua.

Lea Guido, Minister of Social Welfare in Nicaragua's post-revolutionary government, remembers how at first women served largely in support roles:

> We set up clinics—well, maybe the word 'clinic' is a bit much, but we did organise houses where medical attention could be meted out during the war. We gave intensive first-aid courses in semi-underground conditions. We promoted massive inoculation programmes, knowing we'd have thousands of wounded.[22]

Dora Maria Tellez, military commander during the liberation war, recalls that as women were mobilised as combatants relationships between women and men began to change:

> Personal relationships changed. In general, I think they improved... Women participated in our revolution, not in the kitchens, but as combatants. In the political leadership, this gives us a very different experience. Of course, they played other roles during the war, acquired tremendous moral authority, so that any man—even in intimate relationships—had to respect them. A man would be hard put to lift a hand or mistreat a woman combatant.

Just the fact of being combatants together, however, did not erase the inequities between Nicaraguan men and women:

> The problem of male chauvinism was evident among comrades... Some men harboured distinctly sexist attitudes toward women. They believed that women were for domestic tasks alone, and that they shouldn't go beyond being messengers. There were lots of arguments. Some comrades were open to dealing with sexism. Others remained closed. Some said women were no good in the mountains, but they were only good 'for screwing', that they created conflict—sexual conflict. But there were also men with very good positions... it's been a long struggle! We won those battles through discussions and by women comrades demonstrating their ability and their resistance.

Today at Managua's Carlos Aguero Military School, Nicaraguan women are training to serve as both rank and file soldiers and as officers in what has become the post-revolution state military force. After Somoza's defeat, officials of the new Sandanista government debated whether male and female soldiers should be trained together. Nowadays, most women are trained separately. The male director of the military school explains:

> It is not that the women comrades aren't capable... and it's not that we're thinking of excluding women from the army; there are women with excellent military talent, and there is room for them in our ranks, but right now we see the need for training them separately. There are exceptions, of course. There are women who, because of their excellence, must be left in the regular army and given every opportunity to advance. The need to train women separately is not because of any limitations the women have. In fact, you might say it's because of failing on the part of some men. Our army has many new soldiers, comrades who haven't had the experience of fighting alongside women, and they aren't always able to relate to a woman as just another soldier. They still tend to see them as women.

Running through the military school commandant's explanation is the implicit understanding of the post-revolutionary army as basically a male institution. There is 'room' for women, women who are outstanding because of their 'excellence' will be 'left' in the regular army. But women will have to accommodate themselves to *men* who enter the military, without regard to whether those men have less experience, less guerrilla background, or less political consciousness. What is 'progressive' is only the amount of room opened up for women in what is being created as a masculine state-authorised institution.

Nonetheless, for many contemporary Nicaraguan women, the military remains an arena for public participation and political activism. By mid-1982 it had 17,000 troops and 30,000 reservists.[23] So long as the revolutionary regime feels endangered by neighbouring Honduran military forces and their formidable American military ally, the Nicaraguan military is likely to be a critically important institution in the country's life.

Nicaraguan women who have remained in the military try to make the most of their limited conditions. Some even claim that separate training courses for women cadets have advantages. Others have gone a step further and formed their own army unit to avoid the sexism that persists in other units and to keep alive a wartime-created self-consciousness among women. A young woman sitting cross-legged on the barrack floor in her khaki fatigues talks about her women's unit, the Juana Elena Mendoza Infantry Comany:

> This company is something we thought up to show our ability and desire to belong to the army. Women want to organise militarily to defend our country. We want to show that women continue to have a role to play, that we are worth something...

7. Rosie the Riveter: Women in Defence Industries

The obsession to produce a perfect weld dominated all throught for months, until I was able to do it... I saw welding as an art, its practitioners fire artists...

When the loudspeakers struck up the heart-catching 'Anchors Aweigh' music, we knew one of ours was sliding down to the sea...

We signed our work occasionally, like artists. I always burned my sign up under the hatch end beam, my favourite welding job. I would not venture to say today how many liberty ships went off to war with a small crocodile etched beneath their hatches.

Kathryn Hulme, *Undiscovered Country*[1]

The industries need the masses as workers, and conversely, as consumers. And since labour in industry is always at the service of the powerful and the powers, among its products prime importance is naturally given to arms (the 'armament race'), which in a mass-consumption economy, find their outlet in mass warfare.

Elsa Morante, *La Storia Romanzo*[2]

Do women really reap lasting gains from wars? Do wars open new doors that give women access to jobs and skills and, ultimately, to independence and security?

Rosie the Riveter, that industrial heroine of the second world war with her goggles, bandanna and confident 'victory smile', came out of and has helped perpetuate a long line of women defence workers who have contributed their labour for the duration.

'For the duration', because her labour and whatever rewards it won her were controlled by military officials who used women workers only for as long as they believed it did not endanger the fundamentally masculine character of warfare and male ex-soldiers' access to the best industrial jobs.

Rosie the Riveter and her sisters were not the first women defence workers. Every time a camp follower cooked a meal for soldiers in order to obtain meagre rations, every time a soldier's wife sewed a uniform in a government garment factory, a woman was contributing her labour to the war machine and, in turn, was becoming economically dependent on that war machine. No prime ministers or Hollywood actors sang her praises, but she was a defence worker 'doing her part'.

Nor was Rosie the Riveter the last of her line. During the last four decades the major industrial powers have not engaged in such total warfare that their officials have had to mobilise women workers to 'release men to fight'. Nevertheless, with much less fanfare than heralded the second world war's women workers, women have been recruited into 'women's jobs' necessary for the spiralling production of sophisticated 'peacetime' armaments. Like the anonymous camp followers in previous centuries, many women today have been made dependent on a militarised economy because of their precarious position in the socio-economic system as a whole. Most notable are women electronics workers, in California, Scotland, Wales, Mexico and South-east Asia, whose employers are increasingly reliant on military contracts for their profits. And, as intriguing as it is to examine the second world war women workers' experiences, valuable understanding about the militarisation of women's work is lost if we stay fixed on the 1940s. The women who sewed uniforms and cooked meals for hundreds of years before the invention of the riveting gun, and the Asian, Hispanic, Welsh and Scottish women today who are straining their eyes to assemble electronic circuitry for the latest weapons, have lessons to offer as well.

First, their experiences suggest that we look beyond 'wartime' to understand what happens when women's work is militarised. Women's work can be militarised in 'peacetime', when it may not be as subject to the sharp rises and falls that catch our attention. Second, these earlier and more recent women defence workers reveal how women in 'feminine' jobs —not just in temporarily feminised 'masculine' jobs—are crucial to the military's use of a country's economy for its own ends. Third, women defence workers in the 1980s alert us to the *international* links between women workers being created by global militarisation. In the past, observers tended to *compare* how wartime defence industries in Britain, America, Japan and Germany treated their women workers. In this decade we need to ask how the militarisation of women's work in both the US and Britain affects the lives of women in Mexico, Taiwan and the Philippines.

Taken all together, what these women down through the centuries make clear is that 'militarised work' stretches far beyond building battleships or assembling rifles. 'Militarised work' refers to *any* labour organised and exploited in the allegedly civilian sector of the economy to produce goods and services that military officials claim they need. From cleaning barracks to typing bureaucratic memos, from wiring missiles to producing television recruiting films, jobs done by women have been militarised. Virtually any job *can* be militarised, that is, made dependent on the military force and its goals.

Furthermore, Crimean camp followers, second world war 'Rosies' and present-day microchip assemblers reveal that *all* military work—not just work done by women—is organised on the basis of gender. If women are *excluded* from certain jobs, it is because the work is 'men's work' and gives men a sense of privilege as men (e.g. aerospace engineering); if women are initially excluded, then *used briefly*, only later to be excluded again (e.g. in shipbuilding) it is again a gendered process; if only women are hired to fill certain militarily dependent jobs, it is because the work has been, traditionally, 'women's work' (e.g. uniform stitching, bureaucratic typing, microelectronic assembling). Consequently, we can't fully understand how military priorities and military spending affect the economy unless we ask how all sexual categories and relationships help promote and sustain military processes.

'For the Duration'

Despite the work that women have done for armed forces down through the ages, it is easiest, perhaps, to see some of the most striking patterns of sexism which organise and impose meaning on that work by looking at those militarised periods officially labelled 'wars'. Wars have beginnings and ends and thus provide us with clearer sign posts for monitoring changing conditions in women's lives.

The American civil war came close to being a 'total' war. So many male clerks were conscripted into the Union army that for the first time the US government hired women to do its clerical work (and found them cheaper and kept many on even after the war). The South was only in the early stages of industrialisation, but the North's blockade stepped up the region's factory production. Southern women made clothing and worked in Confederate munitions factories. In the more industrialised North, many women who went to work in factories during the civil war were wives of soldiers who sought waged employment for the first time because a soldier's pay did not support a wife and children. In Boston alone, an estimated 25,000 women joined the paid work force because of the war. Many of them worked as seamstresses sewing soldiers' uniforms.[3]

When many textile factories in the North were forced to close for lack of Southern cotton, their largely female work forces were laid off. These women textile workers were moved into the garment industry, where government sub-contracts for army uniforms were generating more jobs at low wages.[4] The mechanical sewing machine had just been invented in the 1850s. Though many women seamstresses hoped that learning to use such mechanised technology would earn them higher wages, in fact the emergent garment industry's capitalists organised labour, defined 'skill' and set wages in ways that deprived women of any genuine advancement in the now mechanised industry.

US arsenals, along with textile mills, were America's first large factories. The temporary closing of the cotton mills provided not only garment factories but Northern munitions factory managers with women workers at a time when their male workers were being conscripted and government orders were piling up.[5]

At the large government-run munitions factory in Watertown, Massachusetts, women were hired in great numbers in the early 1860s to meet the Union's wartime needs. Half were daughters of Irish immigrants. The Watertown Arsenal labour force was organised according to gender. Women were clustered in all-female assembly shops, making cylinders for bullets. They were paid on a piece-work basis, while male workers continued to dominate the craft jobs and received a daily or monthly wage. Such differentiated pay schemes not only meant that women earned less than men, but that the *social status* of women was derived from their allegedly more menial tasks.[6] Wartime hardened rather than softened these gender distinctions.

Contrary to wartime myth, most women who came to work at the Watertown Arsenal were not setting out on their own. Two-thirds lived with one or both parents. The arsenal was near their homes and so the women walked back and forth to work each day. It was as *daughters* that most of the arsenal women went to work. They contributed to their family's income, over which they had only minimal control.

Despite their low status in the factory hierarchy, which was built on top of a stratified familial system outside the factory, the Waterdown women defence workers were not passive. In 1864, at the height of the war, the women submitted a pay petition which resulted in their wages being raised from seven and a half cents to nine cents per 100 cylinders assembled. Women workers also voiced their complaints when they came forward as witnesses in formal government hearings. Women protested against the lack of safety precautions in the arsenal. They also called for an end to the harassing behaviour of a male overseer and two other men, whom they accused of 'fooling with the girls'.

Even the slender information we have about the experiences of the women in the Watertown Arsenal in the American civil war indicates striking similarities with what has happened in both major twentieth-century 'total' wars. In all cases the mobilisation of women's labour was a government strategy to free men to fight. Government officials used ethnic and racial strategies in mobilising both male soldiers and female workers.

The government tried to justify the recruitment of women workers without upsetting existing gender ideology and the sexual division of labour. Employers' initially reluctant acceptance of women was followed by efforts to use women's influx into factories as an opportunity to reduce labour costs and accelerate job-cutting factory mechanisation. Women's wartime labour experiences were different according to their positions in the family (as daughters, wives of soldiers, mothers of children) and their place in society's racial or ethnic hierarchy. In the later wars as well, however, some women overcame both their class and racial divisions, and the government's pressure for passive wartime loyalty, to protest at their workplace conditions. And in all cases, politicised women debated among themselves whether participation in the industrial war effort would undermine or strengthen women's individual and collective efforts to gain economic independence and political equality. Each time, after the war, the government launched deliberate programmes to demobilise women workers in order to 'free jobs for our returning boys', and, more fundamentally, to return the social order to its pre-war patriarchal status quo.

The first world war: ballots and bullets

On the eve of the first world war there were approximately 15 million women in Britain. Just under 4 million of them had waged jobs outside their own family, and over one-fourth of them worked for someone else's family as domestic servants.[7] Between 1914 and 1918, at the wartime government's urging, an estimated 792,000 women entered industry for the first time. Many of these women abandoned domestic service, never to return to it again; others went into industry after years of work in garment sweatshops. Women who remained in the traditional trades like garments and textiles were held to their old wages but assigned longer hours for the sake of the war effort. Women entering new industrial jobs enjoyed higher wages than they had as poorly paid domestics, sweated workers or unpaid housewives, but still received lower pay than the men in those jobs, a fact which prompted many male trade unionists to resist women's entry.[8]

Some women leaders of the British suffragist movement,

which had reached a militant peak by 1914, called on women to contribute their labour to the government's war effort in the hope that women would be rewarded with the vote once Germany was defeated. But other suffragists, among them Sylvia Pankhurst, argued that for working-class women the war did *not* open new opportunities. It caused severe dislocations, leaving many women without decent enough employment to feed themselves and their children once the military conscripted their husbands. Furthermore, they claimed, the British government failed to supply adequate child-care facilities to enable many working-class women to take war jobs without endangering the welfare of their children. Poor women who did manage to get jobs were often harassed as prostitutes by police as they walked alone on city streets.[9]

British women's mixed feelings about the opportunities and costs of taking up war work is captured in two poems of the time. Madeline Ida Bedford's poem 'Munition Wages' expresses the confident jauntiness of a woman munitions worker earning better pay than ever before:

Earning high wages? Yus,
  Five quid a week.
A woman, too, mind you,
  I calls it dim sweet.

Ye'are asking some questions—
  But bless yer, here goes:
I spend the whole racket
  On good times and clothes.

Me saving? Elijah!
  Yer do think I'm mad.
I'm acting the lady,
  But—I ain't living bad.

I'm having life's good times.
  See 'ere, it's like this:
The 'oof come o' danger,
  A touch-and-go bizz.

We're all here today, mate,
  Tomorrow—perhaps dead,
If Fate tumbles on us
  And blows up our shed.

Afraid! Are yer kidding?
  With money to spend!
Years back I wore tatters,
  Now—silk stockings, mi friend!

I've bracelets and jewellery,
  Rings envied by friends;
A seargeant to swank with,
  And something to lend.

I drive out in taxis,
  Do theatres in style.
And this is mi verdict—
  It is jolly worth while.

Worth while, for tomorrow
  If I'm blown to the sky,
I'll have repaid mi wages
  In death—and pass by.[10]

Quite a different attitude toward women doing munitions work is expressed by Mary Gabrielle Collins in her poem 'Women at Munitions Making'.

Their hands should minister unto the flame of life,
Their fingers guide
The rosy teat, swelling with milk,
To the eager mouth of the suckling babe
Or smooth with tenderness,
Softly and soothingly,
Or stray among the curls
Of the boy or girls, thrilling to mother love.
But now,
Their hands, their fingers
Are coarsened in munition factories.
Their thoughts, which should fly

Like bees among the sweetest mind flowers,
Gaining nourishment for the thoughts to be,
Are bruised against the law,
'Kill, kill'.
They must take part in defacing and destroying the natural body
Which, certainly during this dispensation
Is the shrine of the spirit.
O God!
Throughout the ages we have seen,
Again and again
Men by Thee created.
Cancelling each other.
And we have marvelled at the seeming annihilation
Of Thy work.
But this goes further,
Taints the fountain head,
Mounts like a poison to the Creator's very heart.
O God!
Must It anew be sacrified on earth?[11]

When women war workers were demobilised at the end of the second world war, to make way for returning male soldiers, many women who had seen the war as a 'great opportunity' were acutely disappointed. Furthermore, although some women were given the vote in 1918, all British adult women did not receive voting rights until 1928, a full decade after the armistice. Similar disappointment was experienced by American women.[12]

'Mobile women' in the second world war

Government manpower strategists used the lesson of the first world war to mobilise women sooner, and on a wider scale, in the second. In Britain, even more than in the US, women were the targets of deliberate mobilisation campaigns. Almost one-third of Britain's total of 12.5 million women worked in industry during the second world war. British wartime employment of women reached a peak of 6 million women in the autumn of 1943.[13] In June 1944, women were 39.4 per cent of the total

British workforce (as compared to the US, where women reached only 34 per cent of the total).[14] The British government, without as large a pool of male university students and unemployed men as America, instituted conscription of women into war industries, a policy American officials avoided.[15]

As did all the major Allied and Axis governments during the second world war, the British government differentiated between single and married women and between women without children and mothers.[16] This was not a new way to structure the labour force. For the past century, not only were women and men recruited, disciplined and rewarded differently, but distinctions were made among women both by employers and by the government.[17] What *was* new was the acuteness and explicitness of the British government's dilemma: it wanted to preserve the distinctions between mothers and other women, especially since the war was so wasteful of human life; yet the very level of violence and length of the conflict meant the preferred gender formula for structuring the labour force became less and less tenable as the war dragged on.

British industry's managers, under pressure from the government, hired more married women with children than it did in the first world war. Eventually, there were 75,000 women with children under 14 years of age working in British industry during the second world war.[18] With 'mothers' becoming a significant production of the industrial labour force, British companies were more pressed than their American counterparts to introduce programmes to relieve working mothers of their double burden. Officially, however, home helpers, factory prepared take-away meals and other innovations were justified on the grounds, not of alleviating women's burdens, but of 'reducing the irregularities in women's factory job performance'.[19]

Nevertheless, despite government pressures and company programmes to permit the use of women with children, the preferred woman worker was single and without ideologically worrying and economically draining encumbrances. For example, in order to lessen their reliance on married women (with or without children) British aircraft factories in the midlands imported single women workers from Scotland and the north-east. In the bureaucracy's jargon, these single female potential workers were known as 'the mobile women'.[20]

Heavy industry feminised

Marjorie Mowlam tells of a woman who works at her university in the north of England. She is in her sixties now and works as a cleaner. But 40 years ago, she worked in a British arms factory. She still talks about that time: it was the best time of her life.[21]

Ruth Wolf was a white foundry worker at the Patterson Foundry in Ohio during the war:

> I loved that job, because I produced something. I wasn't just putting screws into the lock. I knew it was precision work, and required skill. It gave me a self-respect I didn't have before.
>
> Skilled work does wonders for a person's ego. I remember sitting on the subway in New York, going home, and watching black people next to me, who had gotten jobs through the war. They had such an air of dignity about them, of pride in the work they were doing, and I thought, 'Why, I must look just the same!'[22]

Some groups of women were especially open to the government's mobilising propaganda because they were particularly vulnerable to economic exploitation or marginalisation. For example, in the US, wives of servicemen were 'three times more likely to take a job than other wives'.[23]

Just as black women in America had been especially hard hit by the Depression, black women were among those with the highest hopes that the wartime manpower campaigns would open up opportunites for economic security. Precious Mack became a welder at the Kaiser Shipyard in Richmond, California, in the 1940s, but only after making the long bus trip from the South:

> The bus was segregated until we got to some part of Texas. There were empty seats in the front one time, but we didn't dare sit up there 'cause we were raised in the South, and we knew better. We knew to stay in the back half of the bus...

> Things weren't much better when we got to California... we lived in this one-room trailor. One room, honest, with no facilities, no running water, no inside toilet... we had twelve people in our family, and we all lived in that trailor. Four of us went to work at the Kaiser Shipyards. Some of us worked swing shift, or graveyard, while mother was home all the time with six young kids. We'd take turns sleeping, sharing the beds...
>
> It was not much better than home, but at least we had jobs and were making some money.[24]

Propaganda used by the government to mobilise women workers reveals that from the start there was no intention to shake the foundations of society's sexual division of labour. Connie Field's film *The Life and Times of Rosie the Riveter* includes clips from 1940s American government films aimed at the 'mobile woman'—all of them white—are shown using electric tools to make holes in aircraft wings, as the narrator reassures the audience, 'this is just like punching holes in your scouring powder tin'. And, for women, welding fighter planes was 'just like sewing'. The definition of 'women's work' shifted, so that the move from parlour and kitchen to factory floor in wartime would leave the social order intact.[25]

Within British and American factories, work processes were 'feminised', that is, broken down into simpler, more repetitive routines. For women entering plants in the 1940s, jobs and pay rates were better than they had known as unwaged housewives, sharecroppers, domestic servants, clerical or garment workers. But for plant managers, women's entry presented a chance to deskill the work force and cut labour costs. In this sense the war-time sexual division of labour permitted a continuation of the technological transformations of production begun during the first world war.

Propaganda films encouraged women to relate to their new jobs in ways that reinforced, not challenged, their presumed pre-war family dependencies and obligations. One woman worker looks into the camera and tells us, 'I'm an old maid and now I have a family of 16 million to take care of.'[26] Her new job did not mean she had become an independent waged employee in a large impersonal ship or aircraft building firm, she was still simply an 'old maid', and the corporation would be her surrogate family: she was working to support 'our boys'.

Describing soldiers as 'boys' serves to integrate heavy industry work into women's 'natural' role at the same time as it allows those men who are officers to assume 'fatherly' authority over (presumably less adult) men in the ranks. The family myth helps wartime governments to stabilise both the battlefront *and* the home front. Men as well as women have to be convinced by their governments that mobilising women for heavy industry won't upset the social order for which they are being asked to risk their lives.

Under the rubric of maintaining the troops' 'morale'—the site of so much gender politics in the armed forces—the British army designed education programmes for male recruits. The programmes were intended to ensure that the men didn't worry about their wives and 'sweethearts' going astray, wandering beyond the bounds of male authority, while they were off at the front protecting them. Male soldiers were reassured of their masculinity in these education sessions. Women might be called to do factory work, male soldiers were told, but they wouldn't lose their femininity, they wouldn't neglect their children. And, after all, it was only for the duration. Commanders told army instructors to leave the issue of 'women after the war' open and unresolved when talking to the men.[27]

Wanda the Welder

In the American shipbuilding industry, historian Karen Skold has found, entire processes were redesigned by management to incorporate women with as little investment in their training as possible. Rosie the Riveter was more likely to have been a welder.[28] Welding replaced riveting in many stages of shipbuilding because welding was assumed to take less skill, require less training, and threaten skilled male trade unions less. And welders could be paid less than riveters. Where there were still sufficient men in the plant, the process remained more highly skilled and highly paid.

Management—often with male trade unionists' active backing—redesigned production and training processes so that a new sexual division of labour was instituted in heavy industry. The wartime shipbuilding plants in Oregon, Karen Skold discovered, were not the place for radically new relationships between men and women workers.[29] It may not be surprising, consequently, that a 1944 study of 25 American industries found that male workers were making 50 per cent more in hourly wages than women and, in the 80 union contracts studied, only one-third gave women the same entry wage rates as men.[30]

While still depriving women of lasting gains, wartime sometimes allowed women entry to the initial stages of technological revolution. During the second world war the first operational computer (the ENIAC) was developed. Its function was to make the complex calculations required for the success of the Manhattan Project—the secret American operation to develop the first atomic bomb. Even though the computer was a technological breakthrough, the tasks involved in making it work were considered by bomb project managers to be merely 'clerical'. And so it was perfectly natural that one hundred young women were hired to perform this 'women's work'. They designed the programme for the bomb in a few months in the course of 'crawling around the ENIAC's massive frame, locating burnt-out vacuum tubes, shorted connections, and other non-clerical "bugs".'[31]

But after the war, after Trinity, Hiroshima and Nagasaki proved the Manhattan Project's success, computer programming was re-conceptualised; it became 'men's work'. The work was no longer merely clerical; hereafter it was to be thought of as intellectually demanding, creative, and requiring such 'innately' masculine attributes as mathematical and abstract reasoning. From 1945 until the early 1970s, computer programming was a male preserve. Only in the last decade, due to the fragmentation, standardisation and deskilling of the programmer's job, have women been allowed back in the occupation in significant numbers.[32]

In electrical assembly line work, however, managers discovered, through the wartime necessity of hiring women, that processes could be permanently 'feminised'—conceived of as requiring special skills that only women had. This had important implications for defence work's sexual division of labour today, when so many of the newest weapons are based on electronics:

> The experiment [of bringing women into war production work] has shown in some instances the superiority of women to men, in work calling for precision and requiring a high degree of accuracy and care. It has proved the dexterity of women in fine but often rapid moving hand work. In certain aspects of instrument making, in the electrical industries, even in some part of the machine tools industry, management had indicated a high degree of satisfaction with the performance of women which it might not be ready to forego in the future.[33]

Women war workers were subjected to calculated campaigns by government and business officials intent upon using their energies, skills and high expectations in order to optimise military effectiveness. But it would be wrong to imagine that women were passive objects, manoeuvred this way and that, swallowing propaganda without making their own critical assessments.

First of all, as we have seen, policy-makers in business, government and male-run trade unions were not always of the same mind about when and how to mobilise women's labour. Even inside government, divisions emerged as some agencies established specifically to mobilise women became advocates of women's equity. There were also bureaucratic territorial rivalries as military departments attempted to exert control over policy areas that labour departments considered to fall under their jurisdication. Then, too, business executives often were loath to accept women workers, especially black women workers, when being pressed to do so. Executives were more concerned about the integrity of their still male-dominated work forces and the *modus vivendis* that had been hammered out over the years between management and union leaders. These cracks and contradictions in the wartime labour mobilisation process permitted some women to gain more information about how they were being used and what potential opportunities were being denied to them.

Second, women were not totally naive when they entered the new wartime jobs. Many women had had years of work experience—as domestic servants, low level service workers, garment workers and farm hands. Experience had equipped them with a sense of their capacity to cope with oppressive male employers. They had also learned the strategic importance of making common cause with other women on the job or, if possible, with men from ethnic and racial communities low on the workplace pyramid.

Wartime typically increases government's authority to suppress workers' activism, but wartime is rarely a time of total passivity or consensus. American black women protested so they could get hired, and, once hired, could get access to training courses and lavatories with showers.[34] British women in the Land Army, organised to ensure that food production didn't falter, stood up to exploitative farmers.[35] Other women walked off the job when employers—with government officials' agreement—refused to maintain health and safety standards.[36]

Still, if peacetime patriarchy leaves women at a great disadvantage in their struggles to gain security and dignity, wartime patriarchy, so thoroughly imbued with masculine-defined militarist values and controlled by militarily sensitive public institutions, creates conditions in which women's struggles are harder, not easier, to wage in ways that produce genuine and long-lasting improvements for women.

Back to post-war normality: demobilisation of women

Rosie the Riveter—especially when she was confined to welding—wasn't meant to be a pacesetter: she was meant to be a temporarily useful, artificial creation of government's 'manpower' strategists. She was still pictured as a mother or a mother-to-be, even if she had to put aside that natural calling 'for the duration'. When she worked at riveting or welding, she was expected to see that work as an extension of her maternal, feminine instincts and obligations.

Militarists cannot guarantee the social order on their own.

They need patriarchal family structures to assist them in enforcing discipline. It is a dilemma. 'Wartime' is a relatively brief period in which the government can carry on the balancing act between its simultaneous but conflicting needs for mobility and order. Thus as soon as the war is over, the 'mobile woman' is expected to settle down and recommit herself to hearth and home.

Even before the war ended, British and American bureaucratic agencies such as the Ministry for Reconstruction were beginning to plan for the post-war era.[37] Integral to that planning was the ideological reconstruction of motherhood, a construction that would allow the smooth demobilisation of women defence workers and their replacement by returning male soldiers.

Ann Scott James describes Britain's 1945 demobilisation of women:

> As the last guns rumbled and the last all-clear sounded, all the squalor and discomfort and roughness that had seemed fitting for so long began to feel old fashioned.
>
> The Amazons, the women in trousers, the good comrades had had their glorious day. But it was over. Gracious living beckoned once again.[38]

Government propaganda machines which five years before had used pay incentives plus emotional blackmail to rush women into waged labour, now geared up to persuade women themselves that their natural place was back in the kitchen. In 1943, women were being praised for their culinary ingenuity, creating meals that took such a short time to prepare that they could take a factory job and still feed their families nutritious meals. Now propaganda films lured those same women into spending long hours on gourmet dishes that would earn them praise from appreciative husbands. Children who in 1943 were portrayed as cheerfully content in well-staffed day-care centres while their mothers were off contributing to the industrial war effort, were filmed two years later running out into traffic-crowded streets and playing with matches because they didn't have ever-watchful mothers at their sides.[39]

In factory after factory, the female workforce was laid off, even if the technologically simplified production processes remained. In the US, black women were the first to be laid off by management, followed by black men and white women. Women welders became once again cooks or cleaners or unpaid housewives, though frequently not without protest.[40] In Britain, which had a more severe labour shortage after the war, some skilled women workers were retained, but unskilled women workers were forced off the factory floor.[41] Whatever women gain in wartime—and they lose a great deal if they are the targets of male soldiers' occupation, bombing or food rationing—is not under their own control. The gains are temporary, expedient, and reversible.

But what is distinctive about the era in which we are currently living is that militarisation is no longer conceived of as a wartime, short-term anomaly; it is the new normality. *The present post-war era is a militarised peacetime.*

After 30 years of defeminisation, we are entering an era of refeminised defence work, thanks to an electronic revolution in military weaponry. In the 1980s women are being called back to serve the national security strategists. But the present-day 'Rosie' has traded in her confident smile and healthy biceps for obedient concentration and nimble fingers. She is the backbone of the militarised microelectronics industry.

Women in the peacetime military-industrial complex

Women, always the hardest hit by economic recessions, might be tempted in the 1980s to revive the myth of Rosie the Riveter in the face of high unemployment and less obvious but equally devastating under-employment, updating it to fit the militarised 'peacetime' of the 1980s: if the war got us out of the depression in the 1940s, couldn't huge military budgets do the same today? If women went from bread lines, sweatshops, cotton fields and unpaid housework to waged jobs as riveters and welders in the 1940s, shouldn't we, their daughters and granddaughters, take advantage of all the public funds being invested in the production of tanks and missiles to pull ourselves out of the current economic doldrums?

The myth is alluring. It is one on which militarists depend.

Not only does it equate military spending with jobs, it makes a militarised economy appear to be an *aid* to women's liberation: 'the only thing that was bad for the second world war's Rosie was that the war *ended*'. Of course, the myth and its update overlook that it was the fact that the military needed so many thousands of men in its ranks that drove weapons factory managers, stripped of their *preferred* work force, to hire far less preferred workers, women. Had either the American or British government decided to pour so much money directly into civilian production in the early 1940s, (the US government spent $4 million in 1941 alone), the Depression might have receded even faster.[42]

Dollar for dollar, pound for pound, money spent on civilian production and services generates *more* jobs than the same money invested in weapons production. Of all forms of public spending, defence spending is the *least* efficient means of generating jobs. For instance, it has been estimated that whereas $1 billion of public spending for defence in 1973 would have created 45,000 jobs, that same amount of money spent in non-defence areas could have created 70,000 firefighting jobs or 76,000 teaching jobs or 85,000 nursing jobs.[43] A decade later, US Secretary of Defense Casper Weinberger is claiming that nowadays $1 billion of military spending could create 60,000 jobs. Still, American critics noted this newly 'optimistic' calculation still fell far short of the job creation potential of the same dollars spent on social programmes or public works.[44]

Furthermore, since military production processes are heavily oriented toward white collar, technical and skilled blue collar jobs, defence spending does the *least* to generate jobs for those workers most subject to unemployment and underemployment: women and racial minorities. When they do manage, through government anti-discrimination and affirmative action programmes, to get into the higher paying defence jobs, women and minorities remain the most vulnerable to layoffs, layoffs which are frequent in the weapons industry due to the ups and downs integral to an industry so dependent on a single customer.[45]

It is difficult at any time to figure out just how much of a country's job market is dependent on military spending because formal 'defence spending' is not always limited to spending earmarked for the military. Money spent on 'energy development', 'space projects', 'health research' and even 'evaluations of affirmative action' may in fact be designed to serve military objectives.[46]

One obvious way to determine whether one's own job is being militarised is to ask whether one is working for (or economically dependent on someone else who is working for) a major military contractor. In Britain, this would mean asking whether one's economic well-being and job opportunities are *at all* dependent on one of the biggest arms producers: British Aerospace, British Shipbuilders, General Electric Corporation, Plessey, Rolls Royce, Royal Ordnance Factories, Westland Aircraft, British Leyland, EMI, Ferranti, Lucas or Racal Electronics.[47]

The equivalent exercise for an American woman trying to determine *to what extent* her livelihood and job chances are militarised would be to ask whether she is in *any* way affected by the operations of the Pentagon's top defence contractors: McDonnell Douglas, United Technologies, General Dynamics, General Electric, Boeing, Lockheed, Hughs Aircraft, Raytheon, Grumman, Litton Industries, Martin Marietta, Philco or Rockwell International.[48]

An alternative—or, better, additional—question to pose in order to assess realistically how militarily dependent your worklife is becoming is this: How dependent is the *region* where I live on companies whose executives have decided to rely on defence contracts for their profits and viability? British women working in the south-east, midlands, and the north-west regions of England and the Glasgow-Clydebank region of Scotland are surrounded by armaments companies.[49]

These British women workers would have much to share concerning the effects of living in a densely militarised job market with American women living and working in Hartford (Connecticut), Long Island (New York), San Jose and Los Angeles (California), Houston (Texas), Seattle (Washington) and Cambridge (Massachusetts).[50]

In 1960, President Dwight Eisenhower—himself a career

military man—warned of what he saw as a dangerous process gaining a foothold in American life. The process Eisenhower noted was making executives of certain large companies, officials in a few powerful bureaucratic agencies and a handful or pro-military legislators so mutually dependent that, together, they were promoting arms manufacture in order to satisfy their own respective organisational needs, not national security. Because it is fuelled by needs that are, therefore, not purely military, this network is especially visible during 'peacetime'. Eisenhower called this three-headed, mutually reinforcing military spending lobby the 'military-industrial complex'.

Today those behind-closed-doors networks that promote ever higher military arms spending are *international* networks. Companies such as America's General Dynamics, Britain's Rolls Royce and France's Dessault not only compete for the latest NATO order in new jet fighters, they collaborate in an intricate pattern of shifting political-manufacturing alliances.[51]

The military-industrial complex is run by civilian and military elites. In both the US and Britain, it is also an all-male network. Critics of spiralling arms manufacture have called for a break-up of this mutually reinforcing system of support and dependency. Some critics have outlined alternative manufacturing directions that current arms companies could follow if their executives would be more open to workers' suggestions and decision-making influence.[52]

But virtually no analysts—pro or anti—of the military-industrial complex have described the ways in which the network depends on male bonding, male privilege and militarily derived notions of masculinity. There are several dimensions of the intimate relationships that are cultivated between military officials and arms industry executives and scientists that might be more understandable—and thus alterable—if they were examined as one more manifestation of militarism's reliance on and perpetuation of a gender ideology that constructs 'maleness' in a peculiar fashion.

First, approaching the military-industrial complex from the vantage point of gender might reveal why so many men outside the executive suites, technical labs and government offices are so reluctant to challenge the assumptions of 'seriousness' and 'sophistication' of military-industrial spokesmen. Are these men afraid that they, the critics, will somehow be thought 'soft', and less than truly 'serious' as male public figures? Or if they do, as outsiders, take highly critical stands toward defence spending and weapons escalation—as certainly many men have—why do they so often frame their criticisms in a style and language that comes close to emulating that of the male military spending advocates they are challenging?

Second, asking in what ways men *as men* develop such intimate interdependencies might shed light on the oft-mentioned ease with which members of the arms companies and their counterparts in the defence agencies personally relate to one another despite the alleged antipathy between capitalist businessmen and public bureaucrats. Could it be that not simply a mutuality of objective interests is at work, but a more subtle trust based on common experiences (real or imagined) in wartime and/or in the military? Being a 'captain of industry' and a captain of a battleship may have a shared ideological base in patriarchy, which helps compensate for their surface disagreements about the proper role of government.

Third, a feminist approach to the military-industrial complex which makes men visible *as men* might suggest why so many workers in the defence industry, as well as their male union leaders, support management's eager pursuit of more and bigger defence contracts. The defence industries—makers of tanks, armoured vehicles, artillery, planes, ships—have historically relied on an overwhelmingly male work force. 'Rosie the Riveter' was celebrated because she was an anomaly, and a short-lived one at that. Defence manufacturers are typically categorised as 'heavy industry' and heavy industry is thought of in patriarchal societies as the place where men work because they are men. There is a very potent set of ideas conducive to sustaining high military spending on the production of arms. Many male workers imagine that helping to produce tanks is more 'serious', more 'manly' work, than trying to produce, say, buses or hospital equipment.

Some women workers have taken heavy industry's high

status (and consequent high wages) as a given and have sought to improve their own working conditions by gaining entrance on to the factory floor where armaments are being made. Paula Rayman, an American researcher concerned about the militarisation of industry, interviewed women working at Pratt and Whitney, an aircraft engine manufacturing subsidiary of the Pentagon's number two contractor, United Technology. Living in Hartford, a city dominated by 'UT', these women felt that they had little alternative but to try to better their job opportunities within a directly or indirectly militarised company.[53]

Most women in production work (as versus clerical jobs) at UT's Pratt and Whitney subsidiary held blue collar jobs that were defined as semi-skilled and were low paying. Those few women who had gained access into the more skilled, higher-paying jobs were single, young and able to work the shifts less popular with male workers. A Pratt and Whitney executive declared that child-care was a 'private matter' and thus the company provided no child-care facilities for its workers. It may not be surprising, therefore, that only 22 per cent of male workers surveyed, contrasted with over 90 per cent of the women, reported that they had little or no energy at the end of a work day. Without a war draining its male labour, negotiating with a union led by men (International Association of Machinists) who do not see 'women's issues' as a major concern, and with the option of moving production to a more economically depressed region (e.g. Maine) where labour is cheaper and less organised, it is not surprising that Pratt and Whitney and other heavy industry defence firms are less than quick to respond to women workers' needs and aspirations.

'Nimble fingers': the feminisation of electronic weaponry

An estimated 40 per cent of a new navy cruiser is composed of electronics.[54] Roughly speaking, this means that 40 per cent of a navy cruiser is dependent on women's labour, women's labour made cheap.

Today the fastest growing area in the defence industry is 'light industry', not 'heavy industry'. Light industry—textiles, garments, food processing, electronics—always has been the area of manufacturing where women industrial workers have been concentrated because, first, women are supposed to be 'naturally' adept at working with these products and, second, since these industries are labour-intensive and owners maximise profits by keeping wages low, gender ideologies that justify paying women less than men are particularly salient in these industries' hiring strategies. For all its gloss as the frontier industry of the 1980s, the electronics industry is really the latest in a long line of 'light industries' which owe their financial success to the conceptualisation of women workers as able to endure repetition and tedium, as 'naturally' dextrous (and thus not skilled), as careful and precise, as docile, as providers of 'second incomes' in their households, and as first and foremost wives and mothers. If khaki cotton cloth for generations has been the product of these sexist beliefs, so too are the latest electronics-laden navy cruisers.

In the midst of the Falklands war, the *New York Times* carried the headline, 'Electronics Tip the Scales of Combat'.[55] The British-Argentinian battle on the seas and in the air was fought with the newest electronically guided missiles and counter-missiles. The international weapons industrial elite watched carefully. Electronic weapon matched electronic weapon in the South Atlantic; defence contracts hung in the balance. Electronics companies were hailed as the wave of the militarised future. At the same time, electronics companies were becoming more and more dependent on defence contracts. One of the world's biggest, most aggressive microchip producers, National Semiconductor, reported that in 1981, 20 per cent of its profits came from US Defense Department contracts.[56]

Electronic divisions of large arms manufacturers, as well as independent electronics companies, depend on cheap female labour. Tina MacKay works at Lucas Aerospace's Birmingham factory wiring electronic circuits for bombers. Classified as 'semi-skilled' in a company whose predominantly male workforce is mostly categorised as 'skilled', Tina MacKay works in a virtually all-women department. She described her work to Hilary Wainwright:

> We sit in rows like a class-room. Though the foreman sits at the back. They can overlook us better that way. We are separated by such large gaps that we cannot talk unless we shout. Some of the jobs are extremely uncomfortable and tedious. For example, 'lidding' the circuits involves sitting in front of a six foot machine and working with rubber gloves up to your armpits in a vacuum case. You have to put the circuits, the electrodes and the 'lid' together for automatic welding. While the welding is going on you cannot move. You just sit there, your arms sweating, your legs not being able to fit under the table properly and your head going bonkers![57]

While many of the men in these factories—some even may have participated in union efforts to find alternatives to dependency on Ministry of Defence contracts—saw the weapons they were producing as reflections of their own skills, the women performing the lower-paid, dead-end wiring jobs felt far more detached from the actual weaponry. The fact that it was 'sophisticated' weaponry did little to enhance women workers' sense of their skills or social status. Working at Lucas or Ferranti or Plessey was just a job, an economically necessary job. That is, until the Falklands war broke out in the spring of 1982:

> Until the Falklands it was just another job to me. That's when it really came home to me that the things I'm making are going to kill someone; and it might be your own people. The job we do is so far removed from the actual things, that you do not think of it as a lethal occupation—even when you see the actual thing [a missile], on an open day, it does not really register.[58]

Women working today in electrical circuitry departments of large defence industries or in independent electronics factories were there before the Falklands task force set sail and were still there after the task force returned and war fever wound down. Unlike women in the second world war who were mobilised with much government publicity only to be rapidly demobilised when 'the boys came home', Tina MacKay and her co-workers have been hired to supply cheap labour for an industry that is more tied to a general militarisation than to specific wars. Executives of the companies in which these women work see defence contracts as an integral part of the Britain's 'peacetime' economy. And what their own military can't absorb, these companies' executives hope foreign armed forces will purchase (if the American, French and Italian competitors can be beaten).[59]

Furthermore, unlike their foremothers in the first and second world war defence industries, women wiring bombs in the Lucas plant are not causing worrying ideological problems by performing 'men's jobs'. They are hired for those jobs that have for years been structurally set aside as 'women's work' and they can be kept in the assembly line for a long time without upsetting the social order.

On the other hand, as the women who spoke to Hilary Wainwright made clear, it was the very routine, the ordinariness of these women's electrical assembly work that made the outbreak of a war disturbing, in some instances even radicalising. What one week was a tedious, low-paying job that helped pay the rent, the next week became complicity in a system to kill people, something about which many of the women had grave doubts, despite feelings of loyalty to 'our boys' fostered by the government. But any new reservations about producing deadly weapons were very difficult to act upon. A woman classified as 'unskilled' or 'semi-skilled' couldn't quit her current job to seek another, less militarised job as easily as could at least some of the more 'skilled' men in that plant. In addition, while some of their male co-workers were discussing ways to convert their factory to peacetime products, thereby demilitarising their work lives, union organisation in the defence plants tended to replicate the companies' sexual hierarchy, leaving women feeling marginalised even in demilitarisation efforts.

Drive 40 miles west of London along the M4 motorway toward Reading and you enter Berkshire's gentle rural countryside. Here is where Britain's microelectronics industry is being militarised. With government aid, high technology firms are flocking to this congenial region from the economically hard-pressed north. It is the firms' research, design and corporate finance employees—well-paid, white collar, largely male—who are migrating to Berkshire. The microchip assembly lines have been set up elsewhere, at sites near plentiful pools of semi-skilled, unemployed and underemployed women workers—for instance, in Wales and Scotland. There British firms are being joined by foreign microelectronics companies. Both British and foreign managers are in search not just of women workers, but those women workers who live in such economically depressed regions that they can be hired for especially low wages. It is hoped that they feel so vulnerable and will be so grateful for a job that they will not question whether what they are producing is designed to kill people.[60]

Officials in many depressed regions such as Wales or Scotland plan to use their cheap female labour to attract domestic and foreign electronics firms. They dream of their regions becoming the latest 'Silicon Valley'.

The original Silicon Valley, named after a material central to the production of electronic microchips, is located in Santa Clara County, just south of San Francisco. Now the international headquarters for the microelectronics industry, Silicon Valley is a society based on an integrated system of *sexism*, *racism* and *militarism*.[61]

In 1979-80, companies with operations in Santa Clara Valley were awarded $2.3 billion in prime Defense Department contracts[62] for the manufacture of the communications, radar and control mechanisms that increasingly are becoming the heart of such modern weapons as the Trident II and M-X missiles, the B-1B bomber and the Rapid Deployment Force's new Infantry Fight Vehicle. California's financial analysts predict that by 1987 the state of California will get 30 per cent of the nation's defence contract dollars, making an estimated 600,000 Californian workers dependent on the arms industry for their jobs.[63] A large proportion of those militarily dependent workers will be women.

Alice is a 28-year-old white woman who lives with her husband and two children. She works as a wafer-tester for one of Silicon Valley's small firms, Microtech. She is frustrated with the tedium of her job and worries about how few precautions her employers have taken to protect women like herself who routinely work around hazardous chemical and hot furnaces. Still, Alice concludes:

> Women make the best workers at this kind of thing because you have to be patient, you have to be good with your hands, and the work is so tedious. Isn't raising children and doing housework tedious? I mean, women are good at this. And, I guess [women are hired] mainly because the labour is cheap, and you don't have to have a good education behind you to get a good start.[64]

Many of the women working on the benches around Alice are in fact educated, but are newly arrived in the US and have limited English language fluency, making it hard for them to get other, perhaps less militarised jobs. Many of the valley's women workers have emigrated from countries such as Chile and the Philippines, themselves heavily militarised. According to Nina, a 36-year-old Chilean exile who was a trained nurse but now works as an assembler for Davis Instruments, a laser equipment firm, 'People don't know how to put into words the injustices they feel.' The women who work in the electronics plants, Nina feels, are no more than 'little specks' whose labour is used by the companies.[65]

While corporate and technical positions in Silicon Valley are held overwhelmingly by white men, 80 per cent of assembly plant workers are women, a majority of whom are black, Hispanic, or Asian.[66]

When officials in other parts of the US, in Europe, the Caribbean or Asia, dream of creating their *own* Silicon Valleys, they imagine replicating Santa Clara Valley's particular package of conditions: a moderate climate and congenial landscape (to attract the internationally mobile high tech white collar professionals); land available for low, linear assembly plants; easy access to international ports or airfields; a local population that includes women whose ethnic cultures and employment opportunities are such that they can be readily identified by personnel managers as nimble fingered, disciplined and cheap. Not every regional planner has been successful in delivering this special package to the electronics industry's global shoppers.

The Third World equivalent of California's Silicon Valley is the Export Processing Zone. The 'EPZ' is an industrial zone especially created by government elites eager to increase their foreign currency revenues. One of the principal reasons many of these government elites are feeling such a sharp foreign currency pinch in the 1980s is that they have been spending so much on the purchase of expensive police and military equipment hawked by the energetic salesmen from America, USSR, Britain, Italy, France, West Germany and Canada.[67]

The firms being urged to set up factories in the government-paid-for EPZs are foreign firms specialising in light industrial manufacture. One of the biggest attractions Third World government officials hold out to prospective foreign investors is an ample supply of 'cheap', 'docile', 'nimble-fingered' female labour. Electronics firms, many of them actively engaged in weapons production, are among the most frequent tenants of these Export Processing Zones, which are fast becoming part of the international landscape.[68]

The resulting pattern is one in which women electronics workers in countries such as the Philippines, South Korea, Taiwan, Singapore and Indonesia are not merely militarised, they are *triply* militarised. Their labour is exploited so that their governments can go on buying foreign police and military equipment. They live in societies which are made repressive by militarised governments unwilling to confront deep-seated inequities, preferring to rely instead on coercive force and the aid of friendly powers, such as the US, to whom they give military bases. They work on products which themselves either have direct military application or are part of a larger corporate profits formula in which defence contracting plays a central part.[69]

A quick glance at wage differentials suggests why Western owned microelectronics companies take up militarist Third World government offers—all the while remaining on the lookout for a more lucrative pool of cheap 'nimble fingers' elsewhere.

Country	Microelectronics Hourly Wage for Assembly Workers (in US dollars)	Wage and Fringe
US	5.92	8.06
Hong Kong	1.15	1.20
Singapore	0.79	1.25
South Korea	0.63	1.00
Taiwan	0.53	0.80
Malaysia	0.48	0.60
Philippines	0.48	0.50
Indonesia	0.19	0.35

Source: 'Off Shore Assembly', *Global Electronics Information Newsletter*, No. 20, March 1982, p.2.

Although her salary is far below that of a European or American worker, a Philippines electronics worker is often envied by her women friends. First, she has a waged job; 75 per cent of Filipino women do not. Many emigrate to the US, Britain, Canada and Europe in search of jobs. Second, the electronics worker has a job that seems less socially and physically dangerous than working as a 'hostess' or masseuse. Third, compared to a woman sewing jeans or assembling toys, her work space is air conditioned (against the 90°F heat outside), dry and clean. Such favourable conditions are guaranteed by her foreign employer because of the delicacy of the microchips she assembles. Conditions that affect her, rather than the microchips, are treated with less concern. An estimated 95 per cent of electronics workers develop severe eye trouble due to the strain of fixing 50 gold wires to every chip. The company will advance her money for eyeglasses, though it deducts the cost from her salary later. Like most young women electronics workers, after as few as three years, she will have to quit her job because of deteriorating eyesight.

> Migraine, nausea and headaches are bonded with every microchip. [Minda] is also in danger from acids in which components are dipped, and which react to heat. No one

> will have told her or her co-workers of the harmful substances, like TCE, or of her rights not to work with them... Where safety regulations are not applied, Minda's health is available for this industry to dispose of: she can lose her sight, her liver, her fertility—or her job.[70]

These, then, are some of the real costs of a Trident missile or Chieftain tank that remain invisible if we stare fixedly only at government defence budgets or weapons company balance sheets: a spreading international sex division of labour; the reinforcement of pre-existent notions of women's docility and cheapness; cultivation of sexist racism which portrays certain women as especially 'nimbled-fingered'; the thousands of work lives cut short by headaches and chemical infection and deteriorating eyesight.

However, here as in so many of the cases we have looked at, there are *contradictions* and *struggles* that can thwart the use of women for military ends.

The managers of the Western-owned multi-nationals who want to tie their corporate wagons to the military horse are motivated by the desire to maximise profits. In the electronics field, this allegedly requires global shopping to find the most compliant foreign regime which will serve up the cheapest female labour force. The companies will then produce as much of their product as they can in those overseas plants, leaving the 'skilled' design and testing stages to their more expensive workers back in Europe or the US. But government defence officials, usually so eager to meet the needs of their corporate suppliers, are not motivated chiefly by profit. Their goal is to maximise 'national security', and though 'security' and 'profits' do often seem to converge it would be a mistake to think of them as synonymous. Consequently, while their corporate allies want to produce certain goods cheaply in the Philippines or Mexico, the military planners of Western governments want to keep all sensitive defence manufacturing within either their home jurisdictions or, at least, within NATO's territory.

The movement toward reliance on Third World women for the production of strategic weaponry makes these security-conscious officials extremely uneasy.[71] They exert pressure on electronics firms not to move so rapidly to 'off shore production' in their defence manufacturing.

In addition to contradictions, there is struggle. Despite all the obstacles, some Third World women workers in Export Processing Zones have been developing ideas and collective bonds which enable them to begin to protest at their working conditions. In June and July 1982, more than 25,000 workers at the Philippines Bataan Export Processing Zone walked off the job. Women were in the forefront of the unprecedented action, as women make up the overwhelming majority of workers in this zone, which has been the cornerstone of President Ferdinand Marcos's martial and post-martial law development formula. The Philippines government responded with force. It called in the militarised police and decreed that strikes in the microelectronics industry were hereafter illegal. Nevertheless, one executive in a subsidiary of a US electronics firm told an American reporter, 'There is heavy organising going on in our plant and everyone else's.'[72]

By 1981, microelectronics had outpaced the traditional foreign currency earners in the Philippines, coconut products and sugar. It accounted for 40,000 jobs. Most of the firms were American, European or Japanese owned—Fairchild, National Semiconductor, Texas Instruments, Philips, Raytheon. Personnel managers and Philippines government officials imagined the EPZs to be secure enclaves where workers could be more easily controlled and disciplined. But the women who struck in June 1982 had developed quite a different conception of the zone. To them it had come to be seen as a place where thousands of women in different companies worked side by side. The very things that made the zone 'secure', in fact, could also make it a site for political consciousness raising, so that women workers could overcome the pressures for 'docility' and stand up to management's threats and the government's police.

The Bataan workers won concession from the Marcos government in 1982. By autumn there was speculation that the Marcos regime had shelved plans to create a new EPZ.[73] What a year before had seemed a gender-based formula for corporate profits and government control now appeared, in the hands of the women workers, to be a formula for resistance to direct and indirect militarisation.

But resistance is always difficult for women all over the world in the face of the ideological, sexual and economic pressures on them to be dependent, compliant and isolated. Perhaps resistance is especially difficult for women in the militarised job sectors of an increasingly militarised economy. Often, in fact, one of the difficulties hardest to overcome is making the connection between the day-to-day work a woman is doing and the end use of the product. For women are typically are confined to those jobs that are marginalised and distanced from the eventual weaponry. They are wiring complex boards, not designing the tank or fitting the missiles into the aircraft body. That is 'man's work'.

Second, militarisation is occurring today in ways far more subtle than it did back in 1940, so that a woman may not even realise that her job is part of the military's operation. Women are kept away from the inner circles of company policy-making when contracts with defence officials are signed. Tracing the links between a job in an advertising agency (or a bank or an adult education programme) and the military may take time and information resources that many women don't have readily available.

Third, women in certain white collar and professional fields may discover the military connection so late that they cannot face turning down that executive or engineering job in the weapons manufacturing firm. A woman may have fought her way up through a sexist education system only to find out at the end that the only jobs available to her are directly or indirectly dependent on military contracts. Once again, women's struggle for equality can itself be militarised.

On the other hand, it is possible to follow the breadcrumbs of any job back to its military source. According to UN 1981 estimates, 20 per cent of all scientists and engineers in the world were engaged in military-related work.[74] Nevertheless, women at the Massachusetts Institute of Technology, one of America's most prestigious engineering schools and, until recently, a stronghold of technocratic masculinity, in 1982 used their campus feminist group to launch a series of discussions about militarisation and about their non-militarised alternatives as women, as feminists and as young engineers facing job prospects which today come mostly from defence contractors.[75]

It is possible that out of a developing consciousness women workers can begin discussions among themselves about the implications of any such military dependency. And we can all start figuring out why it is that, as *women*, we have not been permitted to know about the militarisation of our hopes and livelihoods sooner, before a war is launched and women are appealed to by male officials to do 'their part' to support 'our boys' sent into battle.

8. Feminism and Militarism

Beyond budgets and origins

There are two approaches to explaining militarisation's effect on women. Each in its own way is intellectually appealing but ultimately inadequate. The first concentrates on the military as an institution with a gargantuan budgetary appetite. Such an approach leads to an examination of defence expenditures, their beneficiaries and their victims. On the one hand, there are the arms manufacturers and their thin layers of privileged male managers, technicians and skilled workers; on the other there are those people, largely women, who are most hurt when social programmes (health, transportation, education, social security) are cut back in order to satisfy the alleged needs of the military and its industrial suppliers.

Adopting this economic approach enables women and men to make the connections *between* guns and butter, to relate the latest tank contract to the understaffed local hospital. This approach compels us to put militarisation into a larger socio-economic context, rather than thinking within the conventionally narrow frameworks of foreign policy or 'national security'. Concentrating on military budgets and the parasitic weapons industry makes the dynamics of the international arms spiral less abstract, more concrete. Unlike men, women get no aesthetic pleasure or rewards of status from talking about 'sophisticated' weaponry or esoteric military strategies. Mobilisation for disarmament can be more broadly based and more open to women's participation when the real costs of armaments become more explicitly related to people's everyday lives and struggles.

But in spite of the advantages of such an approach, in the end regarding militarisation as chiefly an economic-technological phenomenon is inadequate. It leaves untouched, unexplained and unchallenged some of the most powerful ideological and 'private' processes that perpetuate militarisation. The danger is that a military budget cut one year will rise again next year because militarisation's basic causes have been left virtually intact. Disarmament may be too limited an objective. Militarism disarmed is militarism still. The structures of militarisation are only partially dismantled even if nuclear weapons are 'frozen' and arms companies convert to more socially useful products. If ideas entailing men's dominance and women's subservience —patriarchy—remain, the victory over militarism may be surprisingly short-lived. Patriarchal militarism disarmed is only *temporarily* disarmed.

In addition, women taking part in such a narrowly defined anti-militarist movement are all too likely to be marginalised. If the condition of women themselves is not part of the *explanation* of militarism, but only part of the litany of victims of militarism, women's experiences can be ghettoised as 'women's issues', to be assigned significance by male disarmament leaders only as they broaden the base of the movement's public support.

In 1937, on the eve of the second world war, Virginia Woolf wrote what stands still as perhaps the most cogent critique of this narrow approach to militarism. In *Three Guineas* Woolf agreed that many of the contemporary male analyses of escalating military preparations had merit and did indeed warrant popular action.[1] However, Woolf explained, they didn't go far enough or deep enough. Their analyses simply left too much unexplained. Their web of explanation didn't reach out to take in enough of social history. They were trying to leave themselves *as men* out of their explanation of militarism.

As Virginia Woolf saw it, her male contemporaries were acting as if Mussolini's and Hitler's ideas about how society should be ordered had nothing to do with similar views voiced more politely by Church of England clerics or Oxford dons. They were approaching their task as if Britain's generals didn't come from the same patriarchal family environment and didn't benefit from the same patriarchal schools as Britain's male barristers and Members of Parliament. Such 'it's-them-not-us' explanations of militarism simply wouldn't do, concluded Woolf. Women would have to form their own anti-militarist movement. Women would have to *use* their marginalisation to examine with fresh insight the society that was preparing for war with such eagerness. Today, 45 years after Woolf wrote *Three Guineas*, other women are continuing to look at militarism from the vantage point of women, not simply to urge women to join the disarmament campaign, but to provide a fuller explanation of militarism, an explanation that derives from an understanding of women's own lives.[2]

Woolf's approach looked at the problem in terms of social institutions. There is a second approach women have taken when facing the invasion of militarisation into their lives. It starts with women's own experiences and it provokes anger, both of which are politically healthy; but it also can induce paralysis, which is not. This approach conceives of militarism as somehow woven into the very fibre of maleness. Violence against women by men is so pervasive, across so many historical eras and cultural differences, that it seems only explicable by reference to something intrinsic in men *as* men, some fear, some insecurity or aggressiveness which also inclines men to sustain formal institutions—military forces—which embody and legitimise those violent attitudes and behaviours. Chinese foot-binding, seventeenth-century New England witch burnings, 1980s 'Yorkshire Ripper' assaults, the Falklands war and America's imposition of nuclear missiles on Europe all seem rooted in a common source: the intrinsically hostile character of men simply because they are men. And, so this reasoning logically proceeds, not until the qualities of maleness are fundamentally altered is any political, diplomatic or economic reform likely to reverse the threats posed by men as generals, and men as rapists, and men as weapons engineers.

Such an approach has real value, and it would be a mistake to underestimate it. It insists that military ideologies and coercive manoeuvres be discussed *not* simply in terms of technology and economics, but in terms of the sexist structure of the social order. Militarism depends on distorted government budgets, but it also depends on the public denial or trivialisation of wife battering, rape and pornography. Moreover, this approach is valuable for activists insofar as it promotes a more genuinely radical yardstick for gauging the changes that will ensure the *long*-term elimination of the military capacity to shape public priorities in any society. It leads to a conviction that 'personal' relations are so basic to the dynamics which sustain the military's grip on social policy that militarism cannot be pushed back so long as dominance, control and violence are considered 'natural' ordering principles in relations between men and women—i.e. so long as patriarchy is deemed 'normal'. The incidence of wife battering as well as the percentage of the government budget devoted to arms will hereafter have to be monitored by anyone seriously committed to the demilitarisation of society.

Nevertheless, an approach which traces militarism back to patriarchy and patriarchy back to the fundamental quality of maleness can be demoralising and even paralysing. For it implies that only transformation so basic as to alter the very character of men as men can effectively curtail the military invasion of ordinary women's lives.

Perhaps it is possible to be less fixed on the discovery of 'original causes'. It might be more useful to ask: *How* do these values and behaviours get *repeated* generation after generation? What are the *processes* that reproduce the kind of social relations that enhance militarism rather than other social structures and beliefs? Are those processes so totally integrated and so immune to external pressures that they never falter? Or are they full of contradictions and subject to struggles which make them, in fact, much more problematic?[3]

If militarism, and patriarchy as well, depend on explicit processes for their continued existence, then there is more reason to watch what is going on now. At the present militarism *is* being sustained by observable processes. Focussing on process puts *power* back into the picture. It presumes that *decisions* are made by someone, that there were and still are *choices*; some are taken, while others are rejected, and those exercises of power derive from someone's calculation of interest and benefit.

The gendered politics of 'manpower'

Taking women's experiences seriously, looking at the lives of 'ordinary' women, makes it clear that a critical process for armed forces is the acquisition of '*manpower*'. Acquisition of military manpower entails both getting recruits and keeping recruits. Military officials and their civilian allies never have been able to solve this problem once and for all. It has never been enough to tap the supposedly intrinsic domineering or violent qualities in men in order to fill the ranks with soldiers numerous enough, politically reliable enough and technically skilled enough to satisfy the military elite.

Acquisition of manpower has required an elaborate gender ideology and social structure, not just smooth-talking recruiters or strong-armed press gangs. Acquisition of manpower has necessitated that the public believe that wars are fought on something considered the 'battle front' and supported on something called the 'home front'. It has required that male soldiers feel they cannot test their 'manliness' unless they serve in the military, and that proof of passing that test be supplied on the one hand by acts of conquest and on the other hand by thanks from those who have been protected.

On a more mundane level, though no less critical in the processes sustaining militarism, the military manpower must be born and kept alive, even though military forces themselves are organised to kill and wound people. Furthermore, those processes of birth, nurturing and medically resuscitating the potential and actual military manpower must be carried on in ways that don't either divert potential soldiery into caring occupations or, by breaking the link between masculinity and soldiering, deprive the military of its legitimacy in the eyes of the general public that is paying its bills.

Third, a military force needs to have an adequate supply of weapons, clothing, food and shelter to feel it can match whichever opposing military force it currently imagines to be its chief adversary. Yet the very production of those material supplies must be organised in a fashion that doesn't divert too much labour away from soldiering.

Looked at this way, manpower acquisition is not a minor process, overshadowed by questions of budgets and weapons technology. It is a vast and diffuse process that sends ripples throughout any society and even on into foreign societies (where soldiers will find solace or proof in conquest, or where elites will find alternative pools of labour).

In all of these dimensions, furthermore, the military manpower acquisition process is as fraught with troubles in the 1980s as it was in the 1880s or 1580s. Nuclear technology has not made the armed forces' manpower problems vanish. The process of acquisition goes on; it continues to worry military officials and to demand choices and the exercise of power. The processes of military manpower acquisition are *gendered* processes. Military forces past and present have not been able to get, keep and reproduce the sorts of soldiers they imagine they need without drawing on ideological beliefs concerning the different and stratified roles of women and men. Without assurance that women will play their 'proper' roles, the military cannot provide men with the incentives to enlist, obey orders, give orders, fight, kill, re-enlist, and convince their sons to enlist. Ignore gender—the social constructions of 'femininity' and 'masculinity' and the relations between them—and it becomes impossible adequately to explain how military forces have managed to capture and control so much of society's imagination and resources.[4]

Militaries need women—but they need women to behave *as the gender 'women'*. This always requires the exercise of control. Military officials and allies in civilian elites have wielded their power to perpetuate those gendered processes that guarantee the military its manpower. This is what is so strikingly revealed in the experiences of women who have been used as the military's prostitutes, rape victims, wives, widows, social workers, nurses, soldiers, defence workers and mothers.

First, the military institution has needed all of these women to solve problems central to its own continued existence. From fifteenth-century camp followers to twentieth-century electronics workers, looking at women has revealed that military politics never has been the all-male activity it is so typically imagined to be. Second, these women have been needed not simply as undifferentiated workers, but *as the gender 'woman'*, acting in ways women are supposed to act. In other words the military has been dependent on patriarchy. Third, women in all their various military-imposed roles are related to *each other*. If women as military wives will act as the military expects them to act, that in turn helps perpetuate women as defence workers and women as military nurses acting in militarily useful ways. Each reinforces those norms of womanhood on which the military relies.

Finally, guaranteeing that women will act in ways that keep the military's manpower acquisition processes rolling along has not been left to chance. Some women seem too slow in learning 'their place'. Other women openly resist being forced into society's gendered moulds. Still other women, paradoxically, carry the idea of women's different sphere so far as to embarrass the military—asking for 'too much' protection; caring 'too much' about the health of their sons; performing their arms factory jobs with 'too much' enthusiasm. Consequently the military has devised specific policies to maintain control over all women whose services as women it has required. In other words, for centuries military elites have had *policies* regarding women, because they have recognised their dependence on particular gendered social orders. Those policies are knowable. The processes by which those policies are designed, implemented, evaluated and reversed or modified are also knowable. The armed forces' long dependence on women, and the ways they have tried to camouflage that dependence (yet ensure the relationship) *can* be exposed.

Contradictions and military confusion

What becomes surprisingly clear as one examines these military processes is that the military is often very confused. It turns out that the things military commanders want from women just aren't compatible. The military wants women, out of their 'natural caring instincts', to perform as nurses so as to not use up male soldiers in medical tasks, so as to provide a kind of comfort to wounded and maybe resentful soldiers that, as men, they have come to expect, and so as to return those injured soldiers to service as soon as possible. Warfare has changed in ways that make commanders eager to have nurses as close to battlefield violence as possible. But how can women as the gender 'women' be enlisted as military nurses if, as 'women', they are supposed to be excluded from 'the front', from 'combat'?

Similarly, the military needs women as the gender 'women' to provide men with masculinity-reinforcing incentives to endure all the hardships of soldiering. Thus women should, as wives, take up the extra burdens of child care and domestic management out of gratitude for the manly protection their husbands are providing via their military careers. As prostitutes in brothels or massage parlours around military bases overseas, women should interpret womanhood as acceptance of themselves as militarised service objects. But what should the military elite do when Filipino, or Hong Kong women working in exploitative jobs near military bases become convinced of the wifely ideal the military is also promoting, and thus seek to better their condition by marrying an American or British soldier? In so doing, these Asian women provoke in commanders a fear that their institutions will be 'used' and their men will be 'burdened' by alien women.

Contradictions are exposed again when military recruiters attract potential women enlistees with promises of camaraderie among women, 'non-traditional' training and physical exercise. Yet, once such women are soldiers, the same military institution persecutes them for not being heterosexually 'feminine' enough to protect male soldiers' masculine self-confidence.

Military elites are caught again in their own cross-purposes and ideological confusion when they need to socialise successive generations of women married to career officers to dedicate themselves to unpaid labour to sustain the 'military family' and yet refuse to support those loyal military wives in divorce settlements for fear of alienating their senior male officers.

The usual bonding between upper level defence officials and their weapons manufacturing counterparts also turns out to have more cracks than first appears. Men who are corporate executives seek to maximise profits by using the cheapest female labour the world has to offer without regard to state boundaries. Their male military allies might agree to Asia's women being used as prostitutes to satisfy their soldiers' alleged sexual needs, but think 'national security' is jeopardised if those same women are allowed to assemble electronic circuitry for their latest weaponry.

Militarisation is a potent set of processes. But it is not the well-oiled, unstoppable development that is frequently portrayed as being. Sometimes military officials prefer to ignore the consequences of the ideological cracks in the system. They prefer to leave individual women to cope with the cross pressures on their own—by 'confessing' their lesbianism, by getting pregnant to get off the ships, by trying to treat the wiring of missiles as 'just a job', by taking an adult education course to make friends among civilian women, or by silently enduring nightmares of bandaging the hopelessly maimed. Military male elites much prefer to leave it up to individual 'coping', because down through the centuries they have sought to *use* women while all the time *denying* their dependence on women. This is the essence of the 'camp follower' formula. To admit that the military is an institution fundamentally reliant on women (and on a gender ideology) would be to make the military much more vulnerable.

There are times, however, when the military's contradictions around women grow so acute that they threaten to expose not just the weaknesses of the military as an institution, but the hypocrisy running through the entire idea of 'national security'. We are entering just such a period, when those contradictions in the gender system that supports the military are growing. The growth of such contradictions increases the need of military policy-makers to exert even more control over women's lives, but the possibilities for women to challenge the military and militarism also grow.

Military forces in the major powers such as the US and Britain are more than ever before putting a premium on *mobility*. Simultaneously, they are becoming (even where they have access to male conscription laws) increasingly dependent on *long*-term, *voluntary* enlistees. At the same time, military commanders and their civilian technocrats are equipping their forces with more destructive, further-ranging, more rapidly delivered nuclear weapons. Each of these trends is talked about at length in legislative hearings, military journals, officer staff college seminars, and even in the popular press. But almost never are they discussed with reference to military assumptions about gender or, specifically, about women. Instead, they are analysed and debated *as if* the military were so clearly and unavoidably male that there were no need to consider the implications of these three trends for relations between women and men and between the military and women.

But the reality is very different. Down in the middle levels of defence bureaucracies and at the troop level of the uniformed command structure there is plenty of evidence showing just how the trends toward *mobile* tactics, dependence on long-term *voluntary* enlistees, and integration of long-range *nuclear* weapons into conventional war doctrines each requires military institutions to resolve the ideological contradictions about women that they have so far tried to avoid confronting.

First, mobility. Ever since the thirteenth century, male military policy-makers have claimed that women were a drag on military mobility. Women, according to the military gender ideology, may perform vital functions, but they present alternative values and competing loyalties. Whether as wives or sweethearts or nurses or soldiers, women essentially threaten the discipline and male-to-male bonding that are assumed to be critical guarantors of rapid mobilisation (from a peacetime to a wartime footing) and quick field manoeuvres. As British and American military and civilian defence strategies march into this decade, determined to reduce the expense of overseas garrisons while *increasing* their capacities to guarantee alleged national interests reaching global proportions, they are more and more attracted to the model of the 'go-anywhere' military force. To accomplish this, however, will require not just new electronic communications equipment and fast transport, but more control of women so that they cannot 'slow down the march'.

Simultaneously, however, military planners are looking at census projections and finding them bleak, especially if, as in both Britain and the US, there is no conscription to rely on and going back to conscription appears to carry with it grave political risks. Military personnel planners are telling their 'superiors' (and it is at this level only where the requisites for a global mobile force are integrated with requisites for full recruitment quotas) that they cannot get and *keep* the kind (ethnically, educationally, politically) of soldiers they need without using at least some women as soldiers and without guaranteeing prospective male soldiers opportunities for relatively normal family life and/or access to women sexually. Consequently, at the same time as global strategies and field tactics are raising all the more vividly the spectre of women as a drag on troops' mobility, personnel strategies and recruitment tactics are making it imperative to take women's various relationships to men seriously and even to address women's own needs—at least to the point where they will enlist when needed and allow their husbands to enlist and, even more importantly, re-enlist.

Likewise, the armed forces have always presumed that both their own country's officials and businessmen, and foreign officials and businessmen 'hosting' their bases, would co-operate with them in controlling women sexually in ways that make them 'available' to soldiers but not damaging to soldiers' health ('readiness'). But nowadays that mutual dependence between the local officials and businessmen seems more precarious. Where once British and American commanders manipulated the social orders around their colonial bases at will, they are now having to conduct delicate negotiations for leases with independent governments whose officials might seek to ally with great power militarists but who nonetheless have to be far more discreet so as not to appear to be giving away portions of the nation's sovereignty. And some municipal officials at home are beginning to wonder whether economic dependence on bases is such a good idea for their communities after all, especially if it means their now slender budgets are burdened with all the social service demands that a military base imposes. In some cases this reluctance provides an opportunity for women to organise locally in an effort to affect decisions concerning the creation, expansion or renewed leasing of military bases in their own communities.

Finally, the nuclearisation of NATO and Warsaw Pact military doctrine has made virtually meaningless one of the foundations of the military system for controlling women: the mythical dichotomy between 'home front' and 'battle front'. So long as women could be defined as inherently, naturally and intrinsically non-combatants, and therefore as the objects of protection, their labour could be mobilised by government strategists without fear that such mobilisation would shake the social order in which women are the symbols of the hearths and homes the armed forces claim to be defending. Women would work—as mothers, nurses, factory workers—for military prescribed ends, but *whatever* they worked would remain the 'home front'. The realities of warfare, in fact, never quite fit this neat ideological framework, but the processes of propaganda and the processes of bureaucratic labelling together shrouded these awkward facts. They served to deny women's presence in the masculine preserve, 'combat', and to sustain the false image of all men as potential combatants no matter how desk-bound their soldiering.

Nuclear bombs launched by long-range missiles are a reality that even the most deft propagandist cannot camouflage. The need to persuade ordinary people in Greenham Common, England, and Cheyanne, Wyoming, that their 'home front' should be the sites for destructive nuclear-warheaded missiles has made the military pretence of 'rear' and 'front' more transparent than ever. It is not surprising that in both Greenham Common and Cheyanne it is women who are leading the protests against such missile installations.

Furthermore, the civil defence policies of both the American and British governments have been built on the assumption that women's labour can readily mobilised (especially for medical care) as part of a package which makes nuclear war 'thinkable', even 'winnable'. If women couldn't be used in gendered ways, ideas about the thinkability or winnability of a nuclear war would be even more patently absurd. But while such civil defence scenarios as are offered up by the current American and British regimes may be necessary to legitimise the nuclear spiral, at the same time they reveal the artificiality of the 'home front'-battle front dichotomy which has permitted military elites in the past to use women under controlled conditions.

Militarisation and the control of women

Though these contradictions are becoming more acute, military policy-makers will not give up their use of women—they cannot afford to. Instead, they will try to increase their capacity to control women. Ultimately such controls are intended to keep women in the role of camp followers—usable, dispensable, replaceable with other women.

So long as the social order is working as it should in a patriarchy, and so long as military doctrine, technology and recruitment are compatible with that social order, the military does not have to spread its tentacles too deeply into the rest of society. It can let the rest of society's institutions do its work. Women will have enough sons to fill the ranks; men and women will accept life lived in different spheres, with women supportive at home and men active in the public arena; women will cope with dislocation, lack of social services and even violence by drawing on their own ingenuity and private resources; men will identify paid jobs with masculinity while women will see waged work as anomalous or, at most, secondary to their primary mother, daughter and wife responsibilities.

But when, as in this decade, changes in both the patriarchal social order and the military itself make it impossible for the military to count on society, of its own accord, to satisfy the military's particular and ever-expanding needs, military elites and their allies must *take steps* to ensure that such needs are met. Today we are seeing attempts to make more and more of society dependent on, and subject to the control of the military—i.e. the fostering of *militarisation*.

Militarisation is now occurring in Britain and the US in ways intended to guarantee the military the money, brainpower, resources and authority it needs. Militarisation, however, doesn't happen overnight. It can begin slowly and with no war on the horizon, when other issues are demanding women's attention. The process by which the military makes a woman dependent on it—directly or indirectly—for her pay-cheque, her physical security, her education, her reputation in the community, even her own self-esteem advances step by step. It involves specific decisions, choices, uses of power—about family law, government contracts, health care, pensions, job opportunities, scientific research.[4] These decisions can be exposed. With them is exposed the process by which a nervous military is trying to resolve its own contradictions about women.

Women in El Salvador, South Africa, Poland, the Soviet Union, Lebanon, Israel, Philippines, Taiwan, Afghanistan, Argentina and Chile are all enduring determined efforts to militarise their lives, and in ways that are not just *comparable* to the militarisation of British and American women's lives. Today their struggles with military dependence and control are actually *linked to* the militarisation being experienced by women in Britain and America. Policies on the siting of bases, arms trade, joint exercises, national security doctrines that define 'allies' and 'enemies', multi-national bank and corporate lending and investment policies, counter-insurgency training programmes—all involve the British and American armed forces in processes that militarise the lives of women at home *and* women in other countries.

In each country military strategists *need* women. They need women who will act and think as patriarchy expects women to act and think. And they need women whose use can be disguised, so that the military can remain the quintessentially 'masculine' institution, the bastion of 'manliness'.

As the histories of prostitutes, wives, nurses, women soldiers, women insurgents and defence workers suggest, however, there are deep strains. There is a tension between senior commanders' expectations and rank and file male soldiers' expectations. There are embarrassing ideological incongruities, questioned by legislators and the press. Most important of all, there is the capacity of women themselves to analyse their own conditions and to make common cause with other women despite awesome barriers intended to divide them. Perhaps more than in any previous era, we are living at a time when women can draw on their own experiences with the military to expose the military for the contradictory and vulnerable patriarchal institution it is and always has been.

Notes

1. The Military Needs Camp Followers

1. Burton Hacker, 'Women and military institutions in early modern Europe: a reconnaissance', *Signs*, vol.6, no.4, Summer 1981, p.653.
2. Hacker, *op. cit.* p.648.
3. Francis Grose writing in 1801, as quoted by Roy Palmer (ed.), *The Rambling Soldier: Military Life Through Soldiers' Songs and Writing*, Harmondsworth, Penguin, 1977, pp.65-77.
4. Hacker, *op. cit.* p.653.
5. Samuel Hutton, quoted in Palmer, *op. cit.* pp.152-3.
6. Quoted in Hacker, *op. cit.* p.654.
7. I have tried to describe how governments have used and excluded men from different ethnic and racial groups in their militaries in Enloe, *Ethnic Soldiers: State Security in Divided Societies*, Harmondsworth, Penguin 1980, and Athens, Georgia, University of Georgia Press 1980. Also, Enloe, *Police, Military and Ethnicity*, New Brunswick, New Jersey, and London, Transaction Books 1980.
8. Lisa Leghorn describes the various ideological and social structures which allow women's work to go unpaid in *Women's Worth*, Boston, Massachusetts, and London, Routledge & Kegan Paul 1981.
9. Quoted in Hacker, *op. cit.* p.651.
10. *Women Oppose the Nuclear Threat*, stencil (c/o Sisterwrite, 190 Upper Street, London N1) 1981, 'Greenham women on the road', *Spare Rib*, July 1982, pp.18-19. Women's Pentagon Action works through local grassroots groups, for instance, Boston Women's Pentagon Action publishes its own monthly newsletter, *Update*, listing upcoming campaigns, peace fairs, guerrilla theatre, potluck meetings.
11. 'Australia: women in wars', *Spare Rib*, July 1982, p.16.
12. Brenda Thomas, 'Falklands: "brides and sweethearts" bite back',

Spare Rib, August 1982, p.26.

13. Boston feminist activism within the disarmament campaign and the controversy it generated are discussed in Margaret Cerullo with Marla Erlein, 'Peace at any price', *Radical America*, vol.16, nos.1 and 2, January/April 1982; Maida Tilchen, 'Lesbians, gays and the UN Disarmament March', *Gay Community News*, 20 March 1982; Leslie Cagan, 'Feminism and disarmament', in David Dellinger (ed.), *Beyond Survival*, Boston, Massachusetts, South End Press 1983.
14. For Japanese women's reaction to remilitarisation, see Tono Haruhi, 'Women Do Not Allow War!', Tokyo, *AMPO*, vol.13, no.4, 1981, pp.17-20.
15. US Defense Department figures, December 1981.
16. Quote from US veteran of the Vietnam war, in Mark Baker, *Nam*, New York, Quill 1982, pp.33-34.
17. David Harris, 'Draft resistance '80s style', *New York Times Magazine*, 22 August 1982, p.21.
18. US ex-marine who survived the Vietnam war, quoted in Baker, *op. cit.* pp.39-40.

2. The Militarisation of Prostitution

1. The *Observer*, 20 May 1982.
2. Peter Durisch, '...And women must weep', The *Observer*. 30 May 1982.
3. Quoted in Janet Murray (ed.), *Strong Minded Women*, New York and London, Pantheon 1982, p.397.
4. Acton in Murray, *op. cit.*
5. Laura Hapke, *Conventions of Denial in Prostitution: Late Nineteenth Century American Anti-Vice Narrative*, Ann Arbor, University of Michigan, Michigan Occasional Papers in Women's Studies, 1982.
6. Myna Trustram, *Marriage and the Victorian Army at Home: The Regulation of Soldiers' Relationships with Women and the Treatment of Soldiers' Wives*, Ph.D. thesis, Department of Social Administration, University of Bristol, July 1981, pp.357-58.
7. Myna Trustram, 'Distasteful and derogatory? Examining soldiers for venereal disease', in Feminist History Group, *Sexual Dynamics of History*, London, Pluto Press, forthcoming.
8. Trustram, 'Distasteful and derogatory?', *op. cit.*
9. For a discussion of the uses of paternalism in the maintenance of patriarchal structures such as factories, see Judy Lown, 'More a

patriarchy than a factory', in Eva Gamarnikow *et al.*, *Gender, Class and Work*, Heinemann 1983; Trustram, *Marriage and the Victorian Army at Home, op. cit.* p.358.

10. Trustram, *Marriage and the Victorian Army at Home, op. cit.* p.358.
11. Quoted in Murray (ed.), *op. cit.* p.436.
12. Judith Walkowitz, *Prostitution and Victorian Society*, London, Cambridge Unversity Press 1980, p.108. Walkowitz also analyses the political alliances within the repeal movement, alliances which expanded as the Acts themselves expanded to police women, not just for military security but also in the name of social order. See also Nancy Boyd, *Three Victorian Women Who Changed Their World: Josephine Butler, Octavia Hill and Florence Nightingale*, London and New York, Oxford University Press 1982.
13. Kathleen Barry has been especially persuasive in arguing that prostitution is an industry that involves male power used to *create* and *keep* women as prostitutes: Kathleen Barry, *Female Sexual Slavery*, New York, Avon 1979.
14. I was helped in thinking through these questions by a conversation with Myna Trustram, Bristol, May 1982.
15. I am grateful to Jennifer Gould for sharing with me her recent research on the British military's policies toward women in the first world war, in conversation, London, May 1982. Jennifer Gould's Ph.D. dissertation will discuss the wider attitudes and policies surrounding British women's service in the military: *The Woman's Corps: The Establishment of the Women's Military Services in Britain (World War I)*, London, forthcoming. See also Suzann Buckley, 'The failure to resolve the problem of venereal disease among the troops in Britain during World War I', in Brian Bond and Ian Roy (eds.), *War and Society: A Yearbook of Military History*, New York, Holmes and Meier 1977.
16. This is based on information collected and shared by Jennifer Gould, in conversation, London, May 1982.
17. John Ellis, *The Sharp End of War: The Fighting Man in World War II*, London, Corgi Books 1982, p.303.
18. *Ibid.* pp.303-04.
19. *Ibid.* p.304.
20. *Ibid.* p.379.
21. *Ibid.* p.308.
22. For a discussion of both the Paraguayan and the French militaries' policy—especially as the latter's officers' role as

procurers was revealed in a Corsican trial—see Kathleen Barry, *op. cit.* pp.67-70; 70-71.

23. This section is based on Karen Anderson's *Wartime Women: Sex Roles, Family Relations, and the Status of Women During World War II*, Westport, Connecticut, Greenwood Press 1981, pp.104-08.
24. Anderson, *op. cit.* p.108.
25. This second world war linkage between young women's sexuality and state security seems to have its parallel in the 1980s in the growing official alarm in the US over the 'epidemic' of teenage pregnancies. Bureaucratic proposals for control of promiscuous teenage girls are rationalised in terms of 'national security'.
26. This discussion is based on Mikiso Hane, *Peasants, Rebels and Outcasts: The Underside of Modern Japan*, New York, Pantheon 1982, pp.218-25. Hane notes that he, in turn, has relied on the research of a Japanese woman, Morisaki Kazue, author of *Karayuki-san*, Tokyo, Asahi, Shimbunsha, 1976. A feature film based on the life of one of these women sold into prostitution is 'Sandakan 8', 1979 (with English subtitles), distributed in the US by: Kino International Corporation Suite 340, 250 West 57th Street, NY, NY 10019.
27. Mikiso Hane, *op. cit.* p.225. One of the best-known stories is of a woman, sold by her brother, a landless tenant farmer, into debt bondage at the age of ten and forced to work as a prostitute in the town of Sandakan, Borneo, then a British colonial outpost and busy international trading post. Years later she was sought out by a Japanese woman anthropologist. But 1968 she was an old woman and back in Japan (though most *Karayuki* were held in such disrepute that they never were able to go home even if they did manage to get out of the brothels). Her story became the basis of the moving Japanese film, 'Sandakan 8'.
28. *Ibid.* p.225.
29. Susan Brownmiller, *Against Our Will*, New York, Bantam 1976, pp.94-95, describes the French military's system of mobile field brothels in Vietnam.
30. Barry, *op. cit.* p.71.
31. US veteran quoted in Mark Baker, *Nam*, New York, Quill Books, p.53.
32. Barry, *op. cit.* p.72.
33. This information was provided by a social scientist who acted as a consultant on race relations to the US military during the Vietnam

war, conversation with the author, June 1982.
34. Baker, *op. cit.* p.206.
35. *Ibid.* p.321.
36. US veteran quoted in Baker, *op. cit.* pp.208-09.
37. US soldier quoted in Baker, *op. cit.* pp.210-11. For a graphic case study of how the military hierarchy treated such instances of rape during the Vietnam war, see Daniel Lang, *Casualties of War*, New York, McGraw-Hill 1969. For first-hand accounts of what it was like being a black soldier in Vietnam, see Stanley Goff and Robert Sanders with Clark Smith, *Brothers: Black Soldiers in Nam*, San Francisco, Presidio Press 1982.
38. These questions were raised for me by Kathleen Barry in conversation, Cambridge, Massachusetts, September 1982.
39. Stanley Karnow, 'Saigon', *Atlantic Monthly*, November 1981, p.15.
40. 'Vietnam's proposals', *The Asian Record*, August 1982, p.7.
41. This account is based on research done by an anonymous Filipino woman and by Leopoldo M. Moselina, 'Olongapo's R&R industry: a sociological analysis of institutionalised prostitution'. *Makatao: An Interdisciplinary Journal for Students and Practitioners of the Social Sciences* (Asian Social Institute, Manila), vol.1, no.1, January-June 1981. See also *Southeast Asia Chronicle*, special issue no.78, April 1981. Excerpts from Moselina's report, as well as other reports on sex tourism in Thailand, the Philippines and South Korea, appear in 'Tourism and prostitution', *Isis International Bulletin*, no.13, 1979. Also, 'The Tourist Trap', a special issue of *Cultural Survival Quarterly* (11 Divinity Avenue, Cambridge, Massachusetts), vol.6, no.3, Summer 1982.
42. Paul Hutchcroft, 'In the shadow of Subic: castaways of an imperial navy', *Southeast Asia Chronicle*, no.83, 1982, pp.24-25. For a comparison of British and US military forces' effects on prostitution and their common reliance on racism, see David J. Pivar, 'The military, prostitution and colonial peoples: India and the Philippines, 1885-1917', *Journal of Sex Research*, vol.17, no.3, August 1981, pp.256-69.
43. Paul Hutchcroft, 'US bases, US bosses: Filipino workers at Clark and Subic', Tokyo, *AMPO*, vol.14, no.2, 1982, p.37.
44. Hutchcroft, *AMPO*, *op. cit.*
45. *Asia Record*, April 1982.
46. Moselina, *op. cit.* p.10.
47. *Ibid.* p.16.
48. Quoted in Moselina, *op. cit.* p.16.

49. *Loc. cit.*
50. Moselina, *op. cit.* pp.16-17.
51. *Ibid.* p.17.
52. Asian Women's Liberation, Tokyo, has put out a special issue on 'Prostitution Tourism', issue no.3, 1980. For more information also contact: Asian Women's Association, Poste Restante, Shibuya Post Office, Shibuya-ku, Tokyo 1,50, Japan.
53. For more information on women in the Philippines contact: Third World Movement Against the Exploitation of Women, PO Box 1434, Manila-2800, Philippines.
54. Bahai Zain, quoted in Maria C. Villariba, *The Philippines: Canvasses of Women in Crisis*, Change International Reports: Women and Society (29 Great James Street, London WC1N), 1982, p.10.
55. Khin Thitsa, *Providence and Prostitution: Image and Reality for Women in Buddhist Thailand*, Change International Reports, p.15, 1980.
56. *Loc. cit.*
57. John Pilger, 'Thailand: frogmarched into slavery', *New Statesman*, 20 August 1982, pp.10-12. See also, Tim Bond, *The Price of a Child*, London, Anti-Slavery Society 1980.
58. 'Navy R&R threatens Sri Lanka', *Women and Global Corporations*, American Friends Service Committee (1501 Cherry Street, Philadelphia, Pennsylvania 19102), vol.3, nos.1 and 2, p.A-9.
59. Brenda Thomas, 'Falklands: "brides and sweethearts" bite back', *Spare Rib*, August 1982, p.25.

3. Keeping the Home Fires Burning: Military Wives

1. General Sir John Adye in a confidential report to the British Secretary for War, 1881, quoted in Myna Trustram, *Marriage and the Victorian Army at Home: the Regulation of Soldiers' Relationships with Women and the Treatment of Soldiers' Wives*, Ph.D. dissertation, Department of Social Administration, University of Bristol, July 1981, p.63.
2. This came out as an especially significant factor obstructing military wives' identification with the women's movement in the mid-1970s: Lynne R. Dobrofsky and Constance T. Batterson, 'The military wife and feminism', *Signs*, vol.2, no.3, Spring 1977, pp.675-84.
3. In conversation with the author, April 1982.
4. Augustus Stafford MP, quoted by Trustram, *op. cit.* p.332.

5. Brenda Thomas, 'Falklands: "brides and sweethearts" bite back', *Spare Rib*, August 1982, p.24.
6. A good discussion of the historical evolution of this dilemma in Britain is Elizabeth Wilson, *Women and the Welfare State*, New York and London, Tavistock 1977. See also Elizabeth Wilson, 'According to our needs', *New Statesman*, 10 September 1982; Anna Coote and Beatrix Campbell, *Sweet Freedom*, London, Picador 1982. Also Zoe Fairbairns's novel, *Benefits*, London, Virago 1979.
7. Conversation with a civilian nurse who served military wives living in Colchester in the late 1970s, London, May 1982.
8. Jane Smith, 'Little box living', *Spare Rib*, August 1982, p.20.
9. *Ibid.* p.21.
10. Myna Trustram, *op. cit.*.
11. Eighteenth-century British recruiting patter quoted in Roy Palmer (ed.), *The Rambling Soldier*, Harmondsworth, Penguin 1977, p.9. See also Trustram, *op. cit.*
12. Trustram, *op. cit.* p.41.
13. *Ibid.* p.299.
14. Hilary Land, Department of Social Admininstration, University of Bristol, conversation with author, May 1982.
15. Trustram, *op. cit.* p.53.
16. *Ibid.* p.356.
17. Conversation with Shauna Whitworth, research director of the Military Family Resource Center (Springfield, Virginia), a non-governmental but Defense-Department-funded agency specialising in issues concerning US military wives and children, March 1982.
18. Her Majesty's Stationery Office, London 1976.
19. I am grateful to Hilary Land, who was a member of the 1974-76 Committee of Enquiry, for sharing her impressions with men, in conversation, Bristol, May 1982.
20. *Loc. cit.*
21. Conversation with Hilary Land and Miriam David, Department of Social Administration, University of Bristol, May 1982. Information on the relationship between social work and the military in Britain is admittedly sketchy here and deserves more systematic investigation. When I visited the National Institute of Social Work in London in May 1982—in the midst of the Falklands war, when the press and television were filled with stories about military wives and children—the staff told me that the Institute had virtually no connection with the military or with the few

social workers in the Ministry of Defence. One staff member, however, did wonder aloud whether the Falklands war would result in new official interest in expanding military social work.

22. This analysis of the early years of SSFA is based on the research by Myna Trustram, *op. cit.* pp.326-38.
23. John Draper, 'Clients in uniform', *Community Care*, 29 March 1979, p.27.
24. *Ibid.* p.26.
25. *Ibid.* p.27.
26. *Ibid.* p.27-28.
27. *Ibid.* p.27.
28. 'All Things Considered', National Public Television, WGBH Boston, Massachusetts, January 1982.
29. I am not really sure about this. We need to know more about *what* NATO's senior officers share with each other and what they work out on their own. My sense of a relatively low level of official trading of ideas about military wives comes from discussions with Hilary Land and Miriam David in Britain and Shauna Whitworth, of the Military Family Resources Center, in the US. They all believed there was surprisingly little official exchange of ideas and formulas *between* NATO commands in the area of military families and wives policies.
30. The *New York Times*, 31 July 1982.
31. In conversation with Cindy Chin, who helped administer the Boston University Programme, Cambridge, Massachusetts, May 1982.
32. The typically contradictory political role of social workers is discussed in Elizabeth Wilson, *Women and the Welfare State*, *op. cit.* See also Buchi Emecheta's novel, *In the Ditch*, Allison & Busby 1979.
33. A very interesting description of the limits imposed on a social or medical professional working inside the military is: Arlene Kaplan Daniels's analysis of the conflicting roles of the US military psychiatrist, a professional who works mostly with soldiers, not their families. Arlene Kaplan Daniels, 'The social construction of military psychiatric diagnoses', in Hans Peter Dreitzel (ed.), *Recent Sociology*, no.2, New York, Macmillan, 1970, pp.182-205; Polly Toynbee ' "Yes," says the psychiatrist, "we indoctrinate them in the forces. Otherwise they wouldn't fight".' The *Guardian*, November 1982. This interview describes British military psychiatrists' roles in the Falklands war.
34. *Military Family*, vol.2, no.2, March-April 1982, published by the

Military Family Resource Center (6501 Loisdale Court, Suite 900, Springfield, Virginia 22150).

35. *Military Family*, *op. cit.* p.8.
36. *Loc. cit.*
37. In conversation, March 1982.
38. Robert Hickman and Edna Jo Hunter, *Military Retention and Retirement—Reciprocal Family/Organizational Effects*, US Office of Naval Research, San Diego, California 1981.
39. *Soldier*, 11-24 January 1982, p.23.
40. Myna Trustram, *op. cit.* p.68.
41. Susie King Taylor, *Reminiscences of My Life in Camp with the 33rd United States Colored Troops*, (Boston, 1902), quoted in Gerda Learner (ed.), *Black Women in White America*, New York, Vintage Books 1973, pp.240-41.
42. *Ibid.* p.100-01.
43. William Jay Smith, *Army Brat*, New York, Penguin 1982, pp.50, 56-57.
44. See for instance, Edna Jo Hunter *et al.*, *Military Wife Adjustment: An Independent Dependent*, Office of Naval Research, San Diego, California 1981; Edna Jo Hunter and Melissa Pope, *Family Roles in Transition*, US Office of Naval Reseach, San Diego, California 1981.
45. Conversation with the author, Worcester, Massachusetts, October 1981.
46. 'Look after yourself', *Soldier*, 19 April-2 May 1982, p.23.
47. There is a similar quiet rebellion going on among wives of US Foreign Service officers, a rebellion which is causing considerable worry among the US State Department's upper echelon, since it is making foreign service officers harder to move from one overseas post to another.
48. Conversation with the author, March 1982.
49. Adrienne Rich, *Of Woman Born*, London, Virago; New York, Bantam 1977, p.11.
50. 'Abortion Is Illegal', lyrics by Bertolt Brecht, translated by Eric Bentley, quoted in notes of 'Change the World: It Needs It', Labor Records (PO Box 1262, Peter Stuyvesant Station, New York, 10009), 1982.
51. An especially subtle account of the complex trends in a 'post-war era' is contained in Elizabeth Wilson's *Only Halfway to Paradise: Women in Britain, 1945-1968*, London and New York, Tavistock 1980.

52. Among descriptions and analyses of post-war, pre-war and wartime motherhood ideologies are: Denise Riley, 'The free mothers: pronatalism and working mothers at the end of the last war in Britain', *History Workshop Journal*, no.11, Spring 1981, pp.59-119; Jane Lewis, 'The ideology and politics of birth control in inter-war England', *Women's Studies International Quarterly*, vol.2, 1979, pp.33-48; Elizabeth Wilson, *Only Halfway to Paradise*, *op. cit.*; Claudia Koonz, 'Mothers in the fatherland: women in the fatherland', in Renata Bridenthal and Claudia Koonz (eds.), *Becoming Visible: Women in European History*, Boston, Massachusetts, Houghton Mifflin 1977, pp.445-73; Bernice Glatzer Rosenthal, 'Lover on the tractor: women in the Russian Revolution and after', in Bridenthal and Koonz (eds.), *op. cit.* pp.370-99; Maggie McAndrew and Jo Peers, *The New Soviet Women—Model or Myth?* London Change International Reports: Women and Society 1981; 'Women in Eastern Europe', Special Issue of *Connexions: An International Women's Quarterly*, no.5, Summer 1982; Judith Jeffrey Howard, 'Patriot mothers in the post-risorgimento: women after the Italian revolution', in Carol R. Berkin and Clara M. Lovett (eds.), *Women, War and Revolution*, New York, Holmes and Meier 1980, pp.237-58; Nira Yuval Davis, *Israeli Women and Men: Divisions Behind the Unity*, London, Change International Reports: Women and Society 1982; Wayne Roberts, ' "Rocking the cradle for the world": the new woman and maternal feminism', Toronto, 1877-1914', in Linda Keathy (ed.), *A Not Unreasonable Claim: Women and Reform in Canada*, Toronto, The Women's Press 1979, pp.15-46; Leila J. Rupp, *Mobilizing Women for War: German and American Propaganda, 1939-1945*, Princeton University Press 1978.
53. John Faris, 'The all-volunteer force: recruitment from military families', *Armed Forces and Society*, Summer 1981, p.545.
54. Burton Hacker, 'Women and military institutions in early modern Europe: a reconnaissance', *Signs*, vol.6, no.4, Summer 1981, p.652.
55. The US military is facing a rising number of 'military single parents'. By 1981 there were 27,000 single parents in the US Army, one-third of them women. It is questionable whether they are playing the same 'military mothering' role that military wives traditionally have been expected to play.
56. Nancy L. Young, 'The women who pull double duty', *Off Duty Magazine*, America Issue, May 1981, pp.20-21.
57. Franklin Pinch, 'Military manpower and social change', *Armed*

Forces and Society, vol.8, no.4, Summer 1982, p.584. Some military officials define many of these 'soldier-to-soldier' marriages as marriages of convenience, performed only to acquire certain married soldiers' benefits, such as getting out of the barracks; once off base, the two soldiers don't even live with each other: *Youth Policy*, vol.3, no.10, October 1981, pp.67-69.

58. Member of an 1866 British Commission on Recruiting, quoted in Trustram, *op. cit.* p.50.
59. *Ibid.* p.49.
60. Conversation with a civilian nurse who had worked on a British army base where a sizeable number of Maltese military wives lived. London, May 1980.
61. John Draper, *op. cit.* p.27.
62. This black woman is now a social science researcher; she shared these impressions, in conversation, Wingspread, Wisconsin, 5 June 1982.
63. Richard Hope, in conversation with the author, Wingspread, Wisconsin, 5 June 1982.
64. Bok-Lim C. Kim, Army Izuno Okamura, Naomi Ozawa, Virginia Forrest, *Women in Shadows: A Handbook for Service Providers Working With Asian Wives of US Military Personnel*, National Committee Concerned with Asian Wives of US Servicemen (964 La Jolla Rancho Road, La Jolla, California 92037).
65. Kim quoted in Bok-Lim C. Kim *et al.*, *op. cit.* p.15.
66. Kim, *op. cit.* p.53.
67. Its headquarters are 964 La Jolla Rancho Road, La Jolla, California 92037.
68. Kim, *op. cit.* p.87.
69. The *New York Times*, 13 August 1982.
70. 'Falkland fund: inequality even in death', *The Economist*, 7 August 1982. Myna Trustram discusses the variations in Britain philanthropic outpouring that accompanied different wars in *Marriage and the British Victorian Army at Home*, *op. cit.* p.311.
71. *Worcester Sunday Telegram*, Massachusetts, 18 March 1982.
72. EXPOSE (PO Box 3269, Falls Church, Virginia 22043), *Newsletter*, February 1982.
73. Member of EXPOSE in conversation with the author, March 1982. In July 1982, the US House of Representatives passed the Uniformed Services Former Spouses' Protection Act, which returned to the state courts the question of divorce and military benefits. Congressional Representative Patricia Schroeder, a key

supporter of the bill, had been in close communication with the women from EXPOSE. The *New York Times*, 29 July 1982.

74. Conversation with the author, March 1982.
75. Conversation with the author, March 1982.
76. William Jay Smith, *op. cit.* p.117.
77. Kim *et al.*, *op. cit.* p.53.
78. Carson McCullers, *Reflections in a Golden Eye*, Harmondsworth, Penguin 1981.
79. This admittedly speculative analysis was shared with me in conversation by Jalna Hanmer, long active in Britain's Women's Aid, Cambridge, Massachusetts, 13 August 1982.
80. Lillian Tetzlaff, in correspondence, October 1982.
81. Lois A. West, William M. Turner and Ellen Dunwoody, *Wife Abuse in the Armed Forces*, Washington, DC, Center for Women Policy Studies (2000 P Street NW, Suite 508, Washington, DC 20036), 1981, p.4. This study was done under contract for the US Justice Department. One of the most thorough discussions of wife battering and the movement to protect women, drawing especially on the US experience, is Susan Schecter, *Women and Male Violence: The Visions and Struggles of the Battered Women's Movement*, Boston, Massachusetts, South End Press; London, Pluto Press 1983.
82. West *et al.*, *op. cit.*
83. *Hartford Courant*, 17 October 1982. The organisation running the men's anger control group on the Navy base at Groton is the Women's Emergency Shelter in Waterbury, Connecticut.
84. These responses appear in the appendix of West *et al.*, *op. cit.* p.188.
85. West, *op. cit.* p.182.
86. *Loc. cit.*

4. Nursing the Military

1. Burton Hacker, 'Women and military institutions in early modern Europe: a reconnaissance', *Signs*, vol.6, no.4, Summer 1981, p.657.
2. Hacker, *op. cit.* p.662.
3. *Loc. cit.*
4. Eva Gamarnikow, 'Sexual division of labour: the case of nursing', in Annette Kuhn and Ann Maria Wolpe (eds.), *Feminism and Materialism*, London and Boston, Routledge & Kegan Paul 1978. See also Celia Davis (ed.), *Rewriting Nursing History*, Croom Helm 1980.

5. Contemporary account by one of the nurses recruited to work with Nightingale in the Crimea, quoted in 'Capabilities and disabilities of women', *Westminister Review*, January 1909, pp.31-32.
6. This account is drawn from Richard Stites's history of Russian feminism in the nineteenth and early twentieth centuries, *The Women's Liberation Movement in Russia*, Princeton University Press 1978.
7. Quoted by Stites, *op. cit.* p.30.
8. Lawrence James, *Crimea 1854-56*, London, Hayes Kennedy 1981, p.126.
9. The development of French military use of women is described by French military sociologist Michel Martin in *Armed Forces and Society*, vol.8, no.2, Winter 1982.
10. For more on Florence Nightingale, especially her relationship to feminism, see Elaine Showalter, *Signs*, Summer 1981; Susan B. Reverby, *History of Nursing: 1880-1940*, Ph.D, dissertation, Boston University 1982. F.B. Smith, *Florence Nightingale: Reputation and Power*, New York, St Martin's Press 1982.
11. Trustram, *Marriage and the Victorian Army at Home*, Ph.D. thesis, University of Bristol, July 1981, chapter 1.
12. Louisa May Alcott, 'Obtaining Supplies', the first of the short stories collected in Alcott's *Hospital Sketches*, New York, Sagamore Press 1957 (originally published in 1863), p.22.
13. Gerda Lerner, *The Female Experience: An American Documentary*, Indianapolis, Indiana, Bobbs-Merrill, 1977, p.180.
14. Quoted in Rosalyn Baxandall, Linda Gordon and Susan Reverby (eds.), *America's Working Women: A Documentary History, 1600 to the Present*, New York, Vintage Books, 1976, pp.75-76. For the experiences of a woman nurse in the civil war, who fought for hospital reform and use of women, see John Brumgardt (ed.) *Civil War Nurse: The Diary and Letters of Hannah Ropes*, Knoxville, Tennessee, University of Tennessee Press 1982.
15. An intriguing parallel to the process of feminising military nursing has been uncovered by Terry Litterest, an American occupational therapist. Wondering why 'OT' traditionally has been so politically weak, she began to dig into its origins. She discovered that occupational therapy was launched as a profession in the midst of the first world war when a US general wrote home from Europe asking that a contingent of upper-class young women be organised to serve the troops as unpaid volunteers. Their job was

to teach useful skills to seriously wounded soldiers. The US military commanders presumed that women would be best suited to this task because such teaching, it was thought, depended on the OT's ability to uplift the morale of the male troops. They also presumed that OT could be done with minimal training and even less pay. Thus it was alleged appropriate only for affluent, single young women. Five decades after the first world war, Terry Litterest believes, occupational therapists still are being undermined in their efforts to gain greater respect, pay, and policy influence by these original presumptions of a gender-structured military. Conversations with Terry Litterest (Department of Occupational Therapy, Tufts University, Medford, Massachusetts), Cambridge, Massachusetts, Spring 1982.

16. Lesley Merryfinch contributed these insights at a conference of feminists concerned with women in NATO militaries held in Amsterdam in April 1981. The book resulting from the conference is *Loaded Questions: Women in the Militaries*, edited by Wendy Chapkis, Transnational Institute, 20 Paulus Potter Straat, Amsterdam, Holland, 1981, (distributors, London: Pluto Press; Washington, DC: Institute of Policy Studies).
17. This political stance was clearly anticipated by senior women officers from Britain's nursing services at a special seminar on 'Women in the British Military' held under the auspices of the Royal United Services Institute, London, 1978, and attended by male and female officers from several NATO forces as well as from Israel. Excerpts appear in the RUSI *Journal*, 1979.
18. Lorraine Underwood, 'Minority Women and the Military', Women's Equity Action League, Washington, DC, June 1979.
19. I have tried to trace this process as it affects male soldiers in Britain, US, Soviet Union, South Africa, Canada and elsewhere in *Ethnic Soldiers*, Penguin 1980; University of Georgia Press 1980; and in *Police, Military and Ethnicity*, Transaction Books 1980.
20. Darlene Clark Hines (Purdue University), 'Mabel Seaton Stater: The Integration of Black Nurses into the Armed Forces, World War II', Berkshire Conference of Women Historians, Vassar College, June 1981, p.9.
21. This and the quotation that follows come from Hines, *op. cit.*
22. In 1982, the head of the US Army Nurses Corps is a black woman, Hazel Johnson.
23. Vera Brittain, *Testament of Youth*, originally published in 1933, recently has been reissued in Britain by Virago, 1978; and in the

US by Westview Books 1980.
24. Patricia L. Walsh, *Forever Sad the Heart*, New York, Avon 1982.
25. Quoted in a paper Margaret Scobey and Philip Kalish presented to the Inter-University Seminar on Armed Forces and Society, a meeting ground of academic social scientists and military personnel specialists in the US, Britain and other NATO countries, Chicago, Illinois, October 1980.
26. Kalish and Scobey, *op. cit.* p.1.
27. The *Observer*, 25 May 1982.
28. *Navy News*, May 1982, p.3.
29. 'Maxi mash makes it grim', *Soldier*, 11 January 1982, pp.14-15.
30. The *Washington Post*, 25 March 1981.
31. The *Washington Post*, 25 March 1981.
32. The *Washington Post*, 25 March 1981. The following quotations are from the same article. Since then, Lynda Van Devanter has published her own account: *Home Before Morning*, New York, Beaufort Books 1983.
33. David Grumwald, 'Crying need', *Parade Magazine*, The *Boston Globe*, 23 August 1981. A longer interview with Gayle Smith appears in: Al Santoli, *Everything We Had: An Oral History of the Vietnam War*, New York, Bantam 1981. US Vietnam war nurses are also interviewed in Mark Baker, *Nam*, New York, Quill Books 1982.
34. 'Changes in the US Army and Their Impact on Leadership', an unpublished report by David E. Hossen, an officer in the US Army Labor Services Agency, for the Clark University Public Administration Program, July 1981. He cited: US Department of the Army Historical Survey, FY, 1982. I am grateful to Charles Coleman of Clark University for sharing this paper with me.
35. Marilyn Flower and Liz Jacobs, 'War on the wards: making the unthinkable appear routine', *Science for the People*, vol.14, no.3, May-June 1982, pp.8-14. Also: National Public Radio, 'All Things Considered', 7 April 1982.
36. Duncan Campbell, 'Red Cross to mop up after bomb', *New Statesman*, 26 February 1982, p.4.
37. One such anti-nuclear nurses' group is Nurses' Alliance for the Prevention of Nuclear War, Box 319, Chestnut Hill, Massachusetts 02167.

5. 'Some of the Best Soldiers Wear Lipstick'

1. Robert Graves speculates that it is more likely that 'Amazon'

derives from the Armenian word for 'Moon women'; Graves, *Greek Myths*, vol.2, Harmondsworth, Penguin 1955, p.355. I am indebted to Lois Brynes for sharing her research on the origins and evolution of the Amazon myths.

2. One of the most thorough accounts of the history of the Amazon myth is in Simon Shepherd, *Amazons and Warrior Women: Varieties of Feminism in Seventeenth-Century Drama*, New York, St Martin's Press 1981.
3. *Loc. cit.*
4. Mary Daly, *Gyn/Ecology: The Metaphysics of Radical Feminism*, Massachusetts, Beacon Press 1978; Monique Wittig, *Les Guerrilles*, New York, Avon 1973.
5. I am indebted to Serena Hilsinger and Lois Brynes for making sure I visited the Bassae room in the British Museum.
6. Vita Sackville-West, *Saint Joan of Arc*, London, Cobden-Sanderson 1936, pp.169, 181. More contemporary and scholarly investigations of Joan of Arc are: Frances Geis, *Joan of Arc: The Legend and the Reality*, New York, Harper and Row 1981; Marina Warner, *Saint Joan of Arc*, New York, Alfred A. Knopf 1981.
7. Quoted by Geis, *op. cit.* p.192.
8. *Loc. cit.*
9. Geis, *op. cit.* p.167, pp.184ff., 204.
10. Nancy Goldman, 'The Utilization of Women in Combat: The Armed Forces of Great Britain, World War I and World War II', Interuniversity Seminar on Armed Forces and Society, University of Chicago, unpublished manuscript, 1978.
11. 'The Drum Major', reprinted in Roy Palmer (ed.), *The Rambling Soldier*, Harmondsworth, Penguin 1977, p.101.
12. *Ibid.* p.102.
13. *Ibid.* pp.165-66.
14. Lillian Faderman, *Surpassing the Love of Men*, New York, William Morrow 1981, pp.53-54.
15. *Ibid.* pp.51-52.
16. *Ibid.* p.58-60.
17. Linda Grant DePaw, 'Women in combat: the revolutionary war experience', *Armed Forces and Society*, vol.2, no.21, Winter 1981, p.216.
18. Georgina Natzio, 'The future of woman in the armed forces', *Journal of the Royal United Services Institute*, December 1978, vol.123, no.4, p.26.

19. Nancy Loring Goldman and Richard Stites, 'Great Britain and the World Wars' in Nancy Loring Goldman (ed.), *Female Soldiers: Combatants or Non-Combatants*, Westport, Connecticut, and London, Greenwood Press 1982, pp.21-46. Jennifer Gould is currently writing a dissertation on British women in the army in the first world war, London. For a similar tale of twists and turns around the definition of combat, see Sally Van Wagen Keil's history of US women pilots in the second world war, *Those Wonderful Women in Their Flying Machines*, New York, Rawson, Wade 1979.
20. Perhaps the fullest expression of support for women being able to gain equality and 'first-class citizenship' through participation in their country's military is found in the legal brief that the National Organization for Women presented to the US Supreme Court in March 1981 as part of a challenge to the recently re-instituted military registration law which applied exclusively to young men. The challenge was brought on behalf of men, who argued that such one-sex conscription violated men's constitutional rights. But it was supported by the national leadership of NOW, which claimed the law perpetuated US women's second-class citizenship. NOW's brief can be obtained from: NOW Legal Defense and Educational Fund, 132 West 42nd Street, New York, NY 10036.

    A feminist position quite different from that of the equal opportunity advocates is contained in Wendy Chapkis (ed.), *Loaded Questions: Women in the Military*, Transnational Institute, 20 Paulus Potter Straat, Amsterdam, Holland, 1981, (distributors, London: Pluto Press; Washington, DC: Institute of Policy Studies).
21. These figures were cited in the *New York Times*, 19 September 1982. For critical discussions of current nuclear strategic thinking, see Dan Smith, *The Defence of the Realm in the 1980s*, London, Croom Helm 1980; E.P. Thompson and Dan Smith, *Protest and Survive*, Harmondsworth, Penguin, and New York Monthly Review Press, 1980 and 1981; Michael Clark and Majorie Mowlam (eds.), *Debate on Disarmament*, London and Boston, Routledge & Kegan Paul 1982.
22. A good overview of the Reagan administration's conventional-cum-nuclear military plan is Michael T. Klare, 'The Weinberger revolution', *Inquiry*, September 1982.
23. 'Benign neglect', *Newsletter*, no.152, November 1982, Resist (38 Union Square, Somerville, Massachusetts 02143), p.1.

24. Karin Hempel-Soos, 'Karbolmauschen und Stopselmadchen', *Die Zeit*, 9 July 1982; interview with Sibylle Plogstedt, an editor of West Germany's feminist magazine *Courage*, 'German feminism discussed', *Off Our Backs*, October 1982, pp.8-9; conversation with Ulrich Albrecht, UNESCO, Paris, 18 October 1982.
25. A good summary of the discussion of manpower problems is in Franklin Pinch, 'Military manpower and social change', *Armed Forces and Society*, vol.8, no.4, Summer 1982. NATO Military Committee, *Women in the NATO Forces*, NATO headquarters, Brussels 1981 (available from US Department of Defense).
27. Another source of cross-national comparative information on women in militaries is: Nancy Loring Goldman (ed.), *Female Soldiers—Combatant or Non-Combatants: Historical and Contemporary Perspectives*, Westport, Connecticut, Greenwood Press 1982. Eastern European militaries are included in this survey. See also a special issue on 'Women and Men's Wars' of *Women Studies International Forum*, vol.5, no.3/4, 1982, edited by Judith Steihm and published by Pergamon Press, Oxford.
28. International Institute for Strategic Studies, *The Military Balance, 1981-1982*, London 1981, pp.31-33.
29. *Ibid*. p.35.
30. *Ibid*. p.36.
31. A group of feminists met in Amsterdam in April 1981 to consider how NATO militaries used women. In our resultant book, we tried to look specifically at NATO as well as at the more general questions concerning women in the military: Wendy Chapkis (ed.), *Loaded Questions: Women in the Military, op. cit.*
32. Mary Lee Settle, *All the Brave Promises*, New York, Ballantine Books 1980, p.40.
33. Helen Horigan, in conversation, Cambridge, Massachusetts, November 1982; she is currently writing about her experiences for a forthcoming collection by and about lesbian ex-nuns: Rosemary Curb and Nancy Manahan (eds.), *Lesbian Nuns Breaking Silence*, Tallahasee, Florida, Naiad Press, forthcoming.
34. Linda Haymes, 'Why women join the military', *Off Our Backs*, July 1981, p.17.
35. *Ibid*. p.13. A new group has organised to support women military veterans in the US (of whom there are 742,000 in 1982): Women's Veterans Information Network, PO Box 2894, Oakland, California 94608.
36. Conversation with Brenda Moore, now a Ph.D. student at the

University of Chicago, at 'Blacks in the Military Conference', Wingspread, Wisconsin, June 1982.

37. Michel Martin in *Armed Forces and Society* ,vol.8, no.2, Winter 1982.
38. Lorraine Underwood, 'Minority women and the military', Women's Equity Action League (805 15th Street NW, Washington, DC 20005), June 1979. Also: *Black Women in the Armed Forces: A Pictorial History*, Hampton, Virginia, Hampton Institute, Carver Publishing 1975.
39. These figures are from the US Department of Defense Equal Opportunity Office, June 1982, supplied by the Equal Opportunity Office, Office of the Assistant Secretary of Defense (Manpower), 15 October 1982. Such figures are published in June and December of each year and are available to the public upon request.
40. Gloria T. Hull, Patricia Bell Scott and Barbara Smith (eds.), *All the Women Are White, All the Blacks Are Men, But Some of Us Are Brave: Black Women Studies*, Old Westbury, New York, Feminist Press 1982.
41. A new book assessing the status and issue of blacks in the US military (Edwin Dorn, ed., *Who Defend America? Essays on Blacks in the Armed Forces*) is to be published by a black research institute: the Joint Center for Political Studies, 1301 Pennsylvania Avenue NW, Washington, DC, 20004. My own effort to think through the connections between racism and sexism appears in this volume. 'Race and sex in military manpower strategies: comparative lessons from history'.
42. Major Robert L. Nabors, 'Women in the Army: do they measure up?', *Military Review*, October 1982, pp.50-61. Nabors reveals the weakness in each of the standard official arguments for limiting women.
43. This interesting speculation was offered by Brenda Moore, during the 'Blacks in the Military Conference', Wingspread, Wisconsin, June 1982.
44. Nabors, *op. cit.*
45. Interestingly, many men who are firefighters define what they do as 'combat'. Karen Stabiner, 'The storm over women fire fighters', *New York Times Magazine*, 26 September 1982.
46. Judith Steihm has traced this argument. See her book on the introduction of women cadets into the US Air Force Academy in the 1970s: *Bring the Men and Women*, Berkeley, University of California Press 1981, pp.147-77.

47. Winifred Holtby, *Women and a Changing Civilization*, Chicago, Illinois, Academy Press Ltd 1978, pp.123-24.
48. Helen Rogan found this to be the experience of women in the post-second world war army: *Mixed Company*, New York, Putnam 1981, pp.154-55. Rogan's book uses interviews with women to trace the discrimination against women in the US army. She, like many NOW activists, is concerned about equality in the military rather than with militarism itself. Another recent study by a woman historian of the experiences of US women in uniform in the second world war has discovered that military commanders were so worried about public rumours that all army women were sexually promiscuous—with men—that they refused to permit distribution of contraceptives to women personnel, although at the same time such devices were being officially distributed to men: Susan M. Hartmann, *The Home Front and Beyond: American Women in the 1940s*, Boston, Massachusetts, Twayne Publishers 1982, p.39.
49. Derived from figures in an Associated Press report from London, published in *Gay Community News*, Boston, Massachusetts, 27 February 1980; also Jan Parker, 'When you're out, you're out', *Spare Rib*, June 1982, p.6.
50. Especially helpful in working through these contradictions are Lillian Faderman, *Surpassing the Love of Men*, *op. cit.*; Annabel Faraday, 'Liberating lesbian research' in Kenneth Plummer (ed.), *The Making of the Modern Homosexual*, London, Hutchinson 1981, pp.112-29; Adrienne Rich, 'Compulsory heterosexuality and lesbian existence', *Signs*, vol.5, no.4, Summer 1980.
51. *Gay News*, London, no.240, 13-26 May 1982. A new study of gay male officers in the history of the British armed forces is: Frank M. Richardson, *Mars Without Venus: A Study of Some Homosexual Generals*, Edinburgh, Scotland, William Blackwood Publishers 1982 (US distributor, Merrimack Book Service, New Salem, New Hampshire).
52. See *New Statesman*, 30 July 1982, p.2 for argument against the 1967 military exception.
53. Jan Parker, *op. cit.* pp.7-8.
54. *Ibid.*
55. *Ibid.* p.33.
56. Jan Parker *op. cit.* p.33. Writing anonymously to *Spare Rib* after the publication of the three women's story, another lesbian in the WRAC explained, 'Being a lesbian is very difficult. I just say I'm

celibate—blokes give up and reckon I'm queer anyway—but they still haven't got the proof and I don't have to tolerate their wandering hands. The only thing I have to do now is to hide my sexuality and when the time is right tell the army what I think of their system!' 'Letters', *Spare Rib*, August 1982, p.30.

57. *Womanews*, New York, September 1981, p.6.
58. 'Army Dykes', *Off Our Backs*, November 1980, p.9.
59. 'Gay policy leaves military much discretion', *Youth Policy*, vol.3, no.10, October 1981, pp.63-64. At the same time as the US military appears to be increasing its surveillance of suspected lesbians in the ranks, it is becoming concerned about the logistical complexities involved in retaining women soldiers married to male soldiers. By the end of 1981, 'as many as 25 per cent of serving female personnel are married to serving males'. Pinch, *op. cit.* p.584.
60. Quoted in the *New York Times*, 25 July 1982.
61. *Loc. cit.*
62. The following account is based on a series of conversations I participated in with women enlisted sailors aboard a US navy ship docked in an East Coast port. The women wanted their story to be told but asked that their identities and that of their ship be concealed in order to protect those women who still are trying to stay in the navy. Both straight and lesbian women took part in these conversations, September-November 1982.
63. Nina Gilden, *Countering Sexual Harassment: Theory and Applications for the Department of Defense*, prepared for the Deputy Assistant for Defense (for Equal Opportunity), Washington, DC, March 1981.
64. A young women enlisted soldier at Fort Benning, Georgia, quoted in the *Boston Globe*, 29 September 1979. For more extensive interviews with US military women about their experience of harassment, as well as the Pentagon's response to such reports of abuse, see 'Women in the Military', Hearings before the Personnel Subcommittee of the Committee on Armed Services', US House of Representatives, November 1979, Washington, DC Printing Office 1981 (or write directly to the congressional subcommittee).
65. Interview with the author, Boston, Massachusetts, October 1982.
66. Mary Lee Settle, *op. cit.* pp.152-53.
67. The *Boston Globe*, 29 September 1979.
68. The *International Herald Tribune*, 7 March 1980.

69. Quoted in Nina Gilden, *op. cit.* Retired General Jeanne Holm's own book is: *Women in the Military: An Unfinished Revolution*, San Francisco, California, Presidio Press 1982.
70. The *New York Times*, 10 June 1982.
71. *Gay Community News*, Boston, Massachusetts, 16 October 1982.
72. Pinch, *op. cit.* pp.585-86.
73. Quoted in 'The new army', *US News and World Report*, 20 September 1982, p.59. See also Deborah Shapley, 'The army new fighting doctrine', *New York Times Magazine*, 28 November 1982, pp.36-42.
74. Michel Martin, a French sociologist writing in *Armed Forces and Society*, vol.8, no.2, Winter 1982, p.317.
75. I am grateful to Nina Gilden for describing to me the 'tooth-to-tail ratio' and for alerting me to the comparative differences among the services: in conversation, Worcester, Massachusetts, October 1981.
76. Interview with the author, Brighton, Sussex, August 1981.
77. United Kingdom, *Statement on the Defence Estimates*, vol.II, Cmnd 8212-II, London: Her Majesty's Stationery Office, April 1981, p.29. I am grateful to Chris Smith of ADIU, University of Sussex, for sharing this information with me.
78. The *Guardian*, 20 December 1980. I am grateful to Lesley Merryfinch for much of this information.
79. Excerpts from 'The Supreme Court Opinions on Limiting the Military Draft to Men', *The New York Times*, 26 June 1981.
80. Michael Wright, 'The Marine Corps Faces the Future', *New York Times Magazine*, 20 June 1980, p.73.
81. *Women's Report*, London, vol.7, no.3, April-May 1979, p.8.
82. *Loc. cit.* For further debate on the issue, see Hansard, 2 December, pp.193-94.
83. *Loc. cit.*
84. *Navy News*, Ministry of Defence, London, May 1982.
85. For a description of the current sexual division of labour in the Israeli military and an analysis of how it has evolved over the last 40 years, see: Nira Yuval-Davis, 'The Israeli example', in Wendy Chapkis (ed.), *Loaded Questions*, *op. cit.* pp.73-78; Nira Yuval-Davis, *Israeli Women and Men: Divisions Behind the Unity* , Change International Reports: Women and Society, London 1981.
86. 'To Be a Woman Soldier', Shuli Eshel, director, 1981. Information on this provocative film is available from: Shuli Eshel, 42 Shenkin Street, Givatayim 53304, Israel.

87. Office of the Assistant Secretary of Defense (Manpower, Reserve Affairs and Logistics), US Department of Defense, *Background Review: Women in the Military*, Washington, DC, October 1981.
88. Patricia Schroeder, 'Patriotism is not sex specific', *Women's Political Times*, January 1982. Patricia Schroeder is a Democratic Congressional Representative from Colorado and one of the closest monitors of sexual discrimination information clearing house from the same equal opportunity perspective is the Women's Equal Action League (WEAL), (805 15th Street NW, Suite 822, Washington, DC 20005). A new journal intended to monitor and trace the roles of women and the military is: *Minerva: Quarterly Report on Women and the Military*, Linda Grant DePauw, Editor, 1101 S. Arlington Ridge Road, Arlington, Virginia.
89. Quoted in the *Washington Post*, 3 October 1982.
90. Reports of the Defense Department's restriction of jobs open to women include: *The New York Times*, 29 August 1982; *AR News*, Army News Service, Washington, DC, 2 September 1982; *Army Times*, 6 September 1982; Press Conference transcript of appearance of Assistant Secretary of Defense Lawrence Korb on 26 August 1982, Department of Defense Public Relations Office, Washington, DC.
91. The *New York Times*, 29 August 1982.
92. President Reagan's Secretary of Defense, Casper Weinberger, denied that it was unemployment that was temporarily solving his manpower problems. Instead, 'It is again an honor to wear the uniform.' *International Herald Tribune*, 20 October 1982. For a less sanguine analysis of recruitment trends, see the *New York Times*, 13 October 1982.
93. The *Guardian*, 14 October 1982.
94. Ian McEwan, *The Imitation Game*, London: Jonathan Cape 1981; Picador 1982.

6. Women in Liberation Armies

1. Mary Beth Norton, *Liberty's Daughters: The Revolutionary Experience of American Women, 1750-1800*, Boston, Massachusetts, Little Brown 1981; Linda Kerber, *Women of the Republic: Intellect and Ideology in Revolutionary America*, Chapel Hill, North Caroline, University of North Carolina 1980.
2. Darline Gay Levy and Harriet Brauson Applewhite, 'Women of the popular classes in revolutionary Paris, 1789-1795', Mary

Durham Johnson, 'Old wine in new bottles: the institutional changes for women of the people during the French Revolution', Barbara Corrado Pope, 'Revolution and retreat: upper-class French women after 1789', all in: Carol R. Berkin and Clare M. Lovett (eds.), *Women, War and Revolution*, New York and London, Holmes and Meier 1980.

3. For descriptions of women's roles in the Russian Revolution and their post-war experiences, see: Barbara Evans Clements, *Bolshevik Feminist*, Bloomington, Indiana, Indiana University Press 1980; Cathy Porter, *Alexandra Kollantai*, London, Virago 1980; Richard Stites, *The Women's Liberation Movement in Russia*, Princeton University Press 1978; Beatrice Brodsky Farningworth, 'Communist feminism', in Berkin and Lovett (eds.), *op. cit.* pp.145-64; Ann Eliot Griese and Richard Stites, 'Russia: revolution and war', in Nancy Loring Goldman (ed.), *Female Soldiers—Combatants or Non-Combatants: Historical and Contemporary Perspectives*, Westport, Connecticut, and London, Greenwood Press 1982.
4. Susan Woodward, Williams College, presents these findings in her paper presented at a Conference on Women in Eastern Europe, Washington, DC, December 1981. On women partisan fighters, see also: Barbara Jancar, 'Yugoslavian War of Resistance', in Nancy Loring Goldman (ed.), *op. cit.* pp.85-106.
5. Delia Davin, *Woman-Work: Women and the Party in Revolutionary China*, London, Oxford University Press 1979, pp.44-45.
6. *Loc. cit.*
7. *Ibid.* pp.22-23. Delia Davin has a brief but fascinating account of the Chinese Communist Party's attempt to design particular policies to mobilise and support the *wives* of soldiers who joined the Red Army in its earliest build-up in the period of the Jianzi Soviet in the early 1930s. The party's Women's Association was given special responsibility for aiding soldiers' 'dependents' to insure the peasant farms, now short of male labour, would continue to produce food crucial to the survival of the army.
8. Martin Binkin and Shirley Back, *Women and the Military*, Washington, DC, Brookings Institute 1977, p.130.
9. See Stephanie Urdang, *Fighting Two Colonialisms: Women in Guinea-Bissau*, New York, Monthly Review Press 1979; Judy Kimble's review is in *Feminist Review*, no.8, 1981. Also: Stephanie Urdang, ' "Our people will never be free until the women are free as well," women in Guinea-Bissau', *Third World*

Forum (special issue on women in liberation movements), vol.2, no.4, May-July 1976 (Box 159, Stn. G, Montreal, Canada), pp.23-30.

10. Urdang, *op. cit.*; Kimble, *op. cit.*
11. 'Zimbabwe: against the ideology of power', *Isis International Bulletin*, Fall 1981, special issue on women in national liberation movements (including articles on El Salvador, Eritrea, Philippines). A series of interviews with Zimbabwean women who were in the guerrilla forces is available on tape: 'Women Freedom Fighters of Zimbabwe', National Public Radio, 1982 (2025 M Street NW, Washington, DC 20036).

    A recent novel by Nigerian writer Buchi Emecheta, *Destination Biafra*, Allison & Busby 1982, shows how sexual politics are as important as the sexual divisions of labour in shaping women's military experience in periods of nationalism and civil war. Emecheta's heroine is an Oxford-trained Nigerian woman who joined the military during Nigeria's civil war during the 1960s.
12. Michael Rezendes, 'After independence: an African women's movement jolts to a start', The *Boston Phoenix*, 24 August 1982, no.6. In 1982, two politically prominent women in Zimbabwe, the Minister of Community Development and her Deputy Minister, protested their government's official participation in the 'Miss World Contest'. They contended that there should be no 'Miss Zimbabwe', that Zimbabwean women died fighting for their country's liberation and for an end to racist oppression and that the institutionalisation of a 'Miss Zimbabwe' contradicted the principles women had fought for. Despite their protest, the Mugabe government sponsored a 'Miss Zimbabwe' and sent her to London to compete: *Off Our Backs*, April 1982, p.14.
13. The *New York Times* ,17 January 1982. See also Nira Yuval-Davis, *Israeli Women and Men*, Change International Reports, London 1981.
14. Rita Arditti and Estelle Disch, 'Israeli Feminism', *Off Our Backs*, November 1982, pp.8-9. From their discussions with Israeli feminist activists, Arditti's and Disch's analysis suggests that the most effective way to challenge Israeli militarisation is to support Israeli feminism.
15. 'Update: Vietnam', *Southeast Asia Chronicle*, no.83, April 1982, p.27.
16. Jane Hawksley, in conversation, May 1982.
17. Maxine Molyneaux, 'Socialist societies old and new: progress

towards women's emancipation', *Feminist Review*, no.8, 1981; see also her article 'Women and revolution in the People's Democratic Republic of Yemen', *Feminist Review*, no.1, 1979; I am indebted to Jane Hawksley for pointing out to me the theoretical implications of the 'woman fighter with rifle and baby' symbol.

18. Maxine Molyneaux, 'Algeria: socialism for men only?', *Spare Rib*, April 1982. Another helpful analysis of women's struggles for emancipation within a national liberation movement is: Judy Kimble and Elaine Unterhalter, ' "We opened the road for you, you must go forward"—ANC women's struggles, 1912-1982', *Feminist Review*, no.12, Fall 1982, pp.11-36.
19. 'Algerian feminists defeat new family code', *Off Our Backs*, June 1982, p.10.
20. 'Algerian women: myths and liberation', *Connexions: An International Women's Quarterly*, no.2, Fall 1981, p.21. On women fighters, see also Djamila Amrane, 'Algeria: anti-colonial war', in Nancy Loring Goldman (ed.), *op. cit.* pp.123-36.
21. Quoted in 'Women of Palestine: fences, laws, and border patrols', *Connexions: An International Women's Quarterly*, no.2, Fall 1981, p.23. See also Ingela Bendt and James Dowing, *We Shall Return—Women of Palestine*, London, Zed, and Westport, Connecticut, Lawrence Hill 1980.
22. This and others quoted in this section are from Margaret Randall, *Sandino's Daughters: Testimonies of Nicaraguan Women in Struggle*, Vancouver, Canada, New Star Books 1981.
23. 'Sandanistas prepare for the worst', *New Statesman*, 30 April 1982.

7. Rosie the Riveter: Women in Defence Industries

1. Kathryn Hulme, *Undiscovered Country*, Boston, Massachusetts, Little Brown, 1966, pp.181, 184.
2. Elsa Morante's novel of the second world war in Italy has been published in English as *History, A Novel*, New York, Avon 1979, pp.3-4.
3. Susan Estabrook Kennedy, *If All We Did Was to Weep at Home: A History of White Working Class Women in America*, Bloomington, Indiana, Indiana University Press 1979, p.70.
4. According to historian Susan Estabrook Kennedy, 'Women who sewed gray woolen shirts for Union army soldiers received a dollar a dozen from contractors who then sold the same work to

the army for $1.75 dozen.' Kennedy, *op. cit.*

5. Jill Diane Zahniser, 'So Many Decent Girls: Women at Watertown Arsenal, 1861-65', unpublished paper, Women Studies Program, University of Iowa 1980. The following account is based on Jill Diane Zahniser's research.
6. For a fuller account of the processes by which the sexual division of labour in nineteenth-century factories depended on gendered conceptualisations of social status, see Judy Lown, 'The carrot and the stick: the many faces of new paternalism', chapter 6 of *Gender and Class in Industrialisation*, Ph.D. dissertation, Department of Sociology, University of Essex, forthcoming, 1983.
7. Sheila Rowbotham, *Hidden from History*, London, Pluto Press 1973, p.110. See also: Gail Braybon, *Women Workers in the First World War: The British Experience*, Croom Helm 1981.
8. *Ibid.* p.112.
9. *Ibid.* p.114.
10. Madeline Ida Bedford, 'Munitions Wages', reprinted in Catherine Reilly (ed.), *Scars Upon My Heart: Women's Poetry and Verse of the First World War*, Virago 1981, p.7.
11. Mary Gabrielle Collins, 'Women at Munitions Making', reprinted in Reilly, *op. cit.* p.24.
12. US women mobilised specifically for war work also suffered rapid demobilisation after 1918. See David M. Kennedy, *Over Here: The First World War and American Society*, London, Oxford University Press 1980, p.285. Also: Judith McGraw, 'Women and the history of American technology', *Signs*, vol.7, no.4, Summer 1982, p.811. Marine Weiner Greenwald, *Women, War and Work: The Impact of World War I on Women Workers in the US*, Westport, Connecticut, Greenwood Press 1980.
13. Denis Riley, 'The free mothers: pronatlonalism and working mothers in industry at the end of the last war in Britain', *History Workshop Journal*, no.11, Spring 1981, p.64.
14. *The War and Women's Employment: The Experiences of the UK and the US*, Montreal, The International Labor Organization, 1946, p.276. (This report is available in the library of the Women's Research and Resources Centre, London). See also Susan Hartmann, *The Home Front and Beyond: American Women in the 1940s*, Boston, Massachusetts, Twayne 1980.
15. Alan S. Milward, *War, Economy and Society, 1939-1945*, Berkeley, University of California Press 1979, pp.219-20.
16. For description of policies covering women war workers in

Germany and Canada see: Leila J. Rupp, *Mobilizing Women for War: German and American Propaganda 1935-1945*, Princeton University 1978; Ruth Pierson, 'Women's emancipation and the recruitment of women into the labour forces in World War II', in Susan Mann, Trofimenkoff and Alison Prentices (eds.), *The Neglected Majority: Essays in Canadian Women's History*, Toronto, McClelland and Stewart 1977, pp.125-45.

17. For descriptions and analysis of these differentiations in the nineteenth-century labour force, see: Angela John, *By the Sweat of Their Brow: Women Workers at Victoria Coal Mines*, Croom Helm 1980; Jane Humphries, 'Protective legislation, the capitalist state and the working class men: the case of the 1842 Mines Regulation Act', *Feminist Review*, no.7, Spring 1981, pp.1-34. Angela John, 'Letters', *Feminist Review*, no.9, Autumn 1981, pp.106-09; Judy Lown, 'The carrot and the stick', *op. cit.*; Sally Alexander, 'Women's work in nineteenth century London: a study of the years 1820-1850', in Juliet Mitchell and Ann Oakley (eds.), *The Rights and Wrongs of Women*, Harmondsworth, Penguin 1976.
18. Riley, *op. cit.*
19. *The War and Women's Employment*, *op. cit.* pp.279-81.
20. For a description of the debates carried on inside the US government during the second world war over how to use women, and especially for analysis of the efforts of the US Department of Labor's Women's Bureau leaders to gain equity for women workers, see Kennedy, *op. cit.* p.187.
21. From conversation with Marjorie Mowlam, lecturer in politics, University of Newcastle upon Tyne, in London, May 1982. A first-hand account of experiences in a wartime engineering factory is available in: Doris White, *D for Doris, V for Victory*, Wolverton, Milton Keynes, England, Oakleaf Books 1982. See also: S. Fleming and R. Broad (eds.), *Nella's Last War—A Mother's Diary—1939-1945*, London, Sphere 1983.
22. Quoted in the guide book for the film, *The Life and Times of Rosie the Riveter*, Miriam Frank, Marilyn Zeibarth, Connie Field, *The Life and Times of Rosie the Riveter*, Clarity Educational Productions (4560 Horton Street, Emeryville, California 94608) 1982, p.24.
23. Karen Anderson, *Wartime Women: Sex Roles, Family Relations and the Status of Women During World War II*, Westport, Connecticut and London, Greenwood Press 1981, p.91.

24. Miriam Frank *et al.*, *op. cit.* pp.55-56.
25. In addition to the film distributed in both the US and Britain, there is a companion film guide book available which includes a great deal of useful background material and quotes from the five women featured in the film: Miriam Frank, Marily Ziebarth, Connie Field, *The Life and Times of Rosie the Riveter*, *op. cit.*
26. *Rosie the Riveter*, *op. cit.*
27. Patricia Allatt, Department of Sociology, University of Keele, 'Status, class and the social reproduction of masculinity (in World War II)', paper presented at the British Sociological Association Annual Conference, Manchester, April 1982, p.11.
28. Karen Beck Skold, 'The job he left behimd: American women in the ship yards during the World War II', in Carol B. Berkin and Clara M. Lovett, *Women, War and Revolution*, New York, Holmes and Meier 1980, pp;55-72. See also Skold, 'Sex segregation in ship yard occupations during World War II: The case of Portland, Oregon', paper presented at the Berkshire Conference on the History of Women, Vassar College, Poughkeepsie, New York, June 1981. A provocative study of wartime struggles around gender and labour in the US auto industry, is: Ruth Milkman, 'Redefining "women's work": the sexual division of labor in the auto industry during World War II', *Feminist Studies*, vol.8, no.2, Summer 1982, pp.337-72.
29. Skold, 'Sex segregation in ship yard occupations during World War II', *op. cit.*
30. Ruth Milkman, 'Organizing the Sexual Division of Labor', *Socialist Review*, no.49, vol.10, no.1, January-February 1980, pp.130-33.
31. Philip Kraft, quoted by Janine Morgall in 'Typing our way to freedom', *Feminist Review*, no.9, October 1981, p.91.
32. Morgall, *op. cit.* For an analysis of male strategies to preserve their privileges in an occupation undergoing radical technological change, see Cynthia Cockburn's study of British printing compositors: 'The material of male power', *Feminist Review*, no.9, Autumn 1981, pp.41-59; and Cynthia Cockburn, *Brothers*, London, Pluto Press 1983.
33. *The War and Women's Employment*, *op. cit.* p.278.
34. For examples of black women's protests during World War II, see the film, *Rosie the Riveter*; also Miriam Frank, *et. al.*, *op. cit.*; Anderson, *op. cit.*; Rosalyn Baxandall, *Women: A Documentary History*, New York, Vintage, pp.184-287.

35. Carole Jordon, 'Women's Land Army', *Merseyside Women's Paper*, Liverpool, Spring 1982, pp.8-9.
36. Margaret Rhodes, 'Needles and beetles', *Spare Rib*, February 1982.
37. Denise Riley, *op. cit.*; Elizabeth Wilson, *Only Halfway to Paradise: Women in Britain, 1945-1968*, London and New York, Tavistock 1980.
38. Ann Scott James (1952) quoted in Elizabeth Wilson, *op. cit.* pp.83-84.
39. The film *The Life and Times of Rosie the Riveter* includes 1945 film clips which graphically reveal this ideological reversal. See also Andrea Walsh, *Women's Film and Female Experience, 1940-1950*, New York, Praeger 1982.
40. For a case study of the post-war US auto industry, see Nancy Gabin, 'They have placed a penalty on womanhood: the protest actions of women auto workers in Detroit-area UAW Locals, 1945-1947', *Feminist Studies*, vol.8, no.2, Summer 1982, pp.372-98.
41. Denise Riley, *op. cit.* p.81.
42. Marion Anderson, *Bombs and Bread: Black Unemployment and the Pentagon Budget*, Lansing, Michigan, Employment Research Associates 1982, p.1.
43. Estimates derived from Marion Anderson, *The Empty Portbarrel*, cited in 'Guns and Butter', *Newsletter*, no.143, Resist (38 Union Square, Somerville, Massachusetts 02143), p.3.
44. Leonard Silk, 'Cost effective job creation', the *New York Times*, 22 September 1982.
45. Marion Anderson, *Neither Jobs Nor Security: Women's Unemployment and the Pentagon Budget*, Lansing, Michigan, Employment Research Associates 1982; Marion Anderson, *Bombs or Bread: Blacks, Unemployment, and the Pentagon Budget*, *op. cit.*; Emma Rothschild, 'The Philosophy of Reaganism', *New York Review of Books*, 15 April 1982; Emma Rothschild, 'Military expenditure and economic structure', Independent Commission for Disarmament and Security Issues (the Palme Commission), October 1981.
46. In April 1982 the Thatcher government estimated that in 1980-81 240,000 British jobs were directly 'sustained by the defence equipment programme', while 190,000 jobs were indirectly 'sustained': 'In Parliament', *ADIU Report*, University of Sussex, vol.4, no.3, May-June 1982, p.14. In mid-1982 there were 20,000 workers

employed in the Royal Ordnance Factories: 'Ordnance factories to be privatised', *State Research*, London, vol.5, no.31, August/September 1982, p.160. According to the government's Defence White Paper, 1982, 140,000 British jobs were dependent on Britain's exported arms. This was 2,000 fewer jobs than the government claimed in 1981: *Newsletter*, no.55, 21 July 1982, Campaign Against Arms Trade, London, p.4.

47. *War Lords: The UK Arms Industry*, Counter Information Service, London 1982, p.33.
48. 'Defense Contracts: last year's big winners', *Multinational Monitory*, vol.3, no.5, May 1982, p.3.
49. A valuable map is provided in *War Lords, op. cit.*
50. A description of the Grumman Corporation's militarising effects on the economy of Long Island, New York, is available from the Council for Economic Priorities, New York. A study of Connecticut's economic militarisation is Marta Daniels, *Jobs Security and Arms in Connecticut*, Voluntown, Conn., American Friends Service January 1980.
51. For those who would like to read more about the relations between arms manufacturing companies and government's weapons purchasers there is now an impressive array of accessible studies. The following are especially useful in describing the British as well as US military-industrial complexes: Mary Kaldor, *Baroque Arsenal*, New York, Hill and Wang 1981; Mary Kaldor, *The Disintegrating West*, Harmondsworth, Penguin; New York, Hill and Wang 1979; *War Lords, op.cit.*; E.P. Thompson and Dan Smith (eds.), *Protest and Survive*, Harmondsworth, Penguin; New York, Monthly Review Books 1982.

    Descriptions that focus mostly on the US military-industrial complex and how it works include: Gordon Adams, *The Iron Triangle*, New York, Council for Economic Priorities 1981; Paul Brodeur, *The Zapping of America* (about the microwave industry's relations with the US navy), New York, Viking; A. Ernest Fitzgerald, *The High Priests of Waste*, New York, W.W. Norton 1972; Jacques S. Gansler, *The Defense Industry*, Cambridge, Massachusetts, MIT Press 1981; James Fallows, 'The great defense deception', *New York Review of Books*, 28 May 1981, pp.15-19; *Science for the People*, Boston, special issue on militarisation, 1981.
52. British analysts and trade unionists have led the way in studying the possibilities of converting weapons-producing companies to

non-military goods. See especially Hilary Wainwright and Huw Beynon, *The Workers' Report on Vickers*, London, Pluto Press 1979; Hilary Wainwright and David Elliott, *The Lucas Plan*, Allison & Busby 1982; Mary Kaldor, *Baroque Arsenal*, *op. cit.*

53. This discussion is based on an unpublished paper by and subsequent conversations with Paula Rayman, Department of Sociology, Brandeis University, Waltham, Massachusetts, 1982.
54. Economist Lester Thurow cited in 'Reagan's rearmament', *Plowshare Press*, Mountain View, California, January-February 1982, p.4.
55. Drew Middleton, 'Electronics tip the scales of combat', the *New York Times*, 11 May 1982.
56. The *New York Times*, 4 April 1982.
57. Quoted in Hilary Wainwright, 'The women who wire up the weapons', in Dorothy Thompson (ed.), *Over Our Dead Bodies: Women Against the Bomb*, London, Virago 1983. I am grateful to Hilary Wainwright for sharing the typescript of her article with me before publication.
58. *Loc. cit.*
59. General Electric Company (GEC), Racal, Marconi, Plessey and Ferranti are among Britain's biggest electronics companies. All are also major defence contractors and deeply involved in the international arms trade. For a profile of Plessey, see 'Plessey—a company profile', Transnational Information Exchange, no.7/8, October 1980-March 1981, Transnational Institute (20 Paulus Potter Straat, Amsterdam), pp.22-28. See also: 'Plessey Arms Apartheid', Anti-Apartheid Movement, London 1981.
60. For interviews with Welsh women being hired by Sony and other firms newly set up in Wales, see Jenny Vaughan, 'Surviving the recession', *Spare Rib*, April 1982, pp.6-8, 19.
61. Two of the most thorough critical studies of the microelectronics industry are: Dieter Ernst, *Restructuring the World Industry in a Period of Crisis—The Role of Innovation: An Analysis of Recent Developments in the Semi-Conductor Industry*, Vienna, Austria, United Nations Industrial Organization 1982; Lenny Siegel, 'Delicate bonds: the global semiconductor industry', a special issue of *Pacific Research*, (222B View Street, Mountain View, California 94041), January 1981.
62. 'Reagan's Rearmament', *Plowshare Press*, *op. cit.*
63. Dave McFadden, 'California's military build-up', *Plowshare Press*, September-October 1982, p.1. *Plowshare Press* is published

by the Mid-Peninsula Conversion Project, (222C View Street, Mountain View, California 94041). The State of California has published its own study: *The Effect of Increased Military Spending in California*, Office of Economic Policy, Planning and Research, State of California, Sacramento, California, May 1982.

64. Susan S. Green, 'Silicon Valley's women workers', Working Papers of the East-West Cultural Learning Institute, East-West Center, Honolulu, Hawaii 96848, July 1980.

65. Susan Green, *op. cit.* Other papers available in this East-West Center series are: Mary Alison Hancock, 'Electronics industry in New Zealand: exploitation of women and international dependency', and Robert Snow, 'The new international division of labor and the US workforce'.

66. *San Jose Mercury* (San Jose, California), 17 November 1980. In the US as a whole, approximately two-thirds of high tech operatives are women, one-fourth of whom are black, Hispanic, Asian or Native American: *Global Electronic Information Newsletter* ,no.24, September 1982, p.2. This newsletter is an invaluable source of information and critical analysis concerning the conditions affecting women electronics workers all over the world. It is published by the Pacific Studies Center, 222B View Street, Mountain View, California 94041.

67. There is a growing body of information available on the spiralling international arms trade. The following reports are published annually: Ruth Leger Sivard, *World Military and Social Expenditures*, Institute for World Order (777 United Nations Plaza, New York NY 10017): US Arms Control and Disarmament Agency, *World Military Expenditures and Arms Transfers*, Washington, DC; US Department of Defense, *Foreign Military Sales and Military Assistance Facts*, Washington, DC; Stockholm International Peace Research Institute, *Yearbook*, Stockholm, Sweden.

Also of great value are the following independent critical studies: Michael Klare and Cynthia Arnson, *7upplying Repression* (on US *police* equipment sales and assistance), Washington, DC; Institute for Policy Studies 1981; Andrews J. Pierre, *The Global Politics of Arms Sales*, Princeton University Press 1980; Peter Lock and Herbert Wolf, *Registrar of Arms Production in Developing Countries*, Hamburg, Study Group in Armaments and Underdevelopment, University of Hamburg 1977; Milton Leitenberg and Nicole Ball (eds.), *The Structure of the Defence Industry: An International Survey*, Croom Helm, forthcoming,

1983; Ann Schulz, *Military Expenditures and Economic Performance in Iran, 1950-1980*, Worcester, Massachusetts, Department of Government, Clark University, 1982. Also: The *Newsletter* of the Campaign Against the Arms Trade (5 Caledonian Road, London) regularly monitors foreign arms sales by British companies.

68. For feminist analyses of women workers in Third World electronics factories, see: June Nash (ed.), *Women and Men in the International Division of Labor*, Albany, New York, State University of New York Press, 1983; Alıne Wong, *Economic Development and Women's Place; Women in Singapore*, London, Change International Reports 1980; Linda Lim, *Women Workers in Multinational Corporations*, Michigan Occasional Papers in Women's Studies, Ann Arbor, University of Michigan, 1978; Kate Young, Carol Wolkowitz and Roslyn McCullagh (eds.), *Of Marriage and the Market: Women's Subordination in International Perspective*, London, CSE Books 1981.
69. I have explored the link between women's labour and militarisation in 'Women textile workers and the militarisation of Southeast Asia', in June Nash (ed.), *op. cit.*
70. Maria C. Villariba, *The Philippines—Canvasses of Women in Crisis*, Change International Reports: Women and Society, London 1982, p.9.
71. I am grateful to Paula Rayman for alerting me to this growing contradiction.
72. 'Philippines labor', *Global Electronics Information Newsletter*, *op. cit.* issue no.23, July 1982.
73. Salvacia Bulatao, a Philippines activist, in discussion at the Transnational Institute's Conference on Women Textile Workers, Amsterdam, 23 October 1982.
74. Inge Thornssan, Swedish representative on a United Nations study group concerning world military spending, speaking at UNESCO, Paris, 28 October 1982.
75. Communication with the Lesbian-Feminist Alliance, MIT, Cambridge, Massachusetts. What women and men in engineering face in seeking non-defence jobs in militarised America is revealed in the *New York Times*, 'Careers '83', special supplement, 17 October 1982. Virtually every third advertisement by a technician-hiring company or public agency shows missiles, jetfighters or other sophisticated weapons as a symbol of the goods they produce or services they perform. By contrast, the journalists' articles which accompany the advertising of the supplement do

not say a word about this militarising trend in the US job market.

8. Feminism and Militarism

1. Virginia Woolf, *Three Guineas*, London and New York, Harcourt Brace 1938.
2. Cambridge Women's Peace Collective, *My Country Is the Whole World*, London, Pandora Books, forthcoming, 1983: Dorothy Thompson (ed.), *Over Our Dead Bodies: Women Against the Bomb*, London, Virago, forthcoming, 1983; Wendy Chapkis (ed.), *Loaded Questions: Women in the Military*, Transnational Institute, 20 Paulus Potter Straat, Amsterdam, Holland, 1981 (distributors, London: Pluto Press; Washington, DC: Institute of Policy Studies). Leslie Cagan, 'Feminism and disarmament', in David Dellinger (ed.), *Beyond Survival*, Boston, Massachusetts, South End Press 1983; Georgina Ashworth (ed.), *Handbook: Women, Violence and Militarism*, London, Change International Reports: Women and Society, forthcoming, 1983.
3. Two recent articles have helped me in thinking through an approach which concentrates on processes rather than origins: Judy Lown, 'More a patriarchy than a factory', in Eva Gamarnikow *et al.*, *Gender, Class and Work*, Heinemann 1983; Scarlet Friedman, 'Heterosexuality, couples and parenthood: a "natural" cycle?', in Scarlet Friedman and Elizabeth Sarah (eds.), *On the Problem of Men*, London, Women's Press (US distributor: Merrimack Books, New Salem, New Hampshire) 1982, pp.16-17.
4. An especially interesting description of the step-by-step militarisation of an early society which, until militarisation, appeared to have a non-patriarchal state is: Ruby Rohrlich, 'State formation in Sumer and the subjugation of women', in *Feminist Studies*, vol.6, no.1, Spring 1980, pp.77-102.

Index